4/24

SHALOM BOMB

Bernard Kops

SHALOM BOMB

Scenes From My Life

OBERON BOOKS
LONDON

First published in 2000 by Oberon Books Ltd
(incorporating Absolute Classics)
521 Caledonian Road, London N7 9RH
Tel: 020 7607 3637 / Fax: 020 7607 3629
Email: oberon.books@btinternet.com

A catalogue record for this book is available from
the British Library.

ISBN: 1 84002 112 8

Printed in Great Britain by Antony Rowe Ltd, Reading.

1 3 5 7 9 10 8 6 4 2

Photographic Acknowledgements

For permission to reproduce the photographs in this book,
the Publishers would like to thank:

The Museum of London (1); Spillman & Ramsay Ltd. (8, 11);
Oswald Jones, courtesy of Credigion Museum (12); Brigit Barry
(13); Kenny Parker for *Plays & Players* (15, 16, 17, 18); Geraldine
Norman (19); Vaslav, courtesy of The Mander & Mitchenson
Theatre Collection (21); John Darcy Noble (22); Ida Kar,
courtesy of Hulton Getty (23); Ros Asquith (24); BBC (27, 28);
Jocelyn Herbert (32); *Plays & Players* (34, 35); Paul Thompson
(37, 38); Sidney Harris (41); Matthew Thomas (43, 44).

For Erica and the tribe: Adam, Hannah, Abigail, Rebekah, Mark, Terry, Drew, Jessica, Max, Anya and Chloe.

Contents

1. Goodbye Soho, 11
2. The Option, 17
3. Moving, 23
4. Seven Dials, 30
5. The Party, 34
6. Joan and Gerry, 40
7. On Our Way, 47
8. The Opening, 51
9. Coming Back Down to Earth, 56
10. Doing Time at Bristol, 62
11. My Second Coming, 68
12. My Ghosts Return, 74
13. Hobson's Choice, 79
14. Baptism of Fire, 86
15. Waiting for Tynan, 93
16. Lunch with the KGB, 98
17. Absolute Beginners, 104
18. Summoned to Court, 109
19. Arnold's Circus, 115
20. Barricades in West Hampstead, 121
21. Have You Had Your Accident Yet?, 126
22. Bernard, it is Getting Dark, 132
23. Erica by Lethe, 136
24. Slippery Slope, 143
25. O'Flaherty Will Get You Nowhere, 149
26. Take the Money and Run, 155
27. Lindsay, 162
28. The Big Time Beckons, 168
29. One Door Closes, Another Door Closes, 175
30. You'll Never Get Out of Life Alive, 179
31. Can Anyone Direct Me to Where I Am?, 184
32. All the Way Down, 191
33. Exit Downstage, 197
34. Fire in My Head, 204
35. Has Anyone Seen an Old Black Cab?, 209
36. Mr Love and Justice, 213
37. Ezra, 217
38. The World is a Wedding, 222

Also by Bernard Kops, 229

Index, 231

Acknowledgements

I'd like to thank my publisher, James Hogan, for his act of faith, and Sarah Wherry for all her encouragement; Cathy Herbert, my editor, for her dedication and hard work; and Matthew Thomas for his photographs and his time.

Shalom Bomb

I want a bomb, my own private bomb, my shalom bomb.
I'll test it in the morning, when my son awakes,
hot and stretching, smelling beautiful from sleep. Boom! Boom!
Come my son dance naked in the room.
I'll test it on the landing and wake my neighbours,
the masons and the whores and the students who live downstairs.

Oh I must have a bomb and I'll throw open windows and
count down as I whizz around the living room,
on his bike, with him flying angels on my shoulder;
and my wife dancing in her dressing gown.
I want a happy family bomb, a do-it-yourself bomb,
I'll climb on the roof and ignite it there about noon.
My improved design will gong the world and we'll all eat lunch.

My pretty little bomb will play a daytime lullaby and
thank you bomb for now my son falls fast asleep.
My love come close, close the curtains, my lovely bomb, my darling.

My naughty bomb. Burst around us, burst between us, burst within us.

Light up the universe, then linger, linger
while the drone of the world recedes.

Shalom bomb

I want to explode the breasts of my wife
and wake everyone,
to explode over playgrounds and parks, just as children
come from schools. I want a laughter bomb,
filled with sherbet fountains, liquorice allsorts, chocolate kisses,
candy floss,
tinsel and streamers, balloons and fireworks, lucky bags,
bubbles and masks and false noses.

I want my bomb to sprinkle the earth with roses.
I want a one-man-band-bomb. My own bomb.

My live long and die happy bomb. My die peacefully of old age bomb,
in my own bed bomb.
My Om Mane Padme Aum Bomb, My Tiddly Om Pom Bomb.
My goodnight bomb, my sleeptight bomb,
my see you in the morning bomb.
I want my bomb, my own private bomb, my Shalom bomb.

1

Goodbye Soho

So what is it about making a girl pregnant that makes a man feel so pleased with himself? Erica was seven months gone and well into her beatitude. I was thrilled and scared in almost equal parts.

"Do you really want this baby?" she would ask me.

"Of course," I'd reply. "I want a child to respect me. I want a family. I want to be someone. I want immortality. What else is there?"

Other times I was wildly jealous of this woman lying on the bed beside me, so content, with such a cornucopia inside her belly. What immaculate and egotistic creativity. There I was, my thirtieth year to heaven, and I'd done nothing with my life. And there she was, huge, fulfilled, and ever so beautiful.

How delighted with ourselves we were, in our snug flat just behind Camberwell Green, Erica knitting the baby a minute purple garment, so ridiculously small you had to laugh. We walked six inches above the pavement. To hell with the future. We lived each day as it arrived, deliriously happy in each other. We searched through second-hand junk shops for a pram and a playpen, a guitar. For me, it was easy: I was forged in the East End where every day was a joke, where gallows humour was your means of survival. Like that famous Jewish joke. A young man murders his mother and father and is sent before the court.

"Is there anything you would like to say before I pass sentence?" the judge intones.

"Yes, please have mercy on a poor orphan," the young man replies.

All this despite the fearful black headlines of the Cold War. The generals threatened, but we cuddled close.

"Just my luck. Just when everything's going right, the world has to come to an end."

"Fuck them," Erica advised sweetly, with her slight, middle-class voice. "Let's curl up into our own lives."

✻

I was still fragile from my years before Erica. Before her, there had been psychosis and The Benzedrine Nights. Chutzpah had been my only weapon. And there were times, even now, when for no apparent reason an overwhelming darkness would envelop me. It happened anywhere – on the underground, in the park, a café – and I would be completely immobilised. Erica would walk slowly ahead and I would follow her as she coaxed me all the way home. Once there I would descend into uncontrollable crying. She would attempt to comfort me, not knowing the place I was inhabiting and not able to pull me out. But by the morning Fischer-Dieskau would be the bird catcher again and there would be coffee, and hope would return to my world.

One evening I announced to Erica that I would be commencing work on a play, in half an hour. I was itching to create something. My play would contain all the dark humour of my life, I told her. It would be both sad and humorous, significant, and anarchic. All I had to do was look inside myself and shlep out my crazy vision.

Fame was the spur. It always had been. Even as a kid, I'd prayed to the God I didn't believe in: "Please make me famous, and one day I'll return the compliment." A couple of weeks before – and even though they still thought of me as a low-life for having purloined their daughter – my mother and father-in-law had treated us to the Royal Court to see a new play that was causing a stir. It was called *Look Back in Anger*. I'd felt absolutely no affinity for those pathetic creatures and all that squirrel stuff.

"I can do better than that," I told my in-laws, leaving the rest of the audience still applauding. "If he can do it with that crap, so can I."

I was sure that with a little effort everyone would see my true worth, and be amazed and furious at my immediate and spectacular success. I would bathe in the glow of their jealousy. It was sheer jealousy that night that pushed me into direct action: I was determined to show Erica, blossoming with her own creation, that I could be just as clever as her.

There and then I wrote the title, *The Hamlet of Stepney Green*, and after that there was no stopping me. I was just as surprised as my characters when they emerged into the room and performed before me.

"Why are you talking to yourself?" Erica asked me through a yawn the next morning.

"I'm writing a play," I reminded her. "It's all there inside. Just like your baby."

She sat up sharpish. "Our baby!"

I laboured for three days until the birth came rushing towards me. I thought it was perfect. Whoever heard of the need to rewrite in those days?

After a few weeks Adam, our son, arrived. I had never learned to be a proper son and now I had to learn to be a father. We had stayed away from our usual caff for a few weeks – heavily pregnant women usually brought on hysterical laughter amongst the bums and bohemians of Soho – but now we returned, with Adam.

Ironfoot Jack gave us a smiling mouthful of black teeth. "Good to see ya."

I clutched those scribbled pages in my hands. (In case our flat in Camberwell burned down in our absence?) All the usual fingers, the faces, the blaggers were sitting in their usual places. Georgie Dias was weeping into his coffee. He owned the porn shop just along Old Compton, and normally it was impossible to wipe a smile off his ugly face. He was as camp as all get-out, although he had recently declared, "When the heat is on me, it's man, woman or beast." Nobody played it straight in the French Café.

"*La princesa está trieste. ¿Que tendrá la princesa?*" I asked him, for no reason. It was the only bit of Spanish I knew. These were hard times. All we had to impress with was our phoney erudition.

"I've got trouble," Georgie replied. "The vice squad come this morning for their handout, like every Friday, and I'm skint. I've taken nothing this week. Who can afford to buy filth these days? Who can even afford a hard on? Nothing sells. My mags are all crumbling from old age. My naked girls are falling apart, their lovely noonies turning all yellow. The law will come and kick my head in. I'm ruined."

The Countess Eileen de Vismes cooed at my indifferent son.

"We've come to say goodbye, Eileen. We're leaving Soho forever," I told her. We knew we wouldn't be able to return to our old existence with a new baby to look after.

"Leaving Soho? Never! Nobody leaves Soho. Everywhere else is death." She looked to Erica for the truth.

"It's true," Erica said. Everyone always believed her. Nobody ever believed me.

"So what are you going to do? Work for a living?" She spat, elegantly, on the floor.

"Work? What? Never! I haven't committed any crimes. From now on I'm going to write. As a matter of fact, here's my new play. I wrote it this week. Can I read a bit to you?"

But the Countess waved me away and turned back to her coffee. She had lost interest.

Dom Moraes was gentle and quiet as usual. I liked him. He was so affable, so willing to look you straight in the face, and so beautiful with his dreamy eyes and his long eyelashes. Of course, Dom was a poet and so had to be a shit. All poets were shits. The higher the art the greater the shit.

"You've written a play," he observed. "How enterprising of you. But is it a masterpiece? I do hope it's a masterpiece." Dom was a high-caste Indian drop-out. His father was the editor of *The Times of India* and Dom had been educated at the very best public school. His manners were perfect.

"A masterpiece? Possibly," I replied. "Yes, possibly it is."

When Sohocialists made this sort of remark they usually meant it seriously. The ego of people on their uppers knows no bounds. I was made of different stuff – my responses were merely East End survival techniques, but they never twigged this so I fitted in well. If you did show the slightest tinge of reticence, or you were pathetic, they would jump on you and kick your head in, or worse, no one would ever notice you. Everyone was a clever bastard in Soho. You had to brag like hell in order to be shown an ounce of respect, even though nobody believed anyone or anything. You had to play the Soho game: the cruel tongue; the sardonic quip; the outrageous lie. Soho was a great finishing school for all those who were eventually going to top themselves.

"Take it to David Archer. If it's any good he'll know," Dom advised.

I knew all about David Archer. A sort of cottage publisher who liked to go cottaging, he'd just opened a book shop opposite Bertaux in Greek Street. He served coffee there but never wanted anyone to buy a book. Handling cash always seemed to embarrass him. He was extremely rich and owned a third of Wiltshire. He also had an exceptional eye for literary talent even though he knew nothing about literature. He had discovered and published Dylan Thomas and David Gascoyne.

"Yeah! I'll nip round and show him my masterpiece," I agreed. "At the very least he'll give me a cup of coffee."

Frank Norman entered with a swagger, hunched into his Crombie overcoat, no doubt redolent with tales of the latest fingers he'd chivvied.

Frank had a long scar running down the length of his face, and like all supposed tough geezers he had a very sweet manner. He used to reassure me that if ever I needed protection all I had to do was nod and tomorrow you'd be able to buy the offenders straight off the slab round the corner. Only I happened to know that all Frank's crimes were actually petty and pathetic, so the offer wasn't much comfort; the last time he'd been done was for robbing a gas meter.

On our way to David Archer's we came face to face with Lucian the Freud, the grandson of that great madman of Vienna. Who except Lucian Freud could wear such a frightening face? It somehow summed up the icy chill of the world he inhabited.

He didn't smile but tucked a ten bob note into my top pocket. "You both look hungry," he mumbled, and walked briskly away.

Fantastic, I thought, haddock and chips tonight, and a bottle of Chianti. Fish goes straight to the brain and we can do with a bit of sense.

We got to the book shop. It wasn't your usual Charing Cross Road fustian interior. It was clean, sleek and uncluttered. Thin, beautiful volumes were lying around on teak tables from Heals and the smell of coffee greeted us.

David came forward. "You must be Bernard Kops. I've heard a lot about you."

"Only bad, I hope."

"How nice of you to drop in." He bowed towards Erica in best courtier style. "And what a beautiful little baby," he said, edging nervously away from Adam in the pram. He spoke as if he had a pound of plums in his mouth and was as stiff as a guardsman – no doubt he had studied them very closely. Here was another wonderful giver and a lousy taker. It was as if, having inherited a third of Wiltshire, David Archer couldn't wait to give it all away. My heart went out to him immediately.

"Take anything you want, no need to buy. Just take what you want. Take anything," he urged, handing us our free coffee.

A customer who had been perusing the shelves brought a book to the till. David seemed quite put out by this person who dared to offer him actual money. Disgusted with the note, he held it at arm's length and dropped it into the till.

"I hear you've written a play," he said finally. Gossip in Soho travelled even faster than in a Jewish family.

"Yes, I have recently been smitten by Hecuba!" I said. Erica squirmed. She always did at my pretension, and I was pretentious a lot of the time.

"Is it any good?"

"It could be a masterpiece. On the other hand, it could be a dollop of crap." Erica squirmed again. I shot her an outraged expression. I was only telling him the truth.

David jotted down a name and address. I noticed that his arm was withered. All rich people who owned a third of a shire probably had withered arms. There was always a price to pay.

"I know precious nothing about Art, and even less about Drama, but I do have an instinct for faces. I should call this man up immediately. He's an American and a theatre producer. He's living over here and he's looking for talent."

My heart sank into my sandals. Talent was a very questionable word in Soho. If some queer American was after my toches he had it coming to him.

"Before you go," David said, "would you care to take a book? Please! Any one you fancy. No charge, of course."

"May I have two?"

"Absolutely. As many as you like."

I grabbed the thick *Botteghe Oscure* and the latest doorstopper edition of *New Directions.*

David smiled. "What a clever choice. I believe Ezra Pound calls it *Nude Erections.*"

We all laughed, then the words ran out so we left. He watched us through the glass, rather sinisterly, I thought. David was a bizarre creature. This was the man who had started the Parton Press, yet when you met him it was as if he had just emerged from a forest and was suffering his first contact with these things called human beings.

I waved to embarrass him. He wavered back.

"You're a real heartless bastard," Erica said, shaking her head but laughing.

So we took our leave of the Serene Republic, and we didn't look back as we turned the corner into Shaftesbury Avenue. We didn't want to see it crumble before our eyes; all those ridiculous characters turning into pillars of salt.

2

The Option

A few weeks later we changed our minds. We couldn't give it up entirely. Only now we frequented Torino's where a better class of bohemian layabout wasted away his time. Auerbach, Bacon and Freud were regulars, not yet stashing away their millions. John Deakin, camp and acerbic, was always in the corner, and Colin MacInnes looked in four times a day – he and Louis MacNeice would resurrect themselves on Mr and Mrs Molina's coffee. I bumped into David Archer frequently and he seemed much happier now that he had given away all his books and closed up shop. His smile said that he no longer had to open a till and handle filthy money.

Seeing David reminded me that I had a telephone call to make.

I popped my courage into my mouth and stammered into the phone, "Mr Marvin? I've just written a play."

"Anyone who has written a play is good news. Is it a good play?" His American voice was a plush carpet. You just knew he was rich.

"It's very good. It took me three days." I was totally in the dark. I had no idea how long a play should take to write.

"Three whole days? Wow! That's a long time," he said in a twisted sort of tone.

He asked me to introduce myself and I blurted out a lengthy description of my family background: the names of my aunties; the health of my mother – I told him it wasn't so good, she now resided in Plaistow Jewish Cemetery. I told him that my father's first and greatest love was Grand Opera. I told him I came from a long line of socialist fanatics. I told him God was dead and I wasn't feeling so well myself. I told him about all my uncles, always on the make: bookmakers, ticktack men, gamblers, greengrocers, con-men. I told him about my uncle Joe who had a dance band in Amsterdam before the war. "Did you ever hear of Joe Kops and the Hotshots?"

He laughed. "Not offhand."

"And I believe we share the same politics," I said, wanting him to love me all the more, just in case my play wasn't good enough. David Archer had told me that Marvin had come to this country because he was on some sort of McCarthy list.

I told him about Erica and Adam. Finally I told him that David Archer had mentioned him and that he was on the lookout for new, young geniuses.

"And are you a genius?"

I recalled my mother's question, asked almost every day: "If you don't love yourself who is going to love you?" "Maybe. Yes! I probably am a genius." We laughed. He seemed to appreciate that peculiar Esperanto that Jews fall into when not quite sure of the territory. "Don't be a shrinking violet, Bernie," my mother used to say. She had died about six years before, but her mixed metaphors were still in my head. He, too, probably had such a mother. Everyone in New York suffered such mothers, so I'd heard.

"So, when can you come over?" he asked.

"I can come now."

"No, come this evening. I'm baby-sitting and having a few friends over."

Bingo! I put the phone down and laughed. Erica was outside in the rain, pushing Adam backward and forward in the pram and watching me for a sign. Mark Marvin was a marvellous man, I informed her as we walked home. He was dynamic and successful. He wanted me to go to his home that very evening and he was certainly going to buy my play.

"What, without even reading it?"

"Absolutely. We'll be famous. Rich in no time. He's wonderful."

Erica looked at me with that knowing expression. "We mustn't start loving people too quickly," she warned.

"Yes, it's going to be such a problem, being rich," I replied, meaning it.

"Yes, we must be careful. We mustn't spend it all at once," she agreed, not meaning it. We both laughed. We both knew me. I couldn't contain my excitement.

"He's very left wing. He wants to overthrow the government of the United States of America."

"All by himself?"

"Yep, single-handed and he has my approval."

We walked on briskly in the rain, Adam crying and me conducting the air. I was God with my baton, in charge of a vast American orchestra at the Hollywood Bowl, pounding out the notes. Both Erica and I raised our voices to the pissing heavens, joining together for the elegiac climax: "From the mountains to the prairies to the oceans white with foam. God bless America, my home sweet home!" Only a few days before I had seen a dry-cleaned Mormon choir singing that hymn on television.

Later that evening Mark Marvin greeted me at the door of his enormous flat in Bloomsbury.

"BerNARD!" He threw his arms around me as if we had known each other all our lives. "How wonderful of you to come with your wonderful play."

He was pink and plump. Hardly a threat to the continuing existence of the USA, I thought. He led me through to a gargantuan living room where a group of people were sitting. They scrutinised me with benign smiles.

"We've all been waiting for you," Mark said, handing me a glass of wine. "Please, BerNARD. We would love to hear your play." And I suddenly realised that I was expected to read all those ninety-odd pages out loud.

Luckily, I was a show-off. I opened with a few words. "This play is not just a jumble of words put together. It is me. It contains my whole life." Then I grabbed every role by the scruff of the neck and wrung out every ounce of pathos, joy and exaltation that they possessed. I was up there as Sam, the pickled-herring vendor, the first of my many archetypal old men. Sam dies at the end of Act One and I fell on the floor, imagining myself Donald Wolfit on possibly the worst of his off days, although by that time I had almost lost my voice.

I must have been terrible but they applauded. Afterwards there were sandwiches and chocolate éclairs.

One youngish American came forward and thrust out his hand. "Great, son. I'm Sam Wanamaker."

"Thank you, Mr Wanamaker."

"He's famous," the host said. "You heard of him?"

"Who hasn't?" I asked. I hadn't.

An immaculate little man approached us. "Ooh-la-la! I am Tony Mayer, the French Cultural Attaché, and you are very talented. And I, of course, will translate your play into French." Trust a politician to have his hands groping for the main chance.

Two pretty boys came in. Tony's eyes went wild with delight. "Sorry we're late, Mark darling. Have we missed it all?"

Eventually he turned back to me. "I must immediately contact my dear friend Darius Milhaud," he piped. "He must write the music for this play. And Jean... Jean Cocteau, he will love your dark, twisted threnody of joy. You must come to Paris next week. He will love you. He will admire your *splendide* effort."

I loved Cocteau's work. I had seen *Orphée* eight times, but I definitely did not want him to love me. I definitely would not be going next week.

"And my dearest chum, Ionesco. He will just adore your poignant existential vision. He's coming over next week. You know of him, of course."

"Who doesn't?" I didn't, of course. I nodded my delight.

He came close and whispered. "You look so wonderfully scruffy in your impossible clothes, Bernard. Please promise me you will stay ragged as you are and never change. Do not ever shave or smarten yourself. Remember you are you." Then he walked to the door, sighing. "I promised my darling, dear wife, my excellent *amie,* that I would get home early."

It was well past midnight when Tony Mayer finally left, eyeing up the boys on his way.

In a corner another little man was nibbling on a sandwich, hunched into an armchair. He was even smaller than Mark Marvin and me.

"Go over to him," Mark whispered some time later in the evening, "and be nice and friendly. He's a famous drama critic and he writes for the *Sunday Times.* His name is Harold Hobson."

As I approached Hobson gave me his benediction. "I rather liked your play. How original. How folksy."

"Thank you. How kind of you." I simply had to learn the art of ingratiation. "Do you think I have a future, Mr Hobson?"

"Who knows? Do any of us have a future?"

I got the drift. I needed to conjure up a bit more pessimism. "Yeah, I suppose that's in God's hands and he's been rather shtoom of late."

He handed me a card. "I would like you to lunch with me at the Athenaeum. Give me a call." The audience was over.

Sam Wanamaker gave me another slap on the back. "So, young man. What do you do for a living?"

"A living? Who makes a living? I have a bookstall at Cambridge Circus. More like a dying than a living, but I earn a few bob. I intend to make a fortune from my plays." He laughed. You are your work; it's the first thing people ask you at parties.

"I have to make a phone call," I said to Mark.

He nodded toward a door and a moment later I found myself in his bedroom. Even worse, Mark was there with me. A nice, married Yiddisher boy surely couldn't be as bent as old iron, I reasoned silently as he closed the door.

He took out his chequebook. "I'm giving you fifty pounds."

I kept my composure somehow, although fifty pounds was the most money I had ever dreamed of possessing. I took the cheque and stared at it.

"I'm taking an option on your play, BerNARD. I think you have a great future. I shall be your agent and manage everything. All you have to do is write plays. And sign here."

I had a cheque in my fist which proved I was a playwright and had a future of endless joy and riches. I would have signed anything. It could have been my death warrant. I immediately obliged on the dotted line and Mark hugged me and then rejoined his pundits in the other room, all egos blazing about the value of Heidegger and his Silence and whether or not he gave a poultice of comfort to his master, the purveyor of evil. Or was it Wagner?

I dialled Erica. She was suspicious at first so I whispered "Doctor Lotus" and she laughed with delight. Doctor Lotus was our special guardian angel.

"How much?" she asked.

"Fifty nice ones," I whispered. "And on top of that we're going to be rich and famous."

I could hear her roaring incredulously in Camberwell. "Fifty whole pounds! What will we do with all that money?"

"Love will find a way."

"Come home soon. Be careful."

Thus the young Candide Kops left the Bloomsbury flat of his benevolent master and entered the land of make-believe where everyone loved everyone, but carried concealed daggers for the day when their undying affection would turn without warning into murderous rage. Everyone except Candide Kops, who carried nothing except a bunch of withered flowers he found outside Tottenham Court Road underground station.

Erica watched me approach through the curtain. When she opened the door she knew instinctively that something was wrong.

"What is it?"

"I'm afraid. I don't want anything to change with us," I said.

She led me inside and, knowing how to bring us round again to our days of madness and bliss, sang, "There may be trouble ahead..."

She was Ginger and I was Fred as we danced around the small flat. She had on her black dress with huge coloured flowers. I couldn't wait to take it off. I turned off the light with my elbow and grabbed her and kissed her and danced us to our mattress on the floor.

Adam was asleep in the bottom drawer of our small chest of drawers. We couldn't afford a cot. He looked so contained, with his little arms up in the air. Why was he surrendering when he had captured us, I wondered. We lay in the dark, tingling with afterlove and the bubbling thoughts of the things we would buy and the places we would visit when our ship came in; the fruits of success trickling down on to our mattress on the floor.

"It's so exciting. So fantastic. What do you say?"

"Don't let it pull us apart." The moon was falling on her face.

"Never. Never!"

We laughed and made love again. We were so very young.

3

Moving

It was ten in the morning but we were still well away in the land of delights. I was woken up by the telephone ringing in the passage.

"Is that Bernard Kops?" asked a posh voice at the other end. "This is Dick Linklater of the Arts Council." He sounded very friendly. "Are you sitting down?" A funny question. I grunted back. "I'm delighted to tell you you've been awarded five hundred pounds."

"Five hundred pounds!" I was astounded. Was this some French Café joker, getting his revenge on me for having escaped?

"Yes – do you have a bank account?"

Erica appeared with Adam, aware this was a phone call of significance. She stood pressed close to me, wanting to know what all the gasping was about.

"It's an award for your play. It's for you to continue writing. Shall we post it to you?"

"Five hundred pounds," I whispered.

"Five hundred pounds?" Erica echoed, not understanding.

"Yes. We hope it will enable you to live for a year and just write plays. Write another play."

"Who put me up for this, Mr Linklater?"

"Please call me Dick."

"Who put me up for this, Dick?"

"Mark Marvin, the American producer. He believes you are extremely talented and we are very impressed with your work. We'll put the cheque in the post."

"No! Don't post it. Can I call round and pick it up?"

He laughed. "Of course you can."

"I'm coming today. In one hour."

"We shall be delighted to meet you."

I put the phone down. "We're rich!" I cried, and put Erica out of her misery. We put a Yiddish song on the gramophone and whooped with delight. "And just think, no more work forever. Just writing and loving and babies. No more work ever again!"

Peter Schmidt, the painter who lived upstairs, and his girlfriend Cathy came down to find out the news, and soon we were all dancing and singing to express our love of life and the beautiful symmetry of it all.

"I deserve it," I told them. "It took me three whole days to write that play. We should celebrate. I'll buy everyone breakfast."

We decided it would be eggs and bacon and dropped into an Italian greasy spoon, a more salubrious one than usual near the Green. There wasn't a rabbi handy, so I koshered the bacon myself. Later I went to Martin's Bank in St Martin's Lane and sat before the manager. Hard to believe I had never actually set foot in a bank before. I waved the cheque and told him my good news.

"So you're being recognised, Mr Kops."

"Hope not. I'm still wanted for so many crimes."

He guffawed, in a way that only Englishmen can. "I see you write comedy."

"I'd like to draw some immediately, please."

"I'm afraid not, Mr Kops. It will take three days."

"But it's good. It's from the Arts Council. It's government money, and there will be plenty more from now on," I assured him. I just wanted to get my hands on some readies quick.

He smiled, shook his head, then relented and agreed to advance me twenty-five.

I headed straight for Old Compton to rendezvous with Erica at Torino's. When she saw me through the window I yawned like a toff and waved my pristine chequebook. The other faces stared. They didn't seem particularly happy.

"Be careful," my muse muttered when I sat down. "Our good news is another nail in their coffin."

David Litvinoff came in and spotted us in the corner. He was the half-brother of the novelist and my good friend, Emanuel Litvinoff. He asked why we were so happy on such a cold day and was delighted when I told him. He made some notes while Erica and I continued to debate my behaviour outside the window.

"But I like showing off." It seemed to be my only defence.

"People don't want to know your good news, it's human."

"I want to know your good news," David said. "I want to do a story. Don't you want to be in the newspapers? Lovely photo: both of you and Adam."

"Yes," I said. "Please, yes."

"No! Please, no," Erica implored, but we won her round.

"Great!" said David. "I can just see the story all over page two. Impoverished Jewish genius discovered in Soho. Runs pathetic bookstall in Cambridge Circus and suddenly writes a masterpiece."

"No," said Erica, standing up. "If you print that, I'm walking out right now."

I knew she would never, ever leave me, but I always hedge my bets.

"Go easy on the masterpiece bit, David, and whatever you do, don't call me a genius, even if you and I know it's true. Just call me plain brilliant and incredible." Just my luck to fall for a girl who wouldn't let me get away with anything. "I'm going to be famous," I reminded her. I could feel a warm glow spreading all over me. "It proves there is a God after all. He's answered my one prayer."

"To be a wonderful writer maybe, but fame? How can you pray for fame? It could be a terrible affliction." Erica was always the voice of reason. She hadn't been brought up in Stepney where caution wasn't on the menu. I had, and the sun was shining out of my toches and lighting up the whole of Soho.

I gave David all the detail he needed and he made arrangements for us to be photographed a couple of days later.

We were firmly settled at Torino's by this point, surrounded by scribblers. I was in there and halfway through a croissant when I knew that Paul Potts was looking for me – an odour of long-expired Camembert always preceded him. I liked Paul, but I wished I had the courage to tell him that no one would love him if he didn't wash. He was a grand, upper-class Catholic Englishman with a passion for poetry and a love of the down-trodden, now one of them himself and residing at Rowton House, a stinking refuge in Drury Lane for men who had no one, nothing and nowhere.

"I've heard the news," he said. Everyone knew. Good, they could all eat their rotten hearts out. I waited to be congratulated.

"Why you? Why not me?" he continued.

"Because you're a lazy bastard," I explained.

He laughed, and tried to embrace me, as usual playing it both ways. I stopped breathing for a moment so as not to expire.

He let me go and rose to his six feet three inches. "I am Paul Potts, the people's poet, and you dare to utter such lies."

Erica signalled to me to be kind. She always did have a soft spot for the guy.

"Though why they should want to reward you is a mystery. How a stupid, impossible, talentless person like you can find someone to believe in one word you write is hard to imagine; and how they can reward you by giving you money and succour to carry on writing your drivel is even harder. Can you bung me a fiver? Please."

"No! Fuck off."

"You are a Hebrew, descended from kings. Your people brought intellect, morality, thought and poetry to this world. How could they also have given us you? They brought us justice, but where is the justice when the Arts Council of Great Britain reward you for this tripe you have churned out?"

I was enjoying this. He'd never read a single word of my work.

Then he smiled. He was like that, just like English weather. "Buy me a coffee, my dearest Hebraic poet." It was his survival technique that had always melted Erica. "And Bernard, while we're here, I've been thinking. You know you sometimes give me a few quid when you've got it? Well, we both know this can sometimes be awkward. When you refuse me and claim you're skint I am inclined to shout abuse and curses at you across the street. I hate doing this. It's so embarrassing, for me as well as you, and for everyone else in the street. But now that you are a person of fame and substance we can regularise the situation. I suggest you make a regular payment by standing order of five pounds per week from your bank to my newly opened Post Office savings account, and then I can enjoy both our friendship and your most generous and perpetuating donation."

I had to shove my fist into my mouth to keep down the hysteria.

Paul smirked. "Obviously you do not possess the wit, nor the courage, to appreciate such an elegant solution to our problem."

"Paul, I don't have a problem!"

"Please! I'm so sick of the streets and the shitbags of Rowton House. If you must refuse me money, then let me come and stay with you, just for a few days. It would be the act of a truly noble Hebrew."

I laughed. He looked like a pathetic Dickensian waif, and seemed more desperate than usual. "Did you say just for a few days?" My ears could hardly believe my mouth. It was all he needed. He was all over me with gratitude like a slobbering puppy. I fended him off and turned to Erica. "Why don't we let him? Just for a few days." Erica had experienced my brainstorms before. I was looking to her now to reject the idea out of hand.

She was silent. Then she laughed. Paul went to the counter to order us more coffee which I would be paying for.

"Now you really have flipped," she whispered.

"Rachmones! Compassion! Isn't that the basic tenet of our faith?"

"Suddenly you have faith? Jewish faith?"

"The matzo ball doesn't fall far from the tree," I said, trying to sound wise. "I've just had an attack of compassion."

"But he stinks. He'll stink our place out." It seemed we had reversed the order of things.

"So, you make him take a bath every day."

"It's too late for an old dog to learn new tricks."

"I'm an old dog. You taught me new tricks."

"His clothes, Bernard. They're saturated in filth."

"Change his clothes – change his life."

She shook her head, amazed.

"We must give him a chance. Nobody ever gave him a chance." I was getting quite carried away with impulsive generosity. Who knew where it might land me? We were about to give shelter to Soho's Don Quixote.

Paul was chatting to Mrs Molina behind the counter. A whiff of Camembert wafted toward us.

"Erica, you've got to tell him to wash."

"Me? Why me?"

"Because you do all the dirty work, remember? If he doesn't wash he doesn't come."

He returned, smiling.

"Paul, we've been thinking…"

He kissed us both. I held my breath. He danced, sitting in his chair. A five-year-old child living in the skin of a middle-aged man. "When can I move in?

"There's just one little thing you have to do for us first."

"What? Anything."

"You have to wash."

"Wash? I always wash. Why should I wash?"

"Paul! You must promise to have a bath every day."

"Bath? Why?"

"Paul, you stink."

"I stink?" He was astounded. "I stink?" He sniffed at his armpits. "I can't smell a stink."

"I'm telling you just that," Erica replied. God, she was brave. I wanted to hide under the table.

"Nobody has ever told me I stink," he said, on the verge of tears.

"Nobody's had the courage," I chipped in, summoning up some for myself.

"Go and wash somewhere. Have a good bath, and then come to Camberwell and live with us."

He got up and rose to his towering height. "You have hurt me, Erica, beyond understanding. I don't stink. I might smell a little. Nevertheless, to comply with your rules I shall take five baths daily for the few weeks I am with you."

"Few weeks!" I wailed, but he ignored me.

"And I shall move in tomorrow." With that he bowed and left.

That same evening the doorbell rang. It was Paul with a carrier bag of his possessions. He was dressed in green cavalry twill, the perfect English gentleman.

"How nice of you to allow me to come and live with you, albeit for only a month. An act of sheer beauty and delight."

He went into the tiny garden to smoke some weed but left his stink behind. The living room screeched with the sweet smell of a decaying corpse. It screamed as it rushed upstairs and filled the whole house. Cathy and Peter soon came down to investigate its origin. They laughed when we told them the whole ridiculous story – fortunately, they were madly in love and not easily upset.

Paul returned. He yawned, implying it was beddybyes time.

"Paul, did you take a bath?"

"I want to talk to you about that." He filled his pipe with such ceremony as befitted a country squire. Then he closed his eyes and was out like a light.

"He'll never have a bath. We're lumbered." I sighed. The enormity of my mad gesture had come home to roost. We pulled our mattress into the kitchen and slept there.

Next morning when we were barely awake we heard Adam laughing. I staggered into the living room to find Paul and him playing. Adam didn't seem to notice the smell, but then he was just a few months old. Back in bed we groaned and covered ourselves with blankets and laughed like the end of the world.

"Paul, I've run the water. Now will you take a bath?"

"I'm busy. Soon."

It was impossible. He wouldn't allow water anywhere near him.

We were paying the price for sins we had not yet committed.

We got him to sleep in the kitchen for a few nights, but then the stink seemed even more overwhelming, so we decided to put him in the little back room, well out of the way. Then every day we implored him to bathe, and every night agreed that he would certainly bathe tomorrow. He slept and snored like a newborn baby, but we couldn't. We would lie awake, holding our noses. We desisted from love-making. Who could make love with Paul spinning stench through the wall? His noxious cloud had even pervaded the garden. The neighbours would be beginning to think we had buried someone out there.

"I'm going to Spitalfields to contemplate the Hawksmoor church. I'll be back for supper. Incidentally, I love lamb stew," he announced one morning.

We took a walk down the corridor to his room and embarked on an inspection, holding our noses as we opened the door and peered gingerly inside. Lined up along the window ledge, with the sun shining through them, we saw a row of milk bottles, each filled to the brim with a golden liquid.

"Piss! Piss! Piss!" I screamed.

At first it didn't register with Erica. Her sheltered childhood sometimes got in the way of stark reality. It took her a few moments to understand. "Oh my God. He's peed in all the bottles," she said when she'd finally realised. "But why? There's a perfectly good lavatory just outside his door!"

"Poor bastard. Living rough for so long. No one to tell him, no one to look after him. Too much is wrong with Paul, I think."

"He's a useless, lazy bastard. Too lazy even to go to the lavatory in the night."

"We can't live like this."

"Well, he'll never leave. We'll never prise him out of here."

"It's too late for an old dog to learn to piss in the right place."

"So how do we get rid of him?"

Paul had gone too far. There was only one answer: "I've had an idea."

"Yes, we throw him out. We have to do it," she nodded.

"No! We move. Tomorrow." It was like pulling a house down because it needs decorating but it was a solution.

"Brilliant! Yes, we move. We leave the place to him. Anyway, I like moving."

Fond as we were of Paul, compassion could only stretch so far.

4

Seven Dials

The first person to greet us when we got to Torino's was Quentin. Quentin could be waspish and damning if the chemistry wasn't right but he had always been kind to me, especially when I first came to Soho and was so unsure of myself. Being accepted by Quentin gave me instant confidence. He had also taken immediately to Erica.

"You both seem perturbed," he observed. "Where are you hiding your usual ecstatic selves? Sit down and tell me all your woes."

We told him about Paul and the trouble we'd landed ourselves in, and he listened with his usual calm, illustrating the activity with his eyes and fingertips.

"Poor Paul," he said at length. "Poor you." Quentin never stood in judgement.

Roy Wingate and Johnny Noble, otherwise known as Niagara and Victoria Falls, flitted in and floated to our table. They pouted us all a kiss. Quentin asked if they happened to know of a flat going cheap within the Serene Republic.

"Now, that's very odd, Quentin!"

It transpired that Roy's landlady had stopped him on the stairs that very morning and asked him if he knew anyone looking for a place in Monmouth Street.

"Monmouth Street? No!" we hooted. We could hardly believe our luck. Not only would we get to escape from Paul Potts' piss bottles, we would also be going to live in the historic and notorious Seven Dials, birthplace of pornographic broadsheets and vice centre of London for hundreds of years. This was the place where a man still came at twilight to light all the gas lamps, and in the quiet, lonely evening, when all the typists had gone back to Borehamwood, ghosts of pimps and whores and good-time Charlies cavorted around the lampposts. There were cafés, book shops, experimental art galleries, prostitutes, transvestites, pub theatres, things that couldn't be experienced anywhere else in London. And there was Theatreland and Covent Garden market.

In the Seven Dials, we would be coming back down to land in the very beating heart of London.

Later we walked with Quentin along Oxford Street. The crowds pointed and ridiculed and shouted abuse. Quentin went right through them, seemingly oblivious, like a gay Moses, head held high, and led us to our new home. It was bare and perfect, and we could move in immediately.

Paul was staggered by our news. "How could you do this to me? What do I do now? Is there any room for me in your new place?"

"Sadly, no. You can barely swing a cat, if that's the kind of thing that gives you pleasure," I quipped. Some of Quentin's style had rubbed off on me.

"You give me a glimpse of paradise and then you take it away again," Paul cried, but I refused to be moved.

Settling in was immediate and magical, the absence of furniture intentional. It was wonderfully liberating to escape so completely from the East End, bug-ridden, furniture-crammed living rooms of my childhood. Erica and I could finally experience the luxury of being ourselves.

"Remind me never to cross the river ever again," I instructed her on our first night.

Just along Monmouth Street, towards Shaftesbury Avenue, others were also enjoying their freedom. Homosexuals who had previously been peeping out of the closet were now coming right out. They gathered in the As You Like It, the first café that almost dared to speak its name. These were men who were homosexual but weren't screaming queens. Symbols of hope adorned the walls, huge posters of film stars who had somehow survived against all the odds: Judy Garland, Alice Faye, Joan Crawford, Bette Davis, Rita Hayworth, Ann Sheridan, Barbara Stanwyck. I felt a real affinity for the crowd that gathered there – no doubt because we belonged to two persecuted minorities – and Erica and I used to sit in that café for hours at a time, revelling in the polari going on around us.

Apart from the queer café and Torino's, we spent a lot of time in St Giles churchyard, showing off our most remarkable baby boy and reading. I saw myself as a golem about to be activated and felt obliged to lounge around so that I would be ready when inspiration struck. Erica and I embarked on a rich diet of world drama. We produced each new play in our imagination, journeying through Andalusia with Lorca, spending time in pre-revolutionary Russia with Chekhov and Babel, lingering with O'Casey and colluding with Juno to confront the posturing Paycock. We went on our very own Yiddish odyssey through the forest of the *Oresteia* and got well and truly and wonderfully lost. Agamemnon was my uncle Hymie, Clytemnestra my auntie Sarah, Iphigenia my sad cousin Fay. I was Orestes, of course. I had come home to a family reunion to exact a terrible revenge on them all: success and fame.

Once I'd sold my remaining stock, I planned to push my bookstall back to Keeley's Yard and desist from real work forever. It was on my very last weekend of trading that a frumpy little woman came up to my stall and took me by surprise. At first I thought she might be a cleaning lady looking for culture, but then I saw that she was with someone, a nice Jewish boy called Maxwell Shaw who often came along to spend a few bob.

"How's life?" he asked, always one of the first things a Jewish boy asks another.

"Mustn't grumble," I replied, almost always the second thing a Jewish boy says to another. Then I proceeded to show off about all my rotten luck, about having to wait for something to happen after all the wonderful things that had happened to me: a new baby; writing my play; an Arts Council award for five hundred nicker; Mark Marvin recognising my true talent. The charlady seemed to be taking an interest.

"Bernard, have you met Joan Littlewood?"

"Hello," she said and smiled like an owl.

When I'd recovered myself – how could I have known it was Joan Littlewood when she was wearing such a ridiculous hat? – I said hello and told Joan about *The Hamlet of Stepney Green* and about my childhood just up the road from her in Stratford atte Bow. She could see that I was a clever dick but then we were in the same boat, both suffering from a surfeit of ego. She asked me to name my favourite play and I impressed her with a paean of love for the *Oresteia*.

"So why do you think the king obeyed the gods and sacrificed Iphigenia, his daughter?" she quizzed me.

"He was a neurotic Jewish father."

"He was Greek."

"Same difference."

She laughed. "I appreciate your attitude, Bernard, and would love to read your play."

I tried to remain calm and feign only slight interest. I needed to lose the enthusiasm of the amateur. On the other hand, it was common knowledge that this woman was a genius. If she did my play I'd be made. I tried pitching it about halfway. "Thanks. I'll send it to you."

Before she went she said a few words that I've always remembered. "Aeschylus is all about all of us, Bernard, the human family. He is writing about us. Why he has survived all this time is because we recognise ourselves in his work; each new generation sees a reflection of itself. His work tells us the things we already know: the fact that nothing changes." She smiled and walked on, but called back, "Send the play. Don't forget."

Would I ever. I rushed home and blurted out the news.

"Hold on. She may hate it," Erica warned.

Hate it? My play? God, my wife made me furious sometimes. As my safety valve, I knew she was obliged to continually remind me of the dangers of over-enthusiasm, but I wanted to enjoy myself. We definitely had an excuse for a party.

"A party? But why?"

"Because Joan Littlewood is going to read my play and love it! We have so many things to celebrate: us, Adam, this wonderful, if desperately cramped little flat, my play, my award. I want to spend some money, to show off, and to show those hopeless bums that I'm going to do something with my life."

Then I gave her my best shmooze so she'd have to melt.

5

The Party

We thought the Colony Room was a good place to start handing out verbal invitations, and somehow managed to get by Muriel, the guardian angel who sat at the door. We were just inside when Colin MacInnes came in, sucking on a strange fruit I didn't recognise.

"Haven't you ever seen a passion fruit?" he asked, and chucked it over to me. "Try it. They're delicious."

"It's so wrinkled." I threw it back to him.

"Yeah! Just like a black boy's balls," he said, and smiled wickedly. He was pissed. He also seemed to have taken a liking to us. He came over and kissed Erica on the cheek and then turned to me and slobbered kisses all over my face.

"Forgive me. How do you do? I'm Colin MacInnes."

He looked as if the announcement should have an effect but, apart from seeing him at Torino's, we didn't know much about him. Still, I took the opportunity to invite him to our party and explained our reasons for having it.

To our embarrassment, he then announced us to all the denizens of the club. "This is Bernard and Erica Kops, everyone. Bernard has written a play called *The Hamlet of Stepney Green*, and you're all invited to his party."

From this boozy beginning there developed a lasting and crazy friendship between Colin MacInnes and Erica and me. Colin seemed to know about everything: human nature, history, geography, art, literature; and he made it all come alive for us. He also had a fabulously impressive family tree which brought the snob in me right to the surface. When Colin's parents first brought him to England from Australia, the first place he visited was 10 Downing Street, and Mr Asquith the Prime Minster sat Colin on his knee. Burne-Jones was a blood relation; another Ruskin; another Rudyard Kipling. No wonder his tongue and intellect were razor sharp. Yet he always treated us with unbridled adoration. Maybe it was because both he and I took refuge in calling ourselves anarchists, or maybe he just wanted to get close to a couple who didn't argue all the time. And maybe it was because, like Paul Potts, he loved the Hebrews. It seemed to be the thing with some Christian gentlemen.

He also loved the East End and had got himself a place there. He relished the bustle of the Jewish community, the Jewish markets and restaurants – this whole world that I'd spent my youth so desperately trying to escape. It was a far cry from the Australian outback of his youth and the closed, pinched world of Angela Thirkell, his novelist mother whom he detested so much. Walking around the East End with Colin, in the company of Purcell, Hawksmoor, Jack the Ripper, the Huguenots and the Old Nichol, was an enlightening lesson in history.

It was from others that I gradually learned of his prodigious output, his fame and the respect in which he was held. He once gave me a copy of his book, *June in Her Spring*. I was off reading at the time so I slipped it to Erica. When Colin later asked me what I had thought of it, I told him that it was a marvellous evocation of life in rural Australia, and that it was incredibly true and very moving. He cupped my cheeks and kissed me lovingly. I didn't feel the least twinge of guilt – Erica and I were one and the same after all.

Other times he laughed at my opinions. "You are probably the most naive person I have ever met," he said. Although when I told him that I thought the essays he was working on were utterly brilliant, he thought me most intelligent.

Leaving the Colony that night, with Colin halfway down the stairs in pursuit, we almost collided with a figure coming towards us.

"Out of my way! I need a drink." It was Robert Colquhoun. I had seen him and his lover Robert MacBryde hitting each other in the street several times. They had a formidable reputation. "Who the fuck are you?" he growled in best Glasgowese.

"I'm Bernard Kops. A dramatist."

"Well fuck off, you cunt."

"Would you like to come to my party on Saturday?"

"What's it in aid of, you shit pillock?"

"It's on account of getting an Arts Council award."

"Go to fucking hell. Out of my fucking way." He pushed past us and growled his way up the stairs. When he reached Colin he gave him a wet slobbering kiss, smack on the lips.

"Colquhoun's a very talented painter. One of the best," Colin told us a little while later at Torino's. Then he went silent. Then morose. We started off for home.

All the beasts were emerging in Old Compton. Francis Bacon appeared like a creature in a crazy seaside mirror. With him, deep in conversation, was Harry Diamond, soon to be immortalised by Lucian Freud, along with a threatening rubber plant, all his pent-up violence seeping out of the canvas. I approached them both and invited Harry to the party. Bacon always blanked me but Harry was different – there was an unspoken bond between all us East End Jews. Diaspora Umbilica. "Thank you, Bernie. Love to," Harry said, and they continued on their way.

The word got around. A Saturday without a party was like a ship without water, and that night we were all tossing beautifully on an alcoholic sea. My guard was down for once and I was as pissed as the rest. Don Flowerdew was there, in Soho black as usual, oblivious to the crowd and crouched in the corner reading *Maldoror*. The Chava Queen was going through the usual ritual of taking her clothes off and singing "My Yiddisher Momma"; the Countess was quoting Dante in impeccable Italian; Ironfoot Jack was spieling kabbalistic mumbo jumbo on the stairs with his hand up the skirt of a giggling mystery; and three members of the Socialist Party of Great Britain, a third of its entire membership, were arguing about which one of them would be Prime Minister when they got to power.

Robert Colquhoun staggered over at some point early in the evening. "So what's this party for, you lousy little shit?"

"It's because of my award from the Arts Council."

"You're a fucking lousy painter, Bernard."

I laughed. "You're dead right."

This didn't satisfy him, so he began arguing with his lover instead. After a while he slapped MacBryde so hard across the face that blood gushed out his mouth. "My lover! My lover! What have I done to my lover?" he was asking no one in particular when David Archer and Colin MacInnes arrived.

Roy Wingate made a dash across my line of vision for a small blond lad. "Would you care for some marijuana?" he asked him tenderly.

It was so very satisfying to be throwing an average Soho party.

★

Tony Mayer, the Cultural Attaché of the French Embassy whom I'd met at Mark Marvin's, appeared a while later.

"Ooh-la-la!" he chirped as he kissed me on both cheeks. "Bernard! My absolute pleasure." Then he looked more closely and frowned. "But where is your duffel coat? Your sweater? You look far too clean." His eyes were swivelling around the room, goggling the young men, but he kept our conversation going at the same time. "Bernard, I must tell you, before I came this evening Darius Milhaud called me from Paris."

"Who?"

"He loved your play. He wants to compose the music." He grabbed my arm. "It's a great honour. He's a great composer."

"Tell him thanks, but no thanks," I said. I was so bloody-minded in those days. "I want to use Yiddish folk songs." I turned to Erica. "The play is about the death of a community, right? The music must be a traditional threnody of a race that is no more. I don't want a composer, I want a decomposer. All the Jews are dead. They're all gone. They are all decomposers." Who was this morose git talking?

"He's very drunk," Erica explained, looking around alarmed at our Pandora's box, wide open now and full of cavorting strangers. The floor was about to fall in at any moment.

"Jews can't drink," I heard myself spouting as I drank more and more. "Jews can't drink, never. Far too dangerous."

"Jean Cocteau is coming over in a week's time," Tony continued despite me, "and staying with me in Chester Square. You must come to dinner. He would be charmed to meet you. But you must not dress like this. You look really beautiful in your bohemian. Promise?"

"*L'oiseau chante avec ses doigts*," I replied. It was the one line of French I remembered from *Orphée*.

We were interrupted by a furious knocking at the door. I seemed to be the only one to notice, so I went down and answered it.

"Bernard, I'm an actress with Theatre Workshop and I heard Joan and Gerry talking and I know they are doing your play and I wondered if you could put a word in with Joan, because I would just love to be in it and I would do anything, anything, if you would consider having me," she gasped all in one breath, and brought her body up against mine. "I know you are a genius. I will do anything," she whispered in my ear. "I'll do anything, anything, you understand, to be in it. Anything."

It was all too surreal. I pulled away and rushed up the stairs and darted into Adam's room. He wasn't there but the Chava Queen was. She was on top of a young man, on top of a pile of coats. "Fuck me. Fuck," she was crying while the young man underneath gave expression to his primal ecstasy. He opened his eyes and saw me. "Sorry. I'm an accountant," he remarked, before throwing off the Queen, buttoning his flies and rushing out of the room. How did an accountant manage to cross the Stygian river and fall head over heels under a Sohocialist? I followed him sharpish in case I was pulled down as a substitute.

Mark Marvin's face loomed. His laid-back New York sophistication was somehow out of place in this sinking wreck, but he soon started rocking to Elvis Presley. Adam appeared from nowhere, crying. I grabbed him just in time but I was going down and down beneath the surface. "I can't swim!" I screamed.

People danced around me laughing and Erica speeded over with a magnificent breast-stroke and gave me some sexy mouth-to-mouth resuscitation.

"I'll soon have some news for you," Mark said, pulling me to one side. "Joan Littlewood is doing it."

"I'm glad," I replied. "Even great directors need to get their leg over."

Erica gently pulled me to the other room and we collapsed on to the bed. Parties were glimpses of hell. Paul Potts entered our sanctuary to prove it and threw his stinking, greasy coat over me.

"Bernard, please don't ever try to make me believe that you have one iota of talent. You have the head of King David and the intelligence of a flea," he announced and came down to cuddle me, whispering his love song. "Bung us a fiver. No one is watching."

"What's a nice Jewish boy doing amongst all these drunken goyim?" my mother asked from nowhere, shaking her sad head and wagging a bony finger at me.

"Yes, mother, I'm not joining you just yet."

When I woke up the next morning, Erica, Adam and I were curled up together in the basement. I got up and stumbled up the stairs through the wreckage. Everyone had gone except the Chava Queen and her accountant. He was fast asleep, sprawled on the lino, snoring like a pig. The Queen had eye-black smudged all down her face and was crying and staring into a mirror, still singing about her Yiddisher Momma and how she missed her more than ever.

I made a call to Theatre Workshop. I got Gerry Raffles, Joan's partner. Joan wasn't there, he said, but yes, he was able to confirm that they would be producing *The Hamlet of Stepney Green*.

"When?"

"That is yet to be decided. Joan will be in touch to arrange a meeting."

I rushed down to Erica and shook her awake to tell her the good news.

6

Joan and Gerry

A couple of days later Erica and I set out to breathe the holy, radical dust of the Theatre Royal, Stratford East, one of the most creative and prominent drama companies in the world. In our excitement, we left far too early, so we decided to drop off at Whitechapel on the way, to drink in some of the atmosphere that had inspired my play in the first place. Sentimental journeys up to now had always been a dead loss, but with a shining future ahead of me I felt free to enjoy it. What would I ever write about if not this, after all? It was the only world I knew, as sure as matzos fly.

Things were certainly changing fast in Whitechapel, and not for the best. Three hundred thousand Jews had once crammed themselves into these mean streets, but by 1958 only about six thousand remained. The others had moved out along the North-West passage to Willesden, Hendon, Edgware and Golders Green. Their Yiddish love songs, curses and lullabies had all wound down, and the place was dying. Even as we ambled along Old Montague Street to let Adam experience part of his heritage, the backbone of one little school was being ripped apart. The all-night vapour baths in Brick Lane had closed too; the chains on the door were all rusted over.

To cheer me up we made for the little kosher restaurant in Wentworth Street, just opposite the kosher chicken slaughter yard. We passed all the open barrels of pickled cucumber and pickled and shmaltz herrings on the way. It was in this very street that my play's old man Sam Levy makes his living, and his dying, from perpetually dipping his hands into the barrels. We stopped for a moment to look into the execution yard. The slaughterer was having a quick fag, his white apron decorated like a Jackson Pollock, splattered with blood. When we turned round and crossed the road, we found that our little restaurant wasn't there.

"Gonna take a sentimental journey," I sang with half-closed eyes.

"Let's go to Bloom's and have latkes instead," Erica suggested.

The latkes in Bloom's were dead-weight delicious and just the thought of them made us even hungrier. Food was far more important than any of the usual neurotic conversation; it was that stuff that you had once slaved your guts out for, and dreamed about. By the time we got to Aldgate East we were perishing. In the window we watched a man cutting slice upon slice of a great chunk of pickled meat. Latkes and salt beef: perfect partners, as matched as Bernard and Erica, Joan and Gerry.

We'd just about finished the serious business of removing all traces of our food, when out of the window we saw Colin lope past; he lived just round the corner in Hanbury Street. We waved him inside and invited him to join us but he declined. He was on his way back to his pad, he said. It was because of Colin that I knew what "pad" meant. Colin's pad was a small, spartan attic room designed for sleep and work and nothing else. It had a bed, a table, a chair and a typewriter.

"What are you doing in the East?" he asked.

The food was over so I could talk. I told him. The old waiter slouched over, dragging his weary feet, none too happy for witnessing Colin's hello kisses. Such goings-on were not much appreciated in the shtetl. On top of that, Colin waved away the menu and ordered just a lemon tea, which was a terrible insult. The waiters relied on stuffing you to absolute contentment if they were to get any sort of decent tip out of you.

"Be careful," he said. "They're a tricky lot."

"Who? The waiters?"

"No, Theatre Workshop. Joan Littlewood and Gerry Raffles." Colin was always naughty like this, rocking your boat just when it was sailing so serenely. As far as I was concerned Joan Littlewood could sit on the right hand of God. "Malicious rumours abound about them, Bernie, and they must be true."

Only the dead desist from gossip but I protested. "I don't want to know! Joan is a genius and she is directing my play. She has created a whole new theatre style. She has given the theatre back to us, the people, where it belongs."

He laughed. "Bernie, you're a hopeless innocent. Did you know she comes to the East End looking like a frump, but under her snood she actually hides a hairstyle just created by some posh hairdresser in Mayfair?"

"So, why shouldn't a lady make herself beautiful?"

"And the actors work for a pittance. They're all in it together, Joan says, rallying her troops. She says she's one of them, joyously slaving in penury beside them. Meanwhile, she and Gerry retire for the night to Gerry's yacht moored somewhere on the Thames, the *Gerry Dearie*."

"So why can't a socialist own a yacht? Is there a rule book that says it is proscribed for a comrade to possess a yacht? Good luck to them, I say." Colin was the bitchiest I had ever seen him and I wondered if he was harbouring some resentment at my finally getting my play on. But that was crazy. Colin was the last person you would expect to suffer the joys of *schadenfreude*. He was universally successful.

"And when they took the company to Moscow, again it was all hands to the plough. Up the Workers. We all strive together! But all the time Joan and Gerry were living it up in the best state hotel, whilst their actors dossed on the floor of the theatre, after slaving away all day for a pittance. Joan just kept on clobbering them with slogans and the same old crap about all men and women being equal." His eyes twinkled with mischief. "Take no notice of me. I'm just a bitter old queen."

We were not unhappy to see him slope to the door, but he turned back before getting there and came back to the table.

He smiled. "I'm sorry." He was as contrite as a boy who had just broken a window with his catapult.

Joan greeted us warmly and I wondered if she really did have a posh hairstyle under that rather eccentric hat. Could this really be one of the greatest drama directors in the world? Was this the woman who almost single-handed had overturned and eradicated the Theatre of Reassurance? She looked more like an impish schoolboy, a refugee from the *Beano*. Her smile was broad enough to compete with Joe E. Brown. Colin's words of warning, whether they were the truth or malicious lies, made no difference. Joan Littlewood was my saviour, come hell or Highgate. Besides, even if his words were true, that was all to the good. A genius could not be logically understood; the more many-layered and complex she was, the more interesting she had to be. And I was beginning to realise that nobody ever spoke the truth in the theatre. I was perfectly suited to this way of life. My real problem was Erica: she always spoke the truth and expected the truth in return. How many times had I read her a line from my play to be told that it was utterly useless?

"How dare you?" I'd demand. "I know the line is good."

"It's a cliché, Bernard."

"It's perfect. It's beautiful. I feel it."

"Believe me, I'm telling you the truth."

"How dare you tell me truth!" and I'd lose my temper and shout, knowing she was right. Unfortunately, she nearly always was, and in those early days I was often overwhelmed by a crimson fury at realising it.

The foyer was buzzing with young actors, waiting for an audition with Joan. They were locked in a sort of euphoric terror. Joan herself was being pulled from pillar to post, but she found time to have a cup of tea with us. Colin was a real bastard, I decided, denigrating such a worthy, patient, committed and concerned human being.

Over tea she confirmed that she had accepted my play. Apparently I had obeyed all the necessary rules for the making of true drama. "You've somehow discovered that the dramatist must be specific. If he or she attempts universality it becomes preachy and specious, but if you are specific and bring to life your small universe you may well write something universal. O'Casey's little room in Dublin becomes every little room in the world. Your play is a sort of tone poem, a song for a dying community." It all sounded perfect and I puffed up at my own instinctive cleverness. "You have recreated the traditional Yiddish theatre, not the shmaltzy sort of stuff you sometimes see in the Grand Palais," she continued. "And you puncture your action with songs, that's good. That's better than exposition. It's deep in your bones, in your people, in their joys and tribulations. You didn't come from Russia, Russia came from you."

I didn't have the heart to tell her that I didn't come from Russia, or even it from me, but by way of Amsterdam before my father found refuge in Stepney.

Later I sat in the auditorium while this remarkable woman conducted auditions for her next production. Erica stayed in the bar with Adam. I felt privileged. My work was about to be touched by genius.

A young man inched himself to the centre of the stage. Joan asked him what treat he had in store and he nervously declared that he was about to suffer the slings and arrows of Hamlet.

He started to clear his throat when Joan shouted, "No! Fuck that! I don't want any of that!" The poor kid was marooned centre stage, scared shitless.

"Just make us laugh!" she shouted, and he burst out crying and ran off-stage.

I laughed, and hated my reaction.

Joan turned to me. "We want real people, people with guts." There was a madness in her method, but it obviously worked. After all, she infused the British stage for years to come with some of the best actors in the world. I felt out of my depth just watching her.

"How old are you?" Joan demanded of one flouncy bird with too much mascara who had to be forty-plus.

"How old do you want me to be?" was her reply. Joan was very nice to that one.

Later Joan and I rejoined Erica front-of-house. Joan was silent and thoughtful for a time. Then she dropped her bombshell. "Bernard, you must play David in your play. I'm giving you the part."

David was the lead. He WAS the Hamlet of Stepney Green. I was immensely flattered. "You think I can do that? I can act?" I asked, delighted. I turned to Erica. She was not jumping up and down with joy. "Why not?" I demanded. "You know I acted for five years, before I developed a brain and grew up."

"Bernard, you were the biggest ham." The girl who wouldn't say boo to a goose when we first met had obviously found her tongue. As for me, I could already hear the adoring whispers of my future audiences.

"If you can write David, you can act David," Joan reasoned.

"Balls!" Erica replied, for me. "Bernard's writing about a prostitute at the moment. Does that mean he can also play the prostitute?"

I think Joan was rather amused at our division, but I was furious. "Why did you say that?" I demanded when she had left us and gone back inside. "You know I would love to be up there, on the stage. You know I'm a show-off. I would be fantastic."

"You would be laughable."

"Now she won't do my play."

"Don't be ridiculous." The sweet, compliant girl had disappeared and this woman stood there, no longer adoring me without question. I wanted to plead like a little boy but I bit my tongue.

She smiled and gathered Adam, the pram and herself together and hurried for the exit. "I'm going home."

"But I can't come now. Please! It will offend. The future of my play is at stake." I was practically begging.

"Do what you like. See you later." And she was gone.

✱

I returned to the inner sanctum. Joan smiled and I sat down beside her. Another young man walked boldly on to the stage. I could see her wicked expression as she prepared to take the stuffing out of him.

"Make me laugh!" she called.

"Alright then!" the boy shouted back and he took out his shmeckle and pissed all over the stage.

"Marvellous!" Joan rocked with laughter and shouted, "Alright, darling, we'll have you."

Gerry Raffles appeared and looked surprised to see me. He was a nice Jewish boy from a nice, wealthy Jewish family from Manchester and we had met before. I tried to shake his hand but he seemed furious.

"What are you doing here?" he demanded.

"Er…I'm with Joan. She asked me. I'm Bernard Kops."

"I know who you are. No one's allowed in here when Joan's working. Out! How dare you be in here. Get out!"

I had no idea what was going on. I looked at Joan but she just shrugged, so I left.

I phoned Erica, blurted out what had happened and burst into tears.

"Come home now," she said.

"It's all over before it's begun."

"Come home. It'll be alright."

When I got home we cuddled all the way to the bed, but later, in the dark, I worried.

"Maybe tomorrow Theatre Workshop will love me again," I ventured.

"Unfortunately, darling, you're cursed with talent," she said.

"Cursed? Unfortunately? I don't understand."

"Original, first-rate talent is difficult. Second-rate talent is more easily recognised."

"Yes. Exactly. Why don't I just write crap and settle for an easy life?"

"Second-rate talent goes to the top. First-rate talent goes to the madhouse."

"I've been there," I said. "Not going again."

She laughed. "You are what you are, thank God. Let's open some wine."

At that moment I would have gladly given up all my dreams to stay with this woman. If only I could kill the urge to write. We finished the bottle and went silly, tangoing around the room. One half of a bottle of Chianti and I belonged to the universe.

"I wish I could give up this lark," I said.

Erica smiled and didn't believe me. I often wondered why she stayed with me. If I were her I would have left me long ago.

7

On Our Way

A week flew past and we didn't hear a dicky bird from Theatre Workshop. I tried to stay sane but ended up pacing the room like a caged lion on heat. I was certainly hell to live with. I telephoned several times but always to be told that Joan was busy and would call back.

I hadn't heard from Colin for some time either, but his absences were characteristic. He would regularly disappear on love safaris into deepest Notting Hill. When he finally turned up to pay us a visit, he dived ravenously into breakfast, as if to make up for lost time, and I told him my woes, the happenings down at Stratford atte Bow.

"Joan is a genius and now she's gone cold on me," I concluded.

"Beware of left-wingers bearing promises," he advised.

"But, Colin," I protested, "you're left wing."

"I'm way out, man, beyond all wings." Brubeck was playing 'Take Five' on the Third Programme. Colin jigged in his chair, like a shrivelled old balding eagle. "I'm wingless. I think for myself."

"Left wing! Right wing! Two wings flapping the same old bird." Erica had beat us all to the age of cynicism. I still nurtured the hope that the telephone would ring at any moment.

Replenished with breakfast, Colin was now in full flight around the room. "Beware of fucking Marxists. Anarchism's the answer, Bernie. It's a wonderful place to be. On your tod, distanced from all that jargon." He gave us all wet kisses and loped to the door. Nobody ever loped like Colin MacInnes. "Baby, be way out in no-man's land. The air is cleaner out here." And he flapped his wings and flew away.

We carried on waiting for news. I found it hard to deal with the vacuum. Everyone seemed to know that Theatre Workshop was supposed to be doing my play – the tobacconist in Old Compton, the fishmonger in Earlham Street, the undertaker downstairs, Asher the greengrocer in Neal's Yard. "So, when are we going to see this masterpiece of yours?" they asked me. I felt like a pregnant woman who had passed her delivery date. All I could do was apologise sheepishly. Or I invented big lies, like that it was all to do with a big American deal. Sure I was a fraud, but it was easier on my ego. I started crossing over to the other side when I saw a familiar face coming towards me.

Weeks passed and the silence was resounding. My fingers were itching to dial the digits, but Erica always restrained me. Eventually, people stopped asking questions. I began to get used to the idea that fame had approached, taken one look and run the other way. So, I would have to stand behind a bookstall for the rest of my days. There were worse things; it was still better than work. That's what I told myself, anyway. All the time my belly belied my logic. Every time the telephone rang I would run to it.

Then one afternoon, when I was in the middle of baking scones from a packet I'd bought, it rang with a certain tone. Erica got to it before me, which was surprising since she usually avoided the telephone like the plague. She was evacuated to Yorkshire when she was four, not fully understanding that her parents wanted her to survive the German bombs, and she couldn't bear to hear them speaking to her from London, all the time depriving her of their love.

"It's Frank Hauser," she told me. "The Oxford Playhouse."

I answered in a quickly upholstered flat voice, trying to hide any trace of excitement. Hauser spoke really fast, rattling away like a machine gun. He told me he had got my play from the Arts Council and had just finished reading it, and wanted to produce it as soon as possible. One minute you're in the doldrums, the next you're riding high, about to sweep into the halls of fame.

"How soon?"

"Next month?"

"Next month! My God!" Nowadays it takes forever, often longer. Everything has to be scheduled years in advance. You know you'll be dead and long gone before the royalties start to flow. I covered the phone and mouthed the news to Erica, and then arranged to lunch with Frank in a Polish restaurant in Heath Street the following day.

When I put the phone down we danced to our favourite Yiddish record to celebrate. The high male voice sang something like, "Momma, stop shtipping the lodger upstairs. I'm starving. Come down and feed me."

"What about Joan Littlewood?" Erica asked, when we'd worn ourselves out.

"Fuck Joan Littlewood. No! On second thoughts, I'd rather not." I had foregone the uncertainty of waiting for a genius in favour of attaching myself to the certainty of an unknown quantity.

I phoned Joan immediately to break the news and was relieved to be told I'd have to leave a message.

Frank and I fressed eagerly, like two nice Jewish boys, leaving the words till later. I found a few words to compliment the waiter on their delicious gefilte fish. "Of course," I added, "the Jews gave the recipe to the Poles originally."

"On the contrary," the waiter told me, "gefilte fish was invented by the Poles, and the Jews stole it from them."

Our silent war lasted even beyond the strudel, during which he muttered the impossible notion that the Jews had also pinched tailoring from the Poles, plus their dark sense of humour.

Polish waiters aside, I hit it off with Frank Hauser. He seemed an unusually happy and modest man, so much so I wondered how he had survived in the shark-infested waters of theatre.

I was now able to cross the road without having to avoid all the concerned faces. I could even answer their smarmy questions. "Yes, it's going on very soon. I can give you the exact date. We open on May nineteenth this year at the Oxford Playhouse. Make sure you book early."

They were all delighted, of course, but did I denote a trace of disappointment? I was, after all, becoming an expert on subtext.

A few days later we were pulled out of the arms of Murphy by a phone call.

"Bernie, have you seen the *News Chronicle*? Rush out and buy the *News Chronicle*." It was my brother Dave, almost hysterical. Who was I not to listen to my older brother? We rushed out to buy a copy and there on the front page was an enormous photo of Erica, Adam and myself. We looked so beautiful. I stood in the street and almost kissed us. My exciting and wonderful future was now an official and ordained fact, and it could never be unprinted.

We loved Litvinoff's article. We laughed at it between the incessant telephone calls from friends and people I could not recall ever having known. It was the usual Fleet Street tale, the one they never tire of using: rags to riches, the sudden journey from obscurity to fame. They didn't mention the drugs, the addiction, the psychosis after my mother died. Apparently I had just appeared, as if conjured up by Houdini. There was no room for all the poverty and the nightmare of my days in Belmont psychiatric hospital, and for how I reached the end of the road just before Erica appeared. I had died and this was my second coming. I was more than gratified. Not a single piece of my actual work had yet appeared on stage or in print and here I was being loved and hailed.

I didn't actually accost strangers in the street to show them the article, but I did carry the newspaper around with me for a few days, and whip it out, with the joy of a flasher, wanting to see the reaction of my so-called friends. I took cruel enjoyment from searching their faces for a twinge of disappointment.

My best friend before Erica was Jack, an ex-paratrooper who dropped out of the sky one day into the French Café and landed on my table. We were as mad as each other and soon became inseparable. Jack was to become an illustrator, one of the best in the racket. On the afternoon of the *News Chronicle* article, he hugged me with all his strength. "I'm so happy for you, it couldn't happen to a nicer guy. You deserve it all, Bernard," he told me warmly.

Jack was happily married then, but years later I bumped into his wife in Waitrose after they had acrimoniously torn each other apart. I said that I missed seeing her and Jack and she was delighted to enlighten me.

"Remember that day you were all over the *Chronicle*? Well, I was there with him. Guess what? Your best friend Jack got himself into a jealous rage and started jumping all over your photo screaming, 'Why him? Why him? Why not me?' In the end he tore the newspaper apart completely, he was so furious."

8

The Opening

In those days writers, especially dramatists, made good copy. In the late fifties we were popping up all over the place, and strange, a lot of us were Jewish. Maybe it was because we had been tempered in Jewish homes, where if you didn't talk up for yourself you were drowned out by your siblings.

We were the first bubbles on the boiling surface of social change that was taking place. The Victorian era with all its rigid values had only really come to an end around 1945. My father, trapped in desperate poverty and almost blind from a lifetime working as a leather clicker in a shoe factory, had told me that a poor Jewish boy from the East End had no right to be ambitious, but I had refused to accept my place. Then when the Cold War started, we took off. The new writers brought a totally new scenario to the theatre and in our wake new actors emerged, who in turn brought audiences who recognised and identified with the dreams taking place up there on the stage. The Theatre of Reassurance died, and we got the column inches. We were the pop stars of our time. Tight-arsed little English gels from television begged you to appear on *Tonight* or *Late Night Line-Up*. My opinion was sought on world events – what the hell did I know about world events? – on the family, racism, how to make latkes. I just loved shooting the rapids of my big mouth. And I positively bathed in the glow of being recognised in the street.

I even suffered all those new friends, those Sad Boys of the Afternoon, with delight. They hung on my words, and would jump to my command. My shit didn't stink. I was wisdom incarnate. I had become a sort of demi-god because my face had been plastered across the newspapers.

Erica was also excited at the avalanche overtaking us. It meant the end of our day-to-day struggle to survive. It meant identity. It meant we were doing something with our lives.

"What will we do if we wake up and all this has vanished?" I'd ask her.

"We'll return to the bookstall and that will be good enough," she'd say, but I knew she wanted more.

Arnold Wesker came into our lives around that time. He struck me as a man of great charm and enthusiasm. First impressions usually reveal the truth; it's only later that you lose sight of the person. We were often mistaken for each other, probably because we shared a similar background, although Arnold's family was far more politically motivated than mine ever were – when you are as poor as we were you use all your energy just trying to climb out of the shit. We both came from East End Jewish families; we both had fathers who were pretty well defeated by the struggle to survive; and we both had incredible mothers who had somehow survived that struggle. In fact, we each proved to the other that we weren't unique, and I don't think it made either of us particularly comfortable.

Rehearsals started at the Oxford Playhouse. It was do or die time. Erica gave me a hard time by reminding me I was mortal. Our days were full of apprehension, but our nights were serene. As the Talmud whispers in its more intimate moments, "When the bedroom is happy, every room is happy."

The actors loved me, but then actors are always able to switch on their love at a moment's notice, just like children. John Fraser, a beautiful young Scot, was playing David Levy, my crooning hero. Joss Ackland, still fresh from South Africa, took the part of Mr Stone. Harold Lang, God bless him, was Sam, David's father.

I thought Harold was a genius, the way he talked about theatre and about acting. He would spend hours in the dressing room before the curtain making up, with a gaggle of the other actors gathered around his mirror. In my acting days in the fit-up actors only ever talked about the fish and chips their landlady had promised them for dinner, or about their horse which had come in last, but here was a different breed. These were actors with intelligence, who talked about acting and politics, acting and sex, and the subtext of subsex.

I did have a problem with their attempts at a Jewish accent. They were in danger of becoming caricatures, oy vay kids. In those days there were no yardsticks, so it was left to me. I told them to forget trying to produce a Jewish voice, or they would become so fixed on this alone it would choke them. I acted out all my aunts for them. They weren't Jewish characters; they were human beings who happened to be Jewish.

The company, for a time, was just like a family. During the first read-through the actors would sometimes look up from the text, catch my eye and smile and pout me a kiss. I overheard some of them at a tea-break.

"He's like a new O'Casey."

Gosh, I thought, I'm a new O'Casey.

"I'm a new O'Casey," I told Erica later. She hooted.

"You were right. I'm not a new O'Casey," I said a few days later, after hearing the actors discussing me further, "but perhaps I have a soupçon of O'Neill?"

"I've changed my mind," I told Erica the next day. "I'm not like O'Casey. I'm more like a new sort of Jewish Tennessee Williams. Or maybe a new blend of Ionesco and Anski. Or possibly I have a *frisson* of the Clifford Odets."

She tried hard to keep me grounded. "You are you. You are not like anyone else."

Frank Hauser was inspiring, and his energy prodigious. He had the gift of the gab and proved to be a clever sod, but somehow he was kosher. I trusted him from the start – his primary love and enthusiasm was for the text and not for an ism. The only cause he was obsessed with was the cause of theatre and making the play good enough to put before an audience. And he had such a captivating way. He dealt with his actors with dynamic energy and a touch of good old-fashioned shmooze. "Babies! Babies! Please! Listen!" He'd clap his hands and they'd all come to heel. "Listen!"

Frank always called the actors babies and they did seem to need a lot of nuzzling and kissing. One morning I walked into the rehearsal room just as they were about to start and nodded, I thought to everyone.

At coffee break a young girl came over and, admonishing me with a smile, said, "You never said good morning to me. You said good morning to everyone else."

I explained that it had been a collective sort of good morning.

"But you never looked at me when you said it," she said and pouted. "You looked at everyone else."

We checked into Oxford's Randolph Hotel before opening night. When we stepped inside its posh interior, a beatific, roseate glow descended upon me. Little Bernie Kops from the East End had come a long way. What a pity my mother, who defended me against the rest of the family right to the edge of her coffin, still insisting that I would one day release her from poverty and take her to Torquay, wasn't alive to witness this.

When we went into the hotel's sumptuous restaurant I knew I was dreaming. A woman waved us over to her table. She was grand, loud, and ugly beautiful.

"How do you do, Bernard Kops," she said. "I'm Caryl Brahms and this is my friend and writing partner, Ned Sherrin. I am here to review your play tonight and I do hope it is an enormous success."

"Of course it will be a success." Why shouldn't it be, I wondered.

They laughed at my bravado, but I was really big-mouthing my innocence. I had every confidence that nothing could fail. No wonder I would fall so hard in the years to come.

The theatre was crammed that evening: friends, critics, notables. A lot of publicity ballyhoo had preceded this opening. There'd been stories about my background and my present family life and what I ate for breakfast. *Vogue* had done a piece on my 'hooded sense of fate'. They'd all insisted on calling me a barrow boy, although it conjured up an image far from the reality. I had sold second-hand books from a barrow at Cambridge Circus, not cauliflower in Berwick Street.

I had kept my father and my brothers and sisters, and cousins and aunties and uncles away – I didn't fancy a crowd of loud-mouthed East End fans getting up the noses of the critics – but a few of my old Soho friends had hitched up to Oxford for the event, looking rather conspicuous in their bohemian garb against all that respectable academia. I was pulled and pummelled all over the place, introduced to people, trying to be polite, doing crappy small talk. Fenella Fielding wished me luck and kissed me with her eyelashes. I had heard her Hedda Gabler on the radio and thought she was wonderful. I even spotted Richard Burton. He was a friend of Frank's and the theatre and had put money towards the production. I was thrilled. W. H. Auden, with his Clapham Junction face, was already in his cups, surrounded by giggling admirers in the bar. When I was introduced I hoped he'd come up with a memorable line, like, "We must love one another or die," but his handshake was limp and he gazed over my head into the mirror. In the end Erica came and found me and ordered me to stop looking over my shoulder at the famous faces; it smacked of naiveté, she said.

Her hand tightened around mine as the curtain went up and I closed my eyes. I had thought it would be enjoyable but it turned out to be an endurance test. I was somewhere else. The drama flew above my head; only the laughter of the audience gave me hope, but I couldn't be sure whether they were laughing at me or for me.

"Was it good? Is it a success?" I asked Erica when the curtain finally came down. How does one know? Erica was just as nonplussed. The actors taking their call were smiling and looking down in my direction, but then, who could trust little babies?

I saw Colin a few rows ahead. He had a pen and pad in his hand and was sitting amongst the Elders of Fleet Street. He turned round and gave me an antipodean thumbs up and I sent out a warm wave of love to him. His lived-in face was giving nothing away. I would almost have preferred to have been back in Belmont: at least you knew where you were in there. All this was confusion. My knuckles were white from grasping Erica's hands.

Frank had said earlier that no matter what happened, even if the audience called for me, he wouldn't allow me to go up on the stage. But now he grabbed me and pushed me forward.

"Up you go, Bernie."

"But you said..."

"Forget what I said. Get up there."

Who was I to argue? I stumbled and bowed and thanked my wife, Frank and the cast, and from then on the night was a merry-go-round of laughing, kissing and back-slapping.

At one point the gleaming face of a man I had never seen before loomed close. "Mr Kops, I saw your play this evening..."

Oh God, another sycophant, I thought, and braced myself.

"...and I just wanted to tell you I hated it," he said.

We all laughed and drank the fizz. Surely life couldn't get any better than this?

But as the party started to fizzle I became uncharacteristically quiet. People were gently surprised at my change of mood and Erica explained that I was not like other mortals and could often become overwhelmed by good news. Before my mask slipped completely, we left for the Randolph. Everyone waved, showering us with their kisses.

"Was it really successful?" I asked Erica, not for the first time.

"You know it was."

We walked along Oxford's empty night streets and didn't say anything for a while. I had come through failure and somehow survived, but I think we were both wondering if I would be able to cope with success. Even with this remarkable girl beside me, I wasn't sure.

9

Coming Back Down to Earth

They should have hung a notice on me: Do not disturb. He is disturbed enough already. The fear of the previous night had evaporated but, no doubt about it, I was acquiring too many friends too quickly. Everyone loved me, but they didn't know me. I barely knew myself. Only the family made sense in this world.

"A baby does not need my fame, just your milk," I had whispered to Erica when we got back to the hotel, and we went to bed in a spinning boat.

"The gods are smiling," she said.

"Yes, but smiles can cover malevolence. Do the gods have children?" I sounded like an old Yiddish zaydeh.

"You must get down to work," she reminded me.

I closed my eyes, and opened them again to realise I'd been asleep for hours and dawn was creeping across the window. I slipped out of bed and out of the hotel. I wanted to read the reviews before anyone else did in this unreal city. No one was about and no shops were open, but a suspicious constable told me I could get newspapers down at the station. My heart thumped in my chest as I ran all the way; the first demented jogger in England.

I stood in the wind with an open *Times* that threatened to sail me away and I laughed and jumped up and down while the news guy looked on and wondered.

John Russell Taylor's words were a psalm. "Enter a new playwright at the Oxford Playhouse. The pleasure of being the first to see Mr Bernard Kops's play..." I was his forever.

Most of the others were as positive and I marvelled at how clever our drama critics were. Then I dashed back to the hotel and woke everyone, and sang my reviews, falsetto. We danced and then went down for kippers and toast and marmalade.

"It's going to change our way of life," I said.

"Good. We'll cope."

I held my hand over the reviews and spat seven times. In the East End if ever you praised the beauty or the brilliance of a child you had to spit through your fingers seven times and say "Kenain Ahora". This was the magic charm that warded off the evil eye. The Malacha Movis, the Evil One, usually struck when you were off guard, when you thought things were going too well and couldn't be better. I remembered the old yachnas looking upon a beautiful newborn baby and remarking, "Isn't he ugly, poor thing." This was a sure way of deflecting the Evil One to some other poor little bastard. I wasn't at all superstitious but I wasn't in a mood to take chances.

Erica quoted some ancient words of wisdom. "Be careful of what you want because it will surely be yours."

"That's an old Yiddish proverb," I said.

"Actually it's Irish."

"Yiddish! Irish! Same difference. From now on life is going to be a plate of endless potato latkes."

Oxford was marvellously unreal. God, how I envied all those privileged young bastards on their bikes.

Back in London, Colin watched me poring over my reviews, not elated over the good ones and getting upset at the few negatives, or ones that didn't rave.

"Bernie!" he said. "Take my advice. Blow up the good ones and tear up the bad ones. People never remember anyway. You remember far longer than anyone else."

A few weeks later I was invited to speak at Conway Hall with Kenneth Tynan and Alan Bush. I was so flattered. Imagine sharing a platform with one of our most eminent critics, then at the height of his career. I needed to get in with Tynan. *The Hamlet of Stepney Green* was transferring to the Lyric Hammersmith and a good crit from him alone would secure me a place within the Inner Sanctum. I had never heard of Alan Bush but I did a bit of research and discovered that he was a Communist composer who had written an opera about Watt Tyler. He was well respected and his far-left heart was in the right place.

The subject of the symposium was "The Socialist Artist and His Place in Modern Society". So suddenly I was a socialist. A few weeks earlier I had been a Sohocialist. Colin reassured me: "Listen, anarchists are part of the socialist movement. It's just those fucking Marxists who've purloined 'The Internationale' as if it belonged exclusively to them."

Conway Hall in Red Lion Square was packed to its radical rafters. I drank in the sight of the crowded auditorium, a sea of approving, socially committed faces. I was going to be up there for perusal, everyone wondering if I had a brain in my head or if I was just another nine-day wonder, and I couldn't wait to wipe the floor with them.

When it was my turn I danced with words. You have to write to get it right, but shooting your mouth off is very invigorating, besides being a great smokescreen for not getting down to actual work. As I spoke I could feel the energy rising within me. I started experimenting with the cadence of my voice, then the speed of my delivery. I was Michael Foot, Aneurin Bevan, Mussolini, my uncle Hymie. I was Donald Soper, Phil Piratin, Oswald Mosley. I was master of the orator's art. It was hypnotic. Down below I could see Erica smiling. As long as she approved the antics of her naughty little boy, I was okay. I wagged my finger against the assassins of Whitehall and screamed a diatribe, imitating the magical technique of the unique Tony Turner at Speaker's Corner.

I blew it eventually. "Think for yourself!" I declaimed. "If you go with the herd you'll go out with the herd." This had nothing to do with anything, but I was never a person who could mask my true feelings for long. My eyes darted down to my lover girl. I knew I was starting to slip because I could see concern on her face. I was confusing myself. "I can't be sure of my socialism. Sure, I want this whole stinking capitalist structure destroyed no later than the day after tomorrow but..." I moved on to my mother's early death, my father's despair; I railed against their poverty. This kind of talk was never good for me. It brought the sludge of my past with it and the breakdown that had never been resolved. I began to wonder what the shit I was talking about. I knew I wasn't sticking to the point, and I could see Kenneth Tynan getting restless, so I wound down and trundled into silence. I should have been a pair of hands, scuttling across the keyboard of a typewriter.

A question came from the audience. "How committed must an artist be if he wishes to speak for the masses?" Note. In those days artists were always "he".

Alan Bush was in no doubt. "A composer needs to be totally committed to dedicating his endeavours to voice the hopes and dreams of the common man." Tremendous applause.

Kenneth Tynan was also in no doubt. "The writer needs to be absolutely committed, and place all his energies towards the revolution for social change." Wonderful. His words brought a thunderous response. This was music to our prepacked battery of an audience. We should have been down on a building site in East Ham. The men would have jeered us rotten.

It was my turn. First I joked with some East End banter. "What do you want? My honest opinion or the truth?" and then I shot my mouth off again. I was perhaps the most horrified with my answer. "What's all this shit about? A writer, if he is worth anything, is automatically committed. Writing in the first place means commitment. We do not need to impose commitment. If we are not committed we are not writers."

I looked at Tynan for a sign of accord. His face was red and he seemed not at all delighted. I felt elated. Perversely, I wanted this. If the new critics were going to push drama towards their own vision we would surely be creating a new Theatre of Reassurance and we might as well all pack up and go home. I concluded, "In order to be committed a writer needs a typewriter."

I should have been more circumspect and bitten my tongue. Afterwards Tynan strode out without a word, and he went on to slam everything I ever wrote. At some first night he was even overheard remarking to Michael Hastings, "I don't know why I dislike Kops's work so much." He called it sentimental – a convenient term for those who cannot enter the world of normal relationships.

I isolated myself for a time after that and immersed myself in work and family, scorning the badge of left-wing commitment. "Left wing, right wing, two wings flapping the same old bird," I moaned, but I couldn't keep away for long. I was desperate to belong. All the writers out there were coalescing into a group, and I wasn't about to be left out.

"Christopher Logue writes for *Vogue*, which is distressing for Doris Lessing." It was a whirligig of parties and famous names and faces, all connected by the band of comradeship. Writers, actors, musicians, painters were beginning to feel their strength and were taking on the divine right of the Establishment. It was a gang of sorts, though we were all fish of different hue. I knew Arnold from the start, and I especially respected Shelagh Delaney. Doris Lessing also impressed me, with her depth of knowledge and straightforward manner. She was the very last person to indulge in bullshit. I envied Christopher Logue his bold manner and his acerbic tongue. Then there was John Arden, always so intense; Ann Jellicoe, the teacher with ideas and ideals; N. F. Simpson; John Mortimer; and Harold Pinter, who in a previous incarnation published surreal poems in the same little magazines as me, under his earlier name, Harold Pinta.

Out of the blue a call came from the Arts Council. It was Dick Linklater informing me that I had just been appointed resident dramatist to the Bristol Old Vic. I would be the first resident dramatist to be appointed since Elizabethan days. The prospect of leaving Seven Dials did not fill us with joy, although it seemed that I had suggested this very thing when I received my award, obviously on a wave of euphoria. I had an ominous feeling about uprooting myself and burying myself in the provinces – I would be missing all the fun. But everyone was so delighted for me I found it impossible to turn the offer down.

Meanwhile *The Hamlet of Stepney Green* transferred to the Lyric Hammersmith, a beautiful theatre famed for mounting so many historic productions, including two musical plays that particularly moved me: *The Beggar's Opera* by John Gay and *Hassan* by James Elroy Flecker. I felt proud when I stood in the empty auditorium, just breathing in the magical, dusty atmosphere. I had entered the portals of the mighty.

The usual crowd attended first night, together with important hangers-on and familiar celebrity faces from this new world I had so recently uncovered. Only this time, because it was only a tube ride from the East End, I failed to keep my relatives away. They turned up *en masse*: aunties, uncles, dad, brothers, sisters, nephew, nieces. All the women were over made up and all the men were sulking because they had far better things to do. They had got seats in the front stalls in the den of critics, and waved and called over to me, and generally yachnered and noshed away. I died inside. It was straight out of a cartoon by Hogarth.

Peter O'Toole was sitting right in front of me, joking with his mate Jackie McGowan. We exchanged nice words before the curtain. He was already at the Bristol Old Vic where his acting was causing a sensation. He seemed pleased that I was going to be there. I told him about the new play I was writing, *The Dream of Peter Mann*. I told him I was writing it just for him. It was a lie but he was delighted.

When the curtain went up all my family cheered and oohed and ahhhed and I cringed and slid down in my seat. The play went on through my fingertips and I couldn't wait for the curtain. All I could do was watch the obvious discomfort on the faces of the critics.

During the final applause Peter turned round and kissed me and then lifted me bodily and held me up above the audience. I did love Peter, especially when he had his kosher nose. When Peter entered a room his nose went before him. The film producer Sam Spiegel soon circumcised it and Peter got to look burnished and beautiful, just like any other ordinary pop star, but before he entered those deserts of Arabia, Peter was sheer chutzpah.

The reviews were good but not as good as Oxford. One reviewer mentioned that I had filled the theatre with admirers.

A week later we packed and went to Bristol. When we left the train at Temple Meads I heard a terrible noise. It was my heart crashing down into the basement.

10

Doing Time at Bristol

From our very first day in Bristol I was clutched by incurable homesickness. I knew I'd made a wrong move and here we were, sentenced for six months. What should have felt like the start of a great adventure felt more like the beginning of an ordeal. I reasoned that some good had to come out of it all, but I yearned for my Seven Dials, and Old Compton, and having to hide in a doorway to avoid Paul Potts.

We moved into a house in Clifton where Peter O'Toole lived. He was warm and expansive and grand. He had pictures of John Barrymore everywhere. Up until then I had not mixed a great deal with actors socially. I suspected their warmth and instant love, but Peter was different. His was no act. I saw him in the mornings and in the days and in the evenings. He was always the same: courteous and intelligent. And his performances were spectacular. He had such daring. I saw his *Amphitryon, Man and Superman* and *Oh My Papa*.

Peter made Bristol slightly more bearable, but we weren't comfortable, and Adam, now two, did not approve of the move. He seemed to miss his usual space: his small room with his familiar things on the wall, his mobile and his little chair.

The idea was that I would write a new play to be performed at the theatre. I let Peter in on all the ideas I had for this, *The Dream of Peter Mann*. It would be a distant cousin to *Peer Gynt* and *Peter Pan*, with songs. I told him that the hero would crow like a ridiculous and arrogant cock. "Cock-a-doodle-doo!" Peter's cry ripped through the entire house and Clifton Mews outside.

We could not have started at the theatre at a worse time. A tragedy preceded our arrival by a few days. John Moody, the artistic director, and his wife Nell had lost their young son. He had gone swimming in the River Severn and somehow got himself too close to a weir and was swept over and drowned. Nell often used to go down to the weir and just sit there. My curiosity had never heard of good taste back then. I always pursued other people's pain. Figuring that it was better to talk about a loss than avoid it, I asked Nell why she persisted in going to the scene of the tragedy, day after day.

She managed to retain her gentle smile. "If I go down there, and look at the torrent, over and over again, like playing it back," she explained, "maybe this time it will come out differently and he will come back to me."

I met Frank Dunlop, the associate artistic director. He had assisted the great Michael Saint Denis in London and had worked at the Piccolo Theatre in Milan. He was especially inspired by commedia dell'arte, and I was inspired by his productions in Bristol. I shall never forget his production of Carlo Goldoni's *The Servant of Two Masters* and his brilliant idea of getting the comedian Jim Dale to play the lead.

As playwright in residence, I was allowed to wander anywhere in the theatre, to familiarise myself with the planks of stagecraft, and breathe in the atmosphere and the smell of the size on the flats and watch rehearsals, those precious secret moments of building a play. I watched Frank in rehearsal. His energy and inventiveness convinced me that he was exactly the right person to direct my work, and we became good friends. His ideas coalesced with mine. Theatre should be epic, expansive, awash with spectacle, expressionistic and surreal; but within the matrix of the play there should also be a dynamic to which all could relate. The gods must be driven and affected by the ordinary human stories of tragedy and comedy. They too had their pain, their terrible children who never telephoned them. Social drama, on the other hand, was anathema and best kept for that insatiable god called television. The theatre was the place to take chances.

Frank was a pioneer, a leading creative light and inspiration to actors and writers. He had fire. Diplomacy and compromise were not in his vocabulary. His warm smile could turn to rage within seconds. One particular first night when the curtain had just gone up, Frank was still in the foyer in a rage, pacing and red in the face because a few critics had not yet turned up. When one finally arrived Frank let the poor bastard have it and the shrivelling man hurtled into the stalls like a child. It was the first time I felt sorry for a critic.

It was a great source of sadness for Erica and me when much later we fell out of touch. He went on to bigger, more spectacular things with Cliff Richard and others. *Chacun à son goût*. It's the one professional relationship that I really miss.

✱

My own personal fire somehow got lost in Bristol: I came up against my first writer's block. The wall hovered higher than Manhattan and I couldn't see the sky. My second play proved an impossible wayward child that ran out of the house every time I sat down to talk to him. Many times I resigned myself to the thought he had run away for good, but then he would creep back in the middle of the night and give me hope with a tantalising line. By the morning it would be lying on the floor, scrunched up and meaningless. I hung around the flat waiting for inspiration to strike and longing for home, the ream of virgin paper untouched.

"How's it going?" Joan Heal asked me on the stairs one day after we'd been there a couple of months.

"Fantastically. I've almost finished."

"Happy with it?"

"Delirious. I'm driven. You could say it's writing me." I could see Erica dying inside.

"When do you think you can show us a first draft?" John Moody or Nell would gently ask.

"Maybe next week. I just need to twiddle with a few things." I laughed as we passed. Who needed the truth at a time like this? I hadn't even managed a single typed page.

"I might even be able to show you something the day after tomorrow," I called after them.

"Liar," Erica hissed from the side of her mouth.

At least I had the divertissement of the beautiful Theatre Royal, that plush, magical palace where I watched the actors in rehearsal, hoping that some magic would rub off on me and I would be activated into writing.

A young man, intense and funny, often dropped in to chat during the evening. He and Peter were good friends. This was Tom Stoppard, a young reporter on Bristol's *Evening Post*. Tom was clever and amusing and I was not surprised that he shot to such success years later.

He was not wildly in love with his work back then. Like most local reporters he had to write about the things that go on every day: the births, marriages and deaths, the court proceedings, the weddings, the infidelities, the ordinary human happenings, the comedies and the tragedies that strike local communities and that we all find so fascinating. One evening he told us he had been sent to interview

1. Childhood stamping ground, Petticoat Lane, 1950s.

2. My sister Rose's wedding reception in Aldgate, 30 August, 1950. *From left:* my brother-in-law Mick, my mother and father, the bride and the bridegroom, Stan. My sister Phyllis is sitting at the front on the right.

3, 4. Max and Gertie Gordon, Erica's parents.

5. Erica (*in the middle, standing up*), David and Gillian in Charing Cross Gardens with Nanny, *c*.1935.

6. Erica's father's family, Riga, 1930s.

7. The gold and silversmith's that Erica's grandparents owned in Riga before the war.

8. Pushing my barrow along Shaftesbury Avenue.

9. With Erica at my bookstall in Earlham Street, Cambridge Circus.

HUNGRY YOUNG MAN

AND NOW . . . The Hungry Young Man: Soho barrow boy in the open-neck shirt, 30-year-old Bernard Kops. His first play, "The Hamlet of Stepney Green," has just been accepted by Theatre Workshop. America is interested, too. And yesterday he heard that Italian Princess Marguerite Caetani will print three of his poems in her literary review.

As crowds flipped through his second-hand books, he told me: "Soon I shall be able to give up the barrow." Once he nearly threw himself into the river, but, he says, "I'm no angry young man, but hungry for the truth. My wife Erica and I have sacrificed meals so I could write."

His play? "It's about a young man who wants to be a crooner and Prince Hamlet."

▶ Bernard and Erica Kops with their bookstall barrow

● " My play is a poetic sad comedy . . . difficult to explain

Pictures: BILL BECK

10. My splash in the *News Chronicle*.

11. At home in Monmouth Street.

12. With Erica at Torino's.

14. Learning to busk, just in case.

13. Erica and Adam.

The Hamlet of Stepney Green, Lyric Hammersmith, 1958.

15. John Fraser as David Levy.

16. Harold Lang as Sam Levy comforts his son while John Barrard (Solly Segal) and Ruth Meyers (Hava Segal) look on.

18. Harold Lang and John Fraser.

17. Pat Keen as Mrs Stone, John Barrard, and Thelma Ruby as Bessie Levy attempting to make contact with the dead Sam Levy.

19. Soho days. With Frank Norman in Old Compton Street.
John Rety is in the background, on the right.

20. Aldermaston pamphlet.
First printing of my poem
'Shalom Bomb'.

21. *Encore*, Sept/Oct 1958. *Back row, from left to right*: Arnold Wesker, Errol John, me, David Campton.
Front row: N.F. Simpson, Harold Pinter, Ann Jellicoe, John Mortimer.

22. Quentin Crisp in the
As You Like It days.

23. Colin MacInnes in his pad
in Hanbury Street.

24. Paul Potts, the People's Poet, with the Asquiths.

25. The poet, Emanuel Litvinoff.

a woman whose daughter had tragically died that day. He had noticed the woman glancing at a photograph of a girl on the mantelpiece, and he later asked her if there was a photograph of the girl that the newspaper could publish. In her grief, the woman refused. When she left the room for a few minutes Tom quickly swiped the photograph and concealed it. Then he hurried back to the office. He was a cub reporter and merely doing what was expected of him, but he told us that he felt horribly ashamed ever after.

I hated the mews where we were living. It was so silent. One day I went out to the main road with a tape recorder and returned with some noise. I played this non-stop and finally got down to at least some words, but the pressure was enormous. I felt that everyone was expecting me to deliver a work of sheer genius, and soon. As I sat there waiting for inspiration, all that struck was a deeper discontent. There seemed to be no communication between the stock room in the basement and the supply room on the ground floor. That terrible second play. The first had been so easy. I was young and innocent and it shot out of me. Everything I was and believed in gave it substance. In Bristol I was a displaced person. What could I possibly write about in this rootless terrain?

I had other less tangible fears. From our window we could see the great Clifton suspension bridge looming down the road. We were that close. That bridge started to haunt my thoughts and dreams. So many people had thrown themselves off it. Erica picked up on what was going on in my head and said that we would never go anywhere near it, but in the middle of the night I would sweat with fear, trying to keep my eyes open, just in case in my sleep I would be magnetised and sleepwalk towards it and be taken down into the dark waters below. It added to the disconnection of my days. Writing drama became the last thing I wanted to do. I was using all my energy to stay away from that bridge.

I remembered some words of my mother: "There are many ways to get over a wall." So instead of forcing up crap I did the next best thing: I retreated and immersed myself in books on theatre. If I couldn't disgorge I could at least digest. Every day in that tall room I produced a play in my head and I must say, with all modesty, I became the greatest director in the world. Nobody could design a play like me. In that mews I had space, infinity and the best actors in the world. In Bristol I furnished my dreams. Picasso crept into my room one morning; I made him coffee.

He said, "Bernie, a word of advice. Don't go out, seeking your play. Don't go searching for inspiration. Wait till it comes knocking on your door."

His words were comforting but did nothing to lift my homesickness. Bristol was nowhere in my universe. I never connected. It seemed that no humans actually lived there; even Peter O'Toole, Frank Dunlop and Tom Stoppard were just passing through.

When we'd been there about five months, I had to realise that I was never going to come up with the goods. I was never going to finish, or even really get started on, *The Dream of Peter Mann* in Bristol. My discontent became so smouldering that I think the management feared I might self-combust at any moment. They were clearly relieved when I asked if I could terminate our six months contract, and the Kops family quietly slipped away to Temple Meads station.

When we got back to our little flat in Monmouth Street we put Adam to bed and bounced on the bed, whooping with delight. Then we ate chocolate and giggled, and watched the couple opposite in the Shaftesbury Hotel who, just arrived, lost no time yentzing away and, in their dash for the bed, forgot to draw the curtains.

A play has to contain truth, I agreed with myself on that train home from Bristol. So many promising playwrights have fallen by the wayside between their first and second play, because THEY became their drama. A play has to be about something, or it will hover in a miasma of words. On the other hand, too much concentration on theme makes a play an obese main course of exposition. First and foremost, a play should be born through the characters and the dialogue. Too many playwrights are tempted off the pavements by head-hunters and advertising executives with open suitcases crammed with twenty-pound notes, demanding a theme. What is it trying to say, they demand, what's the fucking theme?

The second important thing, I decided, is to organise your writing. Getting caught up in the first draft and constantly rewriting the beginning can only result in frustration. Logic and intellect applied too early gets in the way of truth and power. The thing to do with a first draft is make a dash for the ending so that it emerges complete with all its problems and inconsistencies. At this point it cannot and will not make a lot of sense, but at least it is there, a stepping stone to the next draft. The art of writing drama is in the act of rewriting.

∗

So I created a working practice and was finally able to get down to the real stuff of writing plays. Back in London the Clifton suspension bridge was too far away to threaten me and I was able to sleep my nights without dreams. While I could write I could release the creative side of myself – that creature who loved Erica and life and Adam and the future, and had the strength to curb the self-destructive monster inside me who still roamed around so freely.

11

My Second Coming

I was soon surfing waves of inspiration through the second draft of *The Dream of Peter Mann*. It lent a spring to my step as I made my way along Charing Cross Road towards Legrain's in Gerrard Street. Legrain's had been my first real café, my sanctuary when I was an actor and still living in the East End with my parents. I used to make one glass of coffee last for hours and just watch and listen in those days. The proprietor tolerated me for some reason, even bunged me a slice of cheesecake occasionally. We were waited on by Linda, every straight customer's desire, with legs right up to her bum, and I'd often have to leave the café with a hunched stoop so no one would notice my middle leg.

That was fifteen years before, but it looked like the customers hadn't changed that much. They were all still sat on the same seats: actors, writers, translators, sub-titlers; and the little Jewish dressmakers who had followed the Huguenot silk merchants to Wardour Street a few hundred years before. Even Linda was still there, although her magic no longer worked on me. Erica with the real goods was just a few streets away.

Alun Owen walked in and, spotting me, joined me at my table. Alun was Liverpool Welsh and, despite being an actor, was wildly Celt and very human. We'd been actors together for a while and used to mull over our misfortunes and this lamentable profession that refused to recognise our genius.

He told me he was sick of acting and wanted to be a playwright, and shoved a manuscript across the table. It was a play he had just written called *The Rough and Ready Lot*. He begged me to read it there and then, and stood me a coffee in return. He sat dead opposite while I skimmed down the pages, his eyes on my face trying to read my reaction. It looked to me like it had promise and I told Alun I'd show it to the powers that be at Bristol. Writers rarely push other writers and I think Alun was as surprised as I was by my offer. I didn't have the heart to explain that I was actually no longer working there and that a recommendation coming from me would probably start them all pinching their noses.

I telephoned John Moody that afternoon and he was quite friendly – probably relieved to see me out of the way – and, to cut a long story sideways, not only did they like *The Rough and Ready Lot*, they told me they wanted to put it on.

Even as I dialled Alun's number to tell him the good news, I was asking myself why I'd offered to help him. I was consumed with jealousy, despite myself. Alun would be launched at one of the most beautiful theatres in the world; it should have been me. He went silent at the other end of the phone, and then said that he would love me forever. I couldn't imagine that was going to do me a lot of good.

A few days later I bumped into him along Charing Cross Road. It was the last time I ever saw him. He grabbed me and kissed me and told me his play was scheduled for production at the Bristol Old Vic the next season.

Erica tried to cheer me up. "Listen. It's good to help deserving people."

"Exactly! At my time of life you have no choice but to keep in with the angels."

She laughed. "Your time of life?"

Her derision was good for me, but there was no use pretending my mitzvah had belonged to the highest level of charity.

The play turned out to be a huge success in Bristol and on the basis of that, Alun was chosen to write the Beatles film (their best) *A Hard Day's Night*. Of course, he would have made it anyway, but I like to think I saved him a few years. You could argue that I was responsible for the social revolution: through Alun Owen's immaculate vision the Beatles achieved immortality, the world was changed as a consequence and thus began the Age of Hype. I told Erica how I had changed the world a hundred times. It helped me get over it.

We had a little money trickling in – *The Hamlet of Stepney Green* at Oxford brought in modest royalties to a very immodest young play-wright – so a few weeks later we decided to splash out and move out of Monmouth Street. It was always like that: immediate action. We moved into a huge, empty flat in a mansion block, a spit away from the Reading Room at the British Museum and just a few doors along from Mark Marvin's.

Marvin was another one who worshipped Tynan. When he'd heard about the fracas at Conway Hall he had urged me to be circumspect, which in other words meant I should go crawling and ask Tynan to show me the true path. I secretly agreed that I'd probably gone too far, and I knew of other playwrights who had gone brown-nosing the critics after a bad review, hoping for a good notice next time. To continue to loathe His Imperious Majesty could be highly detrimental to my career, and I was already labelled a suspected leper. I also began to think that I should join in more earnestly with the other writers and start signing political protest letters and all the rest of it.

Erica became increasingly exasperated with me. "Those who come in on the bandwagon, go out on the bandwagon. Think for yourself and the climate will change," she tried to tell me. This little woman wouldn't take shit from anyone.

"But we live in a fascist world," I insisted. "We could be obliterated any moment. Unity is strength."

She shook her head, as if I were a cause that was lost long ago. "Suit yourself."

But I couldn't do that. I wanted Erica to approve. I wanted to convince her. "I hate them but I need them," I kept saying. It went on for days and was our first major row.

"Bernard, you scare me!" she yelled when we'd exhausted ourselves with arguing.

"But I need my friends, my comrades."

"Balls!" she shouted and came at my face with her nails.

"You cow!" I howled and stormed out of the flat, making sure I slammed the door behind me. I wandered along Charing Cross Road, marvelling that this young girl was daring to question my decisions. I still hadn't quite come to terms with it by the time I'd completed a circuit and got back home, but we laughed.

"How can a rich bitch from the City of London School for Girls know everything?" I shouted from the kitchen. "And how can she bear to stay with a person who is always wrong?"

"Go to hell," she shouted back from the bathroom.

"Fuck you," I hurled back at her.

"Yes, please." She emerged in her Japanese kimono. Adam was now fast asleep, and we made love. Anger is a sensational aphrodisiac.

"Erica," I said later in the dark, "I really am going to change the world."

"First learn to change your socks."

*

70

One afternoon not long after, I opened out the *Evening Standard* and found Mark Marvin splashed all over the front page. Or rather splattered upon the pavements of Manhattan; he'd jumped from the first floor of an office building. My agent had abandoned me and I was outraged. He'd opened a window and turned himself into a kishke omelette without giving me a thought. Not just me. I couldn't understand how he could do such a thing to Blanche, his loving and beautiful wife.

I re-enacted Marvin's death dive in the dark, under my blankets. As far as I was concerned, I'd been in his pocket when he'd jumped. Since he owned part of me, I felt justified to stop him in flight to record the details. Did you take your jacket off? Did you take your car keys? Are your flies done up? Did you shit yourself? I wanted to see his expression; his pink podgy face before it turned into strawberry jam.

"One door closes, another door closes," Erica concluded. I'd been trying to deal with the practicalities of it all. Besides deserting me, Mark had left my business affairs in a real mess.

I got on with cooking dinner. Erica was a great commis to my head chef. "Darling, I've decided I really am a good socialist, deep in my heart."

She smiled. "Congratulations," and turned up Alfred Deller so that the room was drowned with "Waley Waley".

"Don't you want me to have a successful career?" I shouted. She didn't seem to hear.

If my marriage was on the rocks I couldn't blame myself. Besides, there was no time to work on relationships, there was marching to be done. It was time to sing "Where have all the flowers gone?" It was time to write letters to *The Times*. The in-crowd were branching out and hurling themselves at the smirky Establishment. I couldn't honestly see the Ruling Classes shaking in their shoes at the protestations of the angry brigade, but I was committed to The Cause nonetheless.

Erica stayed in the background pitying me. She came along to the marches to keep an eye on things and stop me making an utter imbecile of myself, and I was grateful for the sudden whiff of her perfume. "So, you're not leaving me today?" I'd ask her.

"The day's not over yet." We still managed to laugh.

One evening Frank Dunlop, no longer at Bristol but trying to make a name for himself independently, came to see us with clarion news.

He had been beavering away behind my back and had fixed things so that *The Dream of Peter Mann* would be going to the Edinburgh Festival.

Almost as soon as we knew, Colin appeared at the door and loped towards me for a kiss and a cuddle. He seemed to smell good news. He saw our beaming faces.

"And why aren't you marching with your banal comrades?" he asked when I'd told him.

"Haven't you heard? The Cold War's gone. I've abolished it."

"I thought I saw something slinking down the road and disappearing round the corner."

He was already on the floor building bricks with Adam. I brought out the wine and we clinked glasses.

For a period after that Frank dropped in every day. We all worked together while the wind howled outside. You couldn't slip a sheet of typing paper between us, and the winter, pounding and scratching at the windows, was jealous to be left out of things.

Then one slushy day Erica happened upon a travel article in the *Observer.* It was a feature on a little place called Nerja on the south coast of Spain. The travel writer wrote, "I fear by telling you of this peaceful, unspoiled oasis I will spoil it forever," and we felt obliged to get there before it was overrun by a plague of tourists.

I refused to fly – I would rather have died – so we embarked on a sea voyage on a liner going to Australia. On the way it pulled into Gibraltar where flowers were in bloom, people strolled the streets, and we had to shade our eyes from the sun. From there we got a taxi and sped around the nightmare bends beyond Malaga and all the way along the Costa del Sol. It was night when we arrived at our oasis. We stood in the chirping twilight by the edge of the sea where the Moorish sultans had once looked back wistfully to Africa. And at midnight we sat in the small town square and the gypsies came winding down the cobbled streets, strumming guitars and singing. It was George Borrow come to life.

That first night we stayed at the hotel in the square but we didn't have to look very far in the morning to find an enormous old house to rent, with disbelief at the ridiculously low price. "Perhaps we can stay here forever," I tried to say in my laughable Spanish. The sun shone straight down and we tanned ourselves in the garden, three doors along from where Federico Garcia Lorca's brother lived. In the evening we breathed in the thick aroma of jasmine as we slipped into pristine white sheets and I tuned in to the World Service on our small battery set. The weather man told us of raging blizzards that were sweeping England. It was the most cheering news we had heard in a long time.

12

My Ghosts Return

The enormous old house turned out to have a damp problem and at night insects fressed on our blood, so we moved to a little house up in the mountains. We now looked down on Nerja, nestling in the arms of the sea.

But even then, our Spanish honeymoon didn't last long, although at first the sound of the sea and the sun were all we thought we needed. Every morning we were woken by the sound of the goats as they came tinkling across the cobbles, and the scent of the mountain herbs would waft down and mingle with the smell of burning toast for breakfast. After breakfast we'd take a walk down into the town and drink coffee in the little square and read *The Times*, paying special attention to the weather reports. "Snow and ice blanketing London. This is the life."

Nerja enjoyed sunshine almost all the year round, even with Franco in power. The Civil Guard patrolled, incongruous in ominous uniforms. "*Buenos días*," they nodded and I smiled back, but they sent a chill right through me. I was getting to know my Lorca and the Spanish, and the Civil Guard.

One morning a handsome, suntanned German tourist crossed the square and sat close by us at the café, where Adam was supervising an imaginary battle with two toy soldiers. The German was just about five years older than me, deep in the age of responsibility where one is supposed to know what one is doing. I wondered what he had been doing in the war. In what Panzer division? In what Einsatzgruppen? How much of the dust of my relatives had he turned into egg-timers?

He smiled across and asked us where we came from. The universe, we told him, and he laughed, not quite understanding. Adam went close to his table and the Handsome Hun smoothed his hand across his hair.

"*Schön. Schön.*"

I pulled Adam away. "Take your fucking hand off my son's head," I growled, and he continued to smile.

Erica now pulled me away. "You're mad," she hissed.

"Yes, I'm mad. Fuck you, holocaust. Get off my back."

That same day we went down to the beach. It was unseasonably hot and we read while Adam splashed in the sea. It seemed like only a few minutes had passed when I looked up and Adam was not there. My heart thumped. I screamed. Erica ran towards the water and a man came up from the skyline to meet her. Adam was in his arms, gasping for breath. He had ventured way out of his depth and would have certainly drowned – we didn't know it at the time but apparently the beach was notorious for claiming children.

"Thank you," I said. What do you say to a sheepish man who has just rescued your genes, your only sure bit of immortality? The man was almost apologising for having saved our most precious possession.

"My pleasure," he replied and, embarrassed, walked quickly away.

We gathered our things together. "Going so soon?" The guy who owned the *merendero* seemed sad.

I tried to explain. "Yes. This is one of the most dangerous beaches in Spain. And it looks gentle, so peaceful."

We would have gone straight home that day but when we got back to the house there was a postcard from Frank. He was in Cordoba and was coming to see us the next day. We lit a huge welcoming fire with eucalyptus branches, and then took him out to dinner, showing off the wonder of Nerja which in a few years, or even less, would be gone forever.

The gypsies who lived near the caves came into the square, chattering and vivid. They were three times more alive than all the rest of us and I couldn't help feeling drawn to them, this other people who had died alongside the Jews just a few years before. At the time I was overdosing on Lorca and reading his *Deep Song* and I was astounded by the shattering beauty of the gypsy lullabies.

"We have just come from the caves," one gorgeous girl said, flashing her chiaroscuro smile at me.

"Thank you," I replied, at a loss for words for the second time that day.

In the middle of that night we were woken up choking on our kishkes to find that the house was filling up with smoke. In a panic we all rushed outside to gasp for oxygen and then dashed, pathetically, for buckets of water, but it was hopeless. The monster had only just started to roar. The chimney was alight with sparks, and flames were flying upwards and spreading across the wooden roof.

We covered our faces with wet pyjamas and dashed in to retrieve valuables, like the manuscript of *The Dream of Peter Mann*, our wallets, money, traveller's cheques, photos, the record player, and some clothes, while the flames kept licking away, lighting up the night sky. Excited little kids who should have been asleep came running up the mountain to dance around the flaming house, until eventually a little Victorian fire engine chugged towards us and pissed on the flames.

We were all disappointed when the fire was put out and the action was over. I thought we were going to be shot for committing arson by the two slit-eyed Civil Guards who had ambled up from the town. In fact, they were exceedingly civil and offered us cigarettes and suggested we go down to the hotel for the night. When we saw them again a few days later they told us that the examiners had raked over the charred remains and discovered that the builders, with unbelievable stupidity, had built great wooden beams into the chimney. It had only been a question of time.

At the hotel the sheets were crisp and the pillows embraced us. There was a hot shower and the loo was not encrusted with the shit of fifty years. It was bliss. Lying in bed, reading and eating chocolate biscuits, we experienced that kind of contentment that only comes after narrow escapes.

I giggled.

"So, what's wrong?" she asked me.

"Nothing."

"Homesick?"

"No!"

"Liar!" She was the mistress of semiotics. I was homesick to my stomach. In a matter of days we had narrowly escaped two tragedies. Spain was probably the last place on earth that I needed to be.

All that week I had terrible dreams. It was all too familiar. Even as a small child I used to wake in the middle of the night and cry out, terrified by my mortality. My sister Essie, ten years older, would lift me up and bounce away my demons. In the stark, silent night of Nerja, it was Erica who dandled me like a little baby to soothe away the tears rolling down my face, although when this sort of mood enveloped me even she was just a figment of my useless hope.

To survive my nights of the black octopus I've always taken journeys into the past. From our hotel room in Nerja, I lit up forgotten streets, woke up dead neighbours, played draughts and ate chocolate kisses with Josie, my childhood friend, and lifted my dead cousin Jackie out of his little coffin and played hide and seek with him.

Mr Adler, a sweet little tailor from Brick Lane, was one of my most persistent ghosts. He often came in the night to measure me up for a wooden overcoat.

He spoke in soft, measured tones. "So, you're a playwright. Should I have heard of you?"

"I doubt it."

"What is a playwright? What is he for?"

"You may well ask. I'm also a poet, for my sins."

"Are you a day poet or a night poet?"

"I don't understand."

Mr Adler had his Brick Lane cosmology all worked out. "Schiller was a day poet, Goethe was a night poet, Shakespeare was a day poet, Baudelaire was a night poet, Blake was a day poet." He shuffled off in his threadbare pyjamas. "The coat will be ready in ten days," he added, and exited through the wallpaper.

A few days later we got on a train in Malaga and began our journey back to the welcoming chill of an early English spring and the cold security of Bloomsbury. Every room rushed towards us, embracing us like orphans who thought they had been abandoned. I resolved not to go mad. Instead I went to the British Museum to get a Reader's ticket and took long daily walks through history. I read *Das Kapital* and wrote anarchist poetry. Sometimes I bumped into Colin and he would drag me to the room where the Elgin marbles were on display. He would stare at them for hours.

"Such beauty can only have been sculpted by the gods," I commented, mainly for his benefit.

"Be quiet!" he barked. "Just sit and look at them. We must find a way of stealing them and getting them back to Greece." Whereas I merely went along with his flights of fantasy, he was always deadly serious.

I was also working with Frank, discussing actors and the text and the meaning of life within the context of my play. It felt good to be a playwright again.

A phone call came from the office of the Russian Ambassador. Would I like to go to a party at the Russian Embassy in Kensington? This sort of invitation always made me feel important. They must have heard

I was getting my second play produced. I was indeed a person of substance.

"What's the party for?" I asked the Ambassador's secretary. How wonderful to consort with the enemy.

"No reason. In the Soviet Union we cherish and celebrate our writers."

In general I was a slob, but for this occasion I cleaned myself up. I had a shave, squeezed deodorant under my armpits, put on a jacket, took Erica's arm and arrived at the doorstep in Kensington.

"Why d'you think we've been invited?" I asked her. She looked tiny on the big step. I remembered when we had first met. I had stood beside her and felt like a giant, even at only five foot four and a half.

"We've been invited because we are important," she told me while we waited.

"Yes, and we're probably even now being photographed by MI5."

"Not that important."

The door opened and the Ambassador came forward to greet us.

"Well, the Russians think we are."

I turned around for a moment to face the bushes where the secret cameras ought to have been and for the sake of the secret microphones I boomed, "In case you do not know, dear gentlemen of Whitehall, I am a playwright and my name is Bernard Kops. And this is my muse and wife, Erica." I gave a full-frontal, mocking smile and followed her into the glittering interior. We were greeted with vodka and caviar.

13

Hobson's Choice

All the gang were there in the huge, glittering room. All the okay names. This was a Cultural Night at the Russian Embassy for the New Intellectual Establishment of Great Britain. First we were treated to a film show. It opened on the empty streets of present-day Moscow. Five cars approached a roundabout.

The Ambassador sitting behind me tapped me on the shoulder. "You see, Mr Kops, we also have our traffic jams."

I was having a hard time keeping awake. We travelled on to Odessa, city of Bialik, Chagall and Babel, where the artistic cream of European Jewry had flourished beyond the reach of the Tsar, although not beyond the reach of the SS who dragged them out of their homes and turned them all into dust.

Erica shook me. "Bernard, wake up."

The film finished and the vodka and caviar girls started doing the rounds again. Those little glasses seemed so innocuous. I knocked back several before Erica's restraining arm could stop me. I was brimming over with confidence.

I could see a group of playwrights gaggling around the Ambassador, all leaning forward, eagerly hanging on to his words. I went over and cut in with what I thought was a good line. "England may not be the best country to live in, but it's the best country to sleep in."

My comrades were not amused, but I was not to be discouraged and told the Ambassador and the cabal that my new play was going to be produced at the Edinburgh Festival. When you're from Stepney Green and you have something to boast about, you tell the world.

None of them congratulated me. Well, they were all self-seeking bastards. Who wasn't? But the Ambassador was expansive and called for more vodka. I could see they would have to carry me out of the place, one way or another. Erica couldn't rescue me; she was marooned with the Ambassador's frump on the other side of the room, missing all the fun.

The others writers drifted off and I decided to play the diplomatic game. After all, this was the Ambassador's residence; everyone lied here.

I launched myself. "The New Writers, the Engineers of the Mind and Soul, the Lovers of Peace, will never fall for the propaganda of the Capitalist lackeys, the Enemies of Peace who oppose the People of the Peace-Loving Democracies. We are here to show our Solidarity with the Workers for International Socialism. Our Common Goal is the Great Ideal. We will strive to achieve True Democracy in our own Wicked Land. I love the Peace-Loving People of Soviet Union. I love the Russian People. My wife's father came from Riga. He fled the tyranny of the Tsar..." The Ambassador's eyes were half closed and he was gently swaying from side to side. I heaped more praise on Pushkin, Gogol, and all the Five-Year Plans. I lauded the Finland Station and the beautiful moustache of Uncle Joe Stalin, the great Dams of Siberia, the Bolshoi Ballet, vodka, socialised medicine.

Erica came up giggling. She was pissed too. "What about Isaac Babel and Mandelstam?" she asked. When she let loose she was far more dangerous than me.

"And Mayakovsky," I added.

The Ambassador hugged me like a long-lost little brother. He stank of garlic. "What is your name, my friend?" His bass voice was dark brown and gravelly.

"Arnold Wesker," I said, and he hugged me more. "In our own humble way we are trying to redress the balance, to achieve truth." This crap I was pouring out. It was beautiful.

"What about Isaac Babel?" Erica asked again.

"You're drunk. You're very drunk. Time to go home," I told her.

"Time to go home. Time to go home. Andy is saying goodbye. Goodbye," she sang.

"I love your idea," the Ambassador said as he held my arm and accompanied us to the door.

"My idea?"

"The one we spoke of earlier. The exchange of a new dramatist between the Soviet Union and your country."

"Oh yes, I remember now," I lied.

"We will be in touch, Mr Wesker."

"I'm Bernard Kops. I was only joking. We're often mistaken for each other."

"We will be in touch, Mr Kops." His great hand descended and strangled my fingers, and then we stepped out into the real world.

"Are you still there?" I asked, as we hurtled through the hazy night toward Bloomsbury.

"Where else would I be?"

We sang all the way along the private road until we reached Notting Hill Gate. "My old man's a dustman, he wears a dustman's hat. He wears gorblimey trousers and he lives in a council flat..."

"Despite all that, my darling, we can be the bridge to peace," I told Erica when we got to bed.

"Just write," she replied. Erica the Oracle. I ranted on while she slept, keeping an eye on the door, wondering when her husband would smash it down and rush in and cut off my shmeckle. Then I remembered that I was her husband; sometimes when our passion was so good I felt that we must be living in sin. With this smug thought I curled into her and fell asleep.

Harold Hobson, the theatre critic of the *Sunday Times*, telephoned me the next day and requested the pleasure of lunching with me at his club. I felt I'd really arrived as I sauntered along Pall Mall, parading my first haircut in ages. I had always admired Men of Letters, those scions of literature who wrote flaming columns of truth and refused to run with the herd, and here I was, making my way into the heart of the intellectual Establishment.

"Careful! The English," Erica warned. "They've been at this game a long time."

"What game?"

"Divide and rule?"

"But I am only divided against myself."

"True."

I would order a Premier Cru white Bordeaux with Dover sole, and when he asked me what wine I wanted with my dessert I would say that half a bottle of Château d'Yquem would suit me down to the ground. Hobson would be amazed at my knowledge of wines. He would never guess that in a previous incarnation I had been a commis wine waiter at Brooks' Club in St James's.

I reached the Athenaeum and looked up admiringly at its magnificent edifice. It was just the sort of place I would bring down on my very first morning of absolute power.

That's what I pretended, anyway. It would have been more honest to admit that this little East End Jew harboured dreams of being accepted by the Inner Sanctum; that he wanted to be loved by the bastards who controlled the world; that he would have been thrilled beyond measure if a missive arrived from Buckingham Palace summoning him to an audience with the Queen. I remember bumping into Arnold one day. He had just returned from some sort of official do and he walked towards me with his hand extended, only half mocking, "Don't touch this hand. It's just shaken the hand of the Queen." We may have been anti-Establishment, but we were all secretly in awe of its big names.

Hobson was charming. I wondered what the hell he was after. Colin, who was never wrong when it came to the ins and outs of the literary jungle, had warned me that there was no such thing as a free fress. I thanked him for his most generous review of *The Hamlet...* and reminded him, in case it had slipped his mind, that he had called me a writer of outstanding talent.

Over the starters, we discussed his recent trip to Paris where he had been hypnotised by the magic of Edwige Feuillère and the sparks she had ignited all over the front stalls. I told him that I had recently seen the Comédie Française perform in London and thought them embalmed in aspic. The critic was not amused; he had loved that particular production. From then on, I tried to curb my tongue, but the wine kept unlocking the mechanism.

"Tell me about Kenneth," he said. "Have you seen him recently?" He obviously meant his greatest rival.

"Kenneth?" I blinked innocently.

"Kenneth Tynan. Aren't you all friends together?" He was obsessed with the fellow. Not only obsessed, he seemed positively threatened by the Venerable Bede.

"What does Kenneth think of your work, Bernard?" he asked. He had been in Paris the week *The Hamlet...* had opened and had missed the review.

"Oh, he thought it was wonderful. He eulogised," I lied into my glass of dessert Malaga. I was learning to create my own truth.

"I'm so glad. It's good to have one's views substantiated by others you respect. Everyone is making such a fuss of Wesker. What do you think about his work?"

"I think he is a very exciting writer. We are very different. Wesker's got a vibrant talent and he deserves his success. I'm content with my own vision. Arnold and I are both journeying towards the same destination but on different paths." I was lying through my teeth. I was not trying to build a new Jerusalem. I had just fallen into the playwright lark and discovered that it was a wonderful way of making a living without actually having to work.

Lunch was over and the waiters were fidgeting to clear the tables. Hobson beamed as he stumbled up to make his exit.

Now he was whispering like a conspirator. "Personally I much prefer your work to Wesker's. You are by far the more talented."

"We are very different. Comparisons are odious. But thank you." Erica had been drumming into me the need to be diplomatic.

"I wish you all the best for Edinburgh."

I thanked him and went out and breathed in the fresh, clean air of Green Park. Ezra Pound travelled with me on the tube home. I mumbled his mantra to protect me. "What thou lovest well remains, the rest is dross, what thou lovest well shall not be wrest from thee." As usual the people in the seats next to me got up and moved away.

After the Edinburgh opening I heard through tribal drums that Harold Hobson remarked to someone, "With regard to Kops and to Wesker, I made a mistake. I backed the wrong horse."

While Frank and Erica were still helping me define and refine *The Dream of Peter Mann*, Penguin, who had published *The Hamlet...* the year before in their anthology *New English Dramatists*, decided to publish it. I nominated Colin to write the introduction and he said he would be honoured.

I fully expected the paean of praise he delivered to delight everyone, but Frank blew his top when he read it and put his foot down. "I absolutely cannot allow this. It's too full of praise. It's obviously written by an uncritical friend. It'll do more harm than good," he raged.

I couldn't see his point; everyone respected Colin and I imagined they'd lap up his words, but Frank was adamant. He told me that people should come and see the play and make up their own minds; they shouldn't be led by the nose. The introduction was too fulsome and, as its first director, he would not allow it.

It was left to me to tell Colin that his introduction would not be needed. I was still a premier league coward in those days so I begged Erica to do the dirty deed. I suspect she hated my cowardice even more than she did the telephone.

"Please, I can't face it," I whimpered from my hiding place underneath the sheets.

Colin was devastated when she told him. He avoided us for weeks.

"What can I say?" I asked him when he finally came round to see us.

"You stabbed me in the back, Bernie."

I asked him how I could make it up to him and he surprised me. He told me that Robert Graves was very ill, recovering from an operation in the general ward of St Thomas's Hospital across the river. "I request that you go and visit him," he said with a wicked twinkle.

"Why would he want to see me?"

"He would love to see you. He's in a bad way. We must show support and solidarity to one of our greatest writers."

I decided to go that afternoon, and so I found myself trying to cross Westminster Bridge. Up until then I had managed to avoid crossing the river. I still suffered from the ridiculous notion that I would be sucked into the water, that my white, dead eyes would be eaten by eels and my flesh by water rats. But I had promised Colin so I slowly zigzagged across. When I had first met Erica I was horrified to learn that she lived on the other side. She always had to hold tightly on to me when we couldn't get a bus over and I would sing Spenser and Eliot, "Sweet Thames, run softly, till I end my song." I might have gone by tube, but the underground also presented incoherent problems for me at the time.

I got to the hospital and presented myself at the bedside of the great man. He looked at me glassily and was obviously in pain. Robert Graves was a giant, a god of my growing up, unswerving in his fight against fascism but now, unshaven and in his pyjamas, he was just another mortal human being.

"Mr Graves, I've brought you something." I handed him a small box of Terry's chocolate almonds.

He hunched himself up and his massive, imperial head tried to smile. "Do I know you? What is your name, boy?"

I told him. He was none the wiser and looked around at the other groaners. "I do so like these ordinary general wards. I don't approve of all that private stuff, do you?" Long pause. "What is it that you do?"

"I'm a dramatist, recently arrived." I felt a real shmuck.

He nodded and patted my hand. "And the very best of luck to you." I had been there three minutes and was already being dismissed.

"Goodbye then, Mr Graves. May you live long and die happy."
And I backed away from the bed, trying not to appear totally
ingratiating.

"What a nice greeting. Is it yours?"

"It's an old East End Jewish saying."

"How very interesting. Goodbye, Bernard Cox. And many thanks
for visiting."

In the end Mervyn Jones wrote the Penguin introduction. It placed me
nicely within the phenomenon of the New Drama and Frank approved.
I was grateful to Mervyn but to me the words were a didactic clump on
the page. Colin's words, like his shmeckle, always stood up.

The Dream of Peter Mann went on a short tour before Edinburgh. We
were all euphoric: director, actors, composer, designer. We felt we
couldn't fail to hit the bull's-eye. Erica and I followed the play as it
moved around. We were wide-eyed novices, hanging on to every
moment, sitting in the corner of every box of every theatre, watching
the tweaking of the text and the acting, alternately stirred, moved and
cowed by Frank Dunlop and his tenacious energy. We bathed in the
magic of the actors, this happy band of brothers and sisters, and we sat
back in admiration as the Family of Theatre brought my dream to life.

14

Baptism of Fire

On tour at Golders Green Hippodrome I felt unusually restless. As soon as the curtain went up, I was waiting for it to come down. I should have been making suits in a sweatshop in Stoke Newington. In the middle of the first act I crept out of the auditorium and paced in the foyer.

A man came rushing out and noticed me. "You've had it also?" he asked.

"No, I wrote it."

He laughed derisively. "God help you."

"He did."

That little man scared the shit out of me. Was this an augury? The ghost of Mr Adler, my Brick Lane tailor, shrugged his response in the empty foyer. Inside the curtain was just descending on Act One and the applause was respectable. I dashed to meet Erica in the bar, my serene and reassuring angel, and Mr Adler slipped away. I wondered whether he would follow us to Edinburgh.

When we arrived I stood staring at the curtain of the Lyceum Theatre and felt that it was too soon for it to go up and reveal my second play. Whom the gods destroy they first make sane. Cold reality was waiting, like an actor, in the wings. After the ballyhoo that had accompanied my first play the critics would all be waiting with knives. Yes, the tour had gone well as tours go, but you could never tell with tours. In the provinces the wind blows in all directions. In Edinburgh I would discover what my play was really made of, one way or another. There was no enjoyment in it. Theatre is like life intensified. Hurdle after hurdle, all eyes upon you. You leap and leap and leap and everyone cheers and then at last you stagger. Everyone gasps, and then starts cheering the runner beside you.

I had gone round and hugged and kissed the cast beforehand. They were wildly friendly and enthusiastic. Tim Hardy and I placed our hands on each other's shoulders. "The play is beautiful," he told me.

"Important. Apposite. It can't fail." How quickly we had all become intimate, and how quickly we would fall apart. These actors I so admired were onions. Peel off one layer to discover their heart and you found another layer underneath, then another. In the end there was nothing, just the smell and the tears. My star was rising and they longed to soar with me and who could blame them. It's the writer who's at the centre of things. He's the first to receive the kicks or the embrace, or both. In those dark days the new breed of actor that aspired to truth, social justice and good collective work was only just beginning to emerge. Unfortunately, most actors were still like little children, all spongy and gooey inside. There was one notable exception in that company, Hermione Baddeley. She was made of different stuff.

In the box I felt exposed. The theatre was jammed to the rafters. All the posh of Edinburgh were there in kilts and dowdy finery. Lord and Lady Harewood chatted intently in the stalls. Beatrice Lillie had come. Edinburgh was expecting a night out, a nice diverting piece of new drama; another well-crafted play from the Theatre of Reassurance.

When the curtain went up two hands clutched at mine. Erica was on one side of me and Frank was on the other. I looked at Frank like a newborn babe at his mother. His smile was meant to be reassuring but it frightened me all the more.

The Dream of Peter Mann is the odyssey of a young man seeking adventure and fame, but whose journey inevitably leads to nuclear destruction. It was the very first play in Britain to bring the atomic bomb to the centre of the action. In those dark days, the Bomb was going to get us all. We saw ourselves teetering on the brink of war and the end of civilisation. The Bomb, the Cold War and the Holocaust were my constant companions. If anyone ever questioned what I was doing with my life, I would throw them the thick black headlines and say, "If this world is sanity, thank God I'm mad." I was writing about things I knew: our folly, the madhouse of the world we had inherited, and the madhouse we were still constructing.

At first it was just two people in the front stalls who quietly got up and shuffled their way out of the theatre. Then a few more, very quietly getting up from their seats and making for the nearest exit. Then two more. And two more. I noticed a slight embarrassed smile on their faces. I looked at Frank. He nodded. "Don't worry," he whispered. I turned to Erica. She squeezed my hand and smiled. I smiled back. Frank smiled. We were all smiling. More and more people were getting up and leaving. The actors were trying their best but they were slowing down, their eyes darting all over the place like in a Japanese No play. It was slowly grinding to a halt. What was it? Was it a fire? Had these people heard the Sirens of Doom? Had I gone mad? I closed my eyes. When I opened them the whole front row of punters was gone. And now the second row, and now the third. All over the auditorium seats were suddenly tipping up and all the bums that had been sitting on them a few minutes before had disappeared. The Pied Piper was obviously outside and the audience was leaving in droves. It was all very quiet, very dainty, very Edinburgh. Erica looked terrified.

"It'll be fine," Frank said, whistling in the dark of our box.

"He who is an optimist hasn't heard the bad news," I replied.

"That's a very good line," he said.

"It's Bertolt Brecht. He came up with it first, unfortunately." If I hadn't quipped I would have howled buckets of tears. "They're leaving because it reminds them of their mortality. They came to be amused, not abused."

I was bathed in sweat. This was a public execution. Frank was no longer smiling.

"This proves the power of the piece," he insisted a moment later.

"I don't want power. I want to be loved." Now tears were running down my cheeks. There were just a few people left in the audience. The actors bravely staggered through to the end, but I hated them and I hated theatre. "Fuck drama! And fuck fucking dramatists!" I wondered what labour exchange I would have to sign on at the following week, if I survived that long.

By now Frank knew and Erica knew and I knew without doubt that this was a disaster. The press would crucify me. I wiped away my tears and saluted the actors standing there, masks of incredulity frozen on their faces. After this they would stand well away from me; *The Dream of Peter Mann* would not be added to their curricula vitae. I was an unmitigated failure, a virus of the most potent kind.

The auditorium was empty except for a few remaining critics, scribbling away, recording the disaster.

"I'm a failure. I'm finished."

"Don't be so stupid! Stupid!"

"It's the end of the world."

Behind every man there's a woman puppet master. "Now smile."

I clamped on my tightest smile. "Good boy."

We went to the first night dirge and everyone commiserated. I growled. I hated them all. There was no way out of my very public humiliation. I just floated through on a blanket of alcohol. Beatrice Lillie, otherwise Lady Peel, entertained the Lord Provost and the good lords and ladies of pishposh Edinburgh. Her imitation of Queen Victoria inspecting the plumbing of Holyroodhouse really shocked them, and it gave us a good chance to slip away.

My fixed smile was still there when we got back to our digs. Adam must have believed my enforced hilarity as I threw him to the ceiling and twisted him around and around. He chortled. He was three years old and he still loved me. The local girl looking after him assumed the play was a raging success. Teetering on the edge of catastrophe, I didn't want to disappoint a baby-minder.

The next day we braved it out and went like Dirk Bogarde up the scaffold to the café opposite the Traverse. All my actors were certainly there but they didn't seem to see me; I was a carrier of the Black Death. I cursed them and spat through my fingers. Then Hermione came in, whispering endearments into the ear of her ferocious little lapdog, and came straight over to our table.

"Be brave, Bernard," she said. "You will live to fight another day."

The black morning lightened by just one degree. Thank God you could rely on at least one righteous person to lift you out of the darkness.

"I'm going back to London. Now," I said to Erica. "I've reached the bottom."

"Then kick against it and you'll come up again," she told me.

We went back to the house we were staying at and I took refuge in the bathroom. I swallowed two tablets of speed which I had secreted in my shoe, left over from my breakdown in 1951. I wasn't about to become a slave to a ridiculous and minute purple heart; I just needed a little chemical assistance to distance myself from the failure and to give me a kick start back into hope.

Later that day I felt wonderful – confident and expansive – although I had to avoid Erica's direct gaze so she wouldn't see my enlarged pupils. I didn't want to give her an ounce of anguish.

But when the phone rang I knew it had to be bad news.

It was my new agent, Dina Lom, in London. "Bernard, I'm afraid they're terrible." My blood ran cold even though I was expecting it.

"I'm afraid they're absolutely, spectacularly terrible. Some of the worst reviews I've ever seen."

There is a complex mix of emotions when you hit rock bottom. You know the truth so you no longer hang on to hope. The effect of the amphetamine was far more intense than it should have been. I was weeping, stretched out on the floor.

Erica was extending her hand, trying to coax me back to standing. "Darling, you have to go to Glasgow."

I couldn't connect. Why did I have to go to Glasgow of all places? I wanted to go home. I looked in my diary. It was 6th September, 1960 and I was due to be interviewed by John Betjeman on some television arts programme. At that moment I needed exposure like I needed another purple heart. I whined like a six-year-old, but there was no point arguing with Erica when she was in this matriarch mood, so I travelled to Glasgow.

Betjeman was waiting for me at the studio. He was the very last person I wanted to meet in this state.

"Have you heard about the reviews?" I asked him. I hoped that my spectacular, public execution had made the producer change his mind so I could get the next train back to Erica. I quoted one review for good measure. "Bernard Kops's fall from success last night was perhaps the most disastrous in the history of British theatre."

Betjeman only soothed and consoled me, but I wasn't to be fooled. I knew how these people in the media operated. Catastrophic demise and humiliating defeat were infinitely more interesting than yet another newly discovered genius. I was going to be made to squirm in front of millions of people.

I couldn't have been more wrong. The old beaver was kind and gentle as he introduced me to his audience and made his own assessment of the play. I had always hated his gentle and refined manner and his sentimental journeys through Metroland; his love of the sort of suburban houses I despised. I hated his whole class. He had probably never known a day's privation in his whole life, and there he was, daring to admire a play that would soon sink without trace.

Later we had coffee and I ate out of his hands, and had to re-evaluate my prejudices.

"The climate will change one day, you'll see. So many writers have been through this experience. Confound them, man. Survive."

He took my Penguin out of his pocket and read out the quote on the front cover. "'A writer of outstanding talent.' Harold Hobson. You can't do better than that. If the book exists the text cannot die. It is not a comfortable play but people can make up their own minds."

As he accompanied me to the street he delivered a small, very Christian-sounding sermon. But no matter, the goyim can also sometimes come up with a few truths. I remember his actual words. "This is your moment of failure, Bernard, but failure well experienced can be success. And remember success can be failure. It's all semantics. It depends on you and on how you respond to events, on whether you have the inner determination to survive or whether you accept the judgement of others and get pushed down by the weight of it all." I could see his message had been pertinent to his own life and I felt like an utter worthless bastard for having pre-judged him. John Betjeman was a good soul, standing there shining against the dark Glasgow sky. I was somewhat lifted on my journey back to Edinburgh.

Unfortunately, my benign mood didn't last long. When I got back to the house I suggested that we go home to London immediately and face the future. We started packing. Erica insisted, however, that I didn't slink away like a thief in the night but that I go down and face the actors and thank them. I laughed derisively and when my apoplexy had subsided I went down to the Lyceum.

None of them was ecstatic to see me. Could I really blame them?

"Goodbye. Thank you," they said.

"My pleasure. Goodbye," I replied and bellowed with laughter. This was good. This was very good. This was all I needed to spur me on. I hated all the momzers.

Erica was trying to calm. "I'll show them!" I told her. "None of them will ever work with me again. If I ever work again." The speed was a long time dying off. "Holocaust came out of acquiescence," I kept repeating. "Now you see it. Now you don't. I will make a whole people vanish before your eyes."

She was concerned. "Yes, it's time to go home."

"Andy is saying goodbye. Goodbye!" I sang.

"Darling! You haven't been taking anything?"

"What? Are you mad? Never. I promised."

She was looking closely at my eyes. Thankfully, my pupils had now returned to normal. "No. You would never do that again. Would you?"

"Never. Absolutely not."

We were walking towards the stage door when Hermione popped out of her dressing room and hugged me.

"Darling, follow your own star and everything will be marvellous again. Wait for the Sundays. You might be pleasantly surprised. I know you will write wonderful, successful plays."

I hugged her back. The choice words of Harold Hobson were digging into my brain. "I backed the wrong horse." He didn't have the courage of his columns.

I needed speed. The taster of the day before had reminded me of its beneficial effects. I planned to go and get a modest supply when we got back to London and reward myself, but only in moderation. Funny thing about drugs, there isn't a time when you don't need your reward. You feel you've earned it when things go well, but you also feel you deserve some sort of compensation when things go against you.

On the train I smiled across at my love who was singing an Israeli lullaby to our restless three-year-old. She was happy to believe that I had surmounted the debacle. As we sped through the rain towards London I couldn't see the way ahead. The high had used up my energy and I nodded forward into sleep.

15

Waiting for Tynan

Strange thing about reviews: when you read them years later, curled, brown cuttings from old newspapers, you laugh. Nothing is more dead than last week's news. Colin had the right idea: blow up the good ones, tear up the bad ones. I kept them all, good or bad, waiting for time to put them in their proper place. Sometimes I changed bad reviews into good ones. Very few people remember how your play was received and those who dwell upon the minutiae are usually the obsessional mad. I could change history. A terrible review from Tynan a year before could be referred to as a fabulous rave. "Surely you saw my wonderful review by Kenneth Tynan in the *Observer* last October?" I'd say.

I had a flop behind me and I was back in the real world. Friends reassured. Second plays were always hell, they told me. *The Dream of Peter Mann* may not have been fully realised but it didn't deserve such a vicious assassination. Colin regaled me with stories about the endless wars between playwrights and critics; how *The Seagull* was hammered on its first night, and how Chekhov was overcome with despair. All writers are obsessed with critics and all critics are obsessed with writers, he told me, and all drama critics are secret drama scribblers who have had their work rejected. Wouldn't anyone be bitter and lurk with a hatchet for a writer with even a sprig of originality?

"Funny," I mused, "when your baby is born, no matter how ugly or deformed it is, everyone comes with gifts to celebrate the birth and tell you how beautiful your baby is. A play brings out the men with cleavers and they set to work chopping your baby to bits."

It was the Saturday night and the next, terrible morning would bring its Sunday newspapers. The dreaded Tynan would pronounce over the land and create and destroy according to his covenant. There was no doubt in my mind that he was about to obliterate my future. I slept on and off that night and in the morning I crept out early.

I wanted to be the first to buy the newspapers and get a chance to familiarise myself with their contents. This would hopefully give me a little poise when the inevitable onslaught of commiseration came. It was six a.m. and I walked slowly towards the main road. It was a bit like following my own funeral. I found the one newspaper stand that was open and paid good money for news of my fall from grace. In an open doorway, I slowly opened each newspaper in turn. The assassins did not disappoint. Each one boomed my death sentence: Guilty! Guilty! Guilty!

In a fit I tore all the newspapers to shreds and a merciful wind blew the pieces along Tottenham Court Road. On my way back to the flat, the roads began to wobble and coagulate. This was definitely a bad sign. I couldn't survive another bout of the horrors, these highs and lows that came even without the aid of drugs. I debated gassing myself so that I could leave a note blaming Kenneth Tynan. There would be a furore in the letters columns of the *Observer* and *The Times* but, unfortunately, and there's the catch, I wouldn't be around to enjoy it.

I prayed in Coptic Street, "If I am spared, dear God, I will give up writing. This is my vow."

And then I saw Nicky, one of my Sad Boys of the Afternoon, walking along the other side. Since Edinburgh, even Nicky, always the most pathetic of them all, had stopped knocking on our door. He lived just around the corner in a furnished pig-sty and he had also been out for the papers. I watched him standing there, transfixed, the open *Observer* in his hands. Nicky was the sort of guy who skimmed through everything and knew every little bit of obscure cultural and showbiz news. He had a mind made entirely out of blotting paper. Who was in, who was out. I was definitely out.

His head was deep inside his open *Observer*, and he was making a gurgling sound as if he was snorting the ink. When he withdrew his head to better enjoy the bliss of my demise, I screamed, "Nicky! Nicky, you bastard! You've read Tynan, you bastard. Bastard! Fuck you for always."

I decided that we would emigrate to Australia. The slow trudge seemed endless, probably because they had tilted the roads upwards. When I finally stood before Erica, I burst into tears. Then I charged into the bedroom, pulled the curtains, jumped on the bed and threw all the blankets over me. I sat there rocking slowly backward and forward like the disturbed child I was.

"Leave me alone. I'm finished. I'm crucified," I sobbed.

"How dare you! Get up. Come out." She pulled me out until I was lying, slobbering on the carpet. "You pathetic creature. Did you write plays for them?"

"No. Go away."

"Who did you write them for?"

"I wrote for me. For us."

"Exactly! You always said history is written by the survivors." She brought me a cup of coffee. "E. M. Forster would be ashamed, seeing you like this."

"What? E. M. Forster? What's he got to do with it?"

It was an incident I'd totally forgotten. My second book of poems, *Poems and Songs*, had been published by Scorpion Press a few years before. E. M. Forster had written to John Rolph the publisher and enclosed a fifty-pound cheque saying, "Please give this to a deserving and promising young writer, but please do not divulge the source of the money." John had decided that I should be the recipient and, of course, also blurted out the identity of the donor. Ever after I had felt that there was a link between the great man and myself.

"You owe it to him to keep your faith and to write no matter what."

"Yes," I whimpered.

"Well, there's the typewriter. Start writing."

"Now?"

"Now!"

"Write what?"

"Write words."

"Yes, beat the bastards." Erica's faith had biblical dimensions. When I hit the rocks like this she was there to haul me out. "Start your new play," she commanded me.

I laughed. "Mine enemies grow older. I'll show the bastards."

On that gloomy Sunday I gathered all my notes together and started on the first draft of *Change for the Angel*, a play about a boy who prays to the Angel of Death to come and take his father. The angel comes as bidden but, ironically, claims the boy's mother not his father. I hammered my way through it and felt as if I was giving kinky old Tynan a knockout blow.

The next day I ambled along Old Compton without a worry in the world. As usual I passed Colman Cohen's, the best cigar shop in London, and as usual the boss came out and called me back. I knew that his greatest delight would be to bring me down and finish me off.

"Bernie, how nice! You're back in London. I saw some terrible reviews in the Sundays. I suppose you'll have to find another profession. Like work for instance." He didn't even attempt to hide his glee.

"Oh? Which reviews did you see?"

He named most of them. "*The Sunday Times, The People, Reynold's News, The Sunday Graphic.*"

"Oh? I'm surprised you missed the one by Kenneth Tynan in the *Observer.* He tore me to pieces. He said my play was probably the worst he'd ever seen. I've got it here. Shall I read it to you?"

"No, thanks. Got to go. Be well." He quickly retreated into the interior of the shop. I felt like I'd triumphed. My new-found technique had come up trumps. Never try and defend work that has so palpably flopped.

I swallowed some speed and rang home to tell Erica that I was feeling much better, and thanked her profusely for me having found her. "I forgive you all my sins," I said.

She smelt a rat immediately. "You haven't taken anything have you?"

"Never. I swear on my mother's life."

"But your mother's dead."

Erica knew everything about my terrible past. My days and nights on the floor, tramping the streets, alone, penniless and gone in the head. We had talked about it all, turned it over again and again. We laughed about those crazy, farcical things I did and I reassured her that those years were dead forever, but I think her fear remained. We both knew how unstable I was just beneath the surface.

I took a walk to Torino's. The same old gang were in there and they cheered my entrance, delighted with my spectacular fall from the dizzy heights of fame and fortune. The one thing the Sohoites could not abide was anyone leaving Soho. "Come 'ere. Give us a kiss, you old cunt." We were all failures together again.

A couple of days later I was walking along Charing Cross Road with Erica and Adam when we bumped into Arnold. In those days, if you walked between Foyles and Leicester Square you were bound to bump into every writer who was still alive. Arnold and I were married by way of the Penguin anthology, *New English Dramatists*, only Arnold was yet to fall from grace. No one had whispered in his ear, "Careful, Whizzy, thou art mortal." After Edinburgh, I couldn't help but resent him. I was jealous of his fame and his acclaim; jealous even of his acolytes, whom I despised.

We stopped to chat and I told him I was writing my third play, *Change for the Angel*, and that it was going to open at the Arts Theatre.

"I admire you, Bernie. If I got the reviews you've just received I would have given up writing."

"In that case, Arnold, you can't be a true artist." I was hurt. I didn't write plays to please the critics or a current climate. I wrote plays because I had no choice.

Change for the Angel also turned out to be a disaster, though I wasn't at all surprised. The preference then was social drama, the sort of theatre that didn't interest me. My taste went towards the epic and expressionistic, but I was a young writer and could still be knocked about by a powerful man at the helm. The director David de Keyser was such a man. During rehearsal I watched as my expressionist style was gradually transformed into stark realism and my beautiful Angel of Death turned into a social worker. The play closed after only a week and, thank God, David decided to return to acting. In my book, he ranks with the great actors of our time.

The auditions, though, are a good memory. *Change for the Angel* has two leading roles, the boy and his brother. We made our mind up quickly on the boy, and Melvyn Hayes went on to give a marvellous performance, but we just couldn't cast the brother. We were about to call it a day when a young man came on the stage and took over. His name was Michael Crawford and he was overflowing with energy and talent. All our frustration and doubt was swept away. It was his first time on any stage, I believe.

So the play died, but I survived, and I came to realise that none of my disasters could finish me as a writer. I was actually being recognised more and more by my two highly publicised failures. "Soon the worm will turn," Erica promised. I just had to survive, to write and rewrite. I had Erica to help me through, and humour to help prick the pomposity that sometimes comes with being a playwright. I was way out there on my own, it was true, but that was probably just the way I wanted it.

16

Lunch with the KGB

Sometimes, even today, I get the feeling that I'm a stranger here on earth. I have a sense of belonging somewhere else, as if I were delivered here by mistake. I was beginning to feel that if I didn't hold on to something, or someone, I would float away. I would joke with the family, "Can someone direct me to where I am?" I started using drugs to help connect me, whereas before I'd been using them to disconnect myself. I was taking one tablet of speed every day, although I was determined not to let my body acquire tolerance. My ego knew no bounds; I was as much in charge of my chemistry as my dreams. The only person who could have helped me was Erica but she was the last person I could tell. Taking drugs is a lonely occupation.

It was morning and I had just swallowed another booster rocket to give me courage to face the word machine. You're always more scared in the morning. My German Olympia was my slave and master. I used to pace the room, giving it sideways glances, before daring to approach the high altar.

That morning the telephone rang and saved me before I got to it. The bass voice at the other end belonged to a Yuri Pavechenko from the Russian Trade Delegation in Highgate.

"Mr Bernard Kops? I would like very much to take you to lunch. Where and when would that be possible?"

The Trade Delegation was that Soviet citadel on Highgate Hill, a mere clenched fist away from Karl, sleeping under his catafalque in Highgate Cemetery. I wondered what they wanted with me, what secret information I could possibly divulge that would help the Soviet Union.

Yuri and I met outside South Kensington underground station. He didn't look lethal. He was poured into an immaculate Savile Row suit. I checked out his hands; they were pink and tiny, not suited to administering karate chops.

He took me to Rasputin's Palace, and we sank down into that plush, pre-Revolutionary ambience. A tape of balalaika music played in the background.

"Do they serve latkes here?" I asked while he murdered his hors d'oeuvres.

He shook his head sadly. "What are latkes?"

"The food of the gods."

"We do not believe in the gods," he said, and moved on to a pyramid of stroganoff; or was it the entrails of a young visionary who refused to sing the right left songs?

I worked my way into a bowl of borscht and got down to business. "Mr Pavechenko, why have you invited me to lunch?"

He stopped eating for a moment. "At the Trade Delegation we arrange for exchanges between the Peace-Loving Soviet Union and your country. We have heard of you and followed your career. We know that the group of writers you are part of is not infected with the propaganda of your government, and we thought you might be interested in certain schemes that we have in mind; schemes that perhaps you could help us initiate, and that will help the cause of peace."

He knocked back some more vodka and I admired his technique. I tried emulating his method and was soon bumping across the ceiling, fleeing the wicked satyrs along with the buxom maidens.

"It would be quite a wonderful holiday as well. The best hotels and the Black Sea resorts. Georgia. Everything taken care of."

"If I helped with this scheme, could my wife possibly come with me?"

"Mr Kops, you could take your grandmother if that is your wish."

It sounded wonderful, just to get away from London. But by then we were on stewed cherries and cream and I was almost totally out of my body. Yuri changed the conversation into what he took care to present as chit-chat. He wanted to know more about the phenomenon of New Drama and the new writers. We all seemed more balanced and less influenced by capitalist propaganda, he said. He wanted to know about my friends because he was new to the country and wanted to familiarise himself with the arts scene. He explained that he was aware that playwrights were quite influential and knew many important people, politicians, for instance. He asked me if I knew any and knocked back yet more vodka.

"Mr Pavechenko, I am a mere dramatist, no one of importance."

He waved away my protestations. "Surely you have been to some gay parties where funny things happened to persons of note?"

This was before the word "gay" had been reinvented; Yuri spoke deliberate and perfect English. "Come. You are being most modest. We in Highgate know your friends mix with famous people."

My instinct to boast, successfully suppressed so far, came rushing to the surface to have its way with me. "Well, I do happen to be on speaking terms with one or two ministers in the government," I lied, and had the satisfaction of his reaction. The cat had got the cream.

I repaired to the loo. There was a phone in the dark passage. Had I been sober I would not have dared to use it and, thank God, Emanuel Litvinoff was in. What he didn't know about the Soviet Union was not worth knowing. I could see Yuri, a real glutton, still stuffing himself in the far corner and I quickly unburdened myself.

Emanuel was furious. "You bloody fool! You're playing with dynamite. The Trade Delegation is notorious. Those people are dangerous. I'll come round and see you later."

I felt great. I was important. I was George Kaplan in the flesh. I might never get out of this place alive. Tomorrow I could be in the headlines and Alfred Hitchcock would take an option.

When I returned, my comrade cracked into smiles and asked whether I would like to write an article for *Kommisol Pravda*.

"What about?"

"Anything. Your friends. Your drama. Your philosophy. How a Lover of Peace can survive in a Capitalist State. Five hundred words."

"How much will I be paid?"

"Five hundred pounds for five hundred words. By return."

"Can I write a thousand words?"

"Maybe for your second article, when we get to know you."

He must have seen the delight I was trying to hide. "We pay our artists well in the Soviet Union. There we truly appreciate the social engineers of the soul."

"I'll deliver them the day after tomorrow," I said and got up to go. He just sat there looking up at me, bloated and smiling. I felt a warm glow of love for Yuri Pavechenko and floated upon its essence towards South Kensington station. I was very, very drunk. No need for more speed today.

Erica must have spied me coming along the road because when I got to the door, it was open and she was there.

"But you never drink," she said.

I blurted out a summary of what had happened. "I'm starting my article right now."

She handed me a cup of camomile tea and I went straight to my Olympia, still pristine after four years of my bashing.

Maybe it was the drink, but the sight of its perfection suddenly galled me beyond reason. I was incensed. "You fucking horrible German machine. Don't you ever go wrong? Can't you just fail to be perfect for once in your life?" I shouted, and then chucked it across the room. It hit the far wall and lay there, lifeless, and was shortly followed by my close acquaintance, Bernard Kops.

When I woke hours later I could hear laughter coming from the kitchen. I stumbled towards my precious typewriter. "My love, my desire, my fear and trepidation, what have I done to you?" I touched the dead machine and it started kicking for dear life. Fraulein was as Germanically efficient as ever.

I went towards the laughter in the kitchen but I listened outside the door first. I was always suspicious of any man alone with Erica. She was so desirable, who could resist making a pass at her? There's a proverb as old as Moses: When the shmeckle stands the brain dies. But it wasn't that kind of laughter. It sounded like Emanuel, remarkably handsome but eminently trustworthy.

"Bernard, why are you loitering?" Erica came out and called me in. She shoved a cup of coffee into my hands and I followed her into the kitchen. Emanuel and I both nodded to each other, smiling like a thousand years, two Yiddish mandarins from the shtetl. I told him more about my meeting with the mysterious Russian and his promise to dish out gold for mere impure thoughts.

"Bernard, you must have nothing more to do with these people. That Trade Delegation is their main nest of spies."

"I know," I said. "But this was perfectly innocent, I assure you."

"You must have been photographed by our Secret Service."

Sometimes I wondered if Emanuel, whom the world knew as a brilliant novelist, knew rather too much. I had a theory that he was actually working for MI5.

He continued, "Anyway, how can you deal with these people, when your own are being persecuted in Russia, the most anti-Semitic country on earth?"

I couldn't resist telling him that Yuri had offered me five hundred pounds in return for just five hundred words.

"That's it! You bloody fool. Don't you dare touch that money. It stinks!"

"I need that money. I can do without all this. It's just a lousy little article about nothing." Like all writers, I was obsessed with money and the getting of it. I would be mad to turn down such an easy offer. "I'm going to write it now. It's a piece of cake."

Emanuel followed me to my Olympia. "It's the oldest and most banal trick in the book." He was really getting on my nerves. "They ask you to write an article about anything, something quite innocuous, and for that they offer you an enormous sum of money. It's called the 'hook' in the spying game. So, for a few hundred words they send you a cheque. It's a fortune. Wonderful. You put the money into your account. It's kosher. Your bank manager smiles. Next thing you know the mask is removed and they start turning the screw. You're ordered to inform them about all sorts of stuff. Rumours, anything you hear or witness no matter how trivial it may seem, sexual peccadilloes of friends and enemies, chit-chat, tittle-tattle, titbits, rumours. You are outraged. You protest. You refuse. Then comes the final turn of the screw. They ask, 'How would British Intelligence react if they knew that a poor playwright had suddenly deposited five hundred pounds in his account from the Moscow Narodny Bank? All that money for a few words about poetry readings in a pub in Old Compton Street.' Come off it, Bernard, you're not that much of an idiot."

He'd convinced me. I was suddenly nervous. "I'm going straight to the powers that be and I'll tell them everything. How do I contact them?"

Emanuel laughed in derision. "You'd be a bloody fool if you did. They'd say, 'Thank you, Mr Kops. You just continue meeting this Yuri and feed him those titbits he desires, and then report back to us. Thank you and good night.' You're in deep and there's no way out. Take my advice. Don't touch this fellow with a barge pole."

I blanched. "Why would they want to use me? I'm hardly important." Erica nearly choked in her coffee.

"Opportunism. Why anyone? They try anyone and everyone."

"Yeah! Every little helps, said the ant pissing into the Atlantic."

"Exactly. They push here, they push there, all over the place. And one day bingo, they land a big sardine." He kissed Erica and, looking lovingly at me, pinched my cheek. "Take care," he said and left.

"Five hundred pounds down the drain." It was all I could think of. "Forget it."

A few hours later, when I had just about recovered, I telephoned Mr Pavechenko.

"Bernard, my friend, finished the article so quickly?"

"Mr Pavechenko, I'm afraid I'm far too busy. Unfortunately, I must decline your kind offer." I didn't wait for his response.

Something was positively stinking and it was me. I was determined not to become another Paul Potts.

"Darling, I've decided to take my annual bath," I called to Erica. It was our usual joke and as usual she ran the water for me. I soaked in bliss, and sang a favourite anarchist song. "The people's flag is getting pink, it's not as red as people think and you, my friends, may kiss my arse, I've got the foreman's job at last." I laughed deliriously. Erica came in and felt my forehead.

17

Absolute Beginners

As usual we were desperate for money. All my life it had been the same. Getting hold of the stuff was a necessary obsession. The Arts Council award and my Edinburgh royalties had been swallowed up long ago and we were flat broke. We'd even had to sell all the jewellery that I'd bought for Erica in Cutler Street over the years.

Erica took Adam to visit her parents at Blackfriars. She usually did this about once a week and would raid their larder and sometimes borrow a few pounds. Now that we had provided them with a grandson, my in-laws had begun to like me a little. I'd even go so far as to say that Erica's mother, usually lost in an existential novel, was secretly quite proud of me.

When Erica returned this week I was astounded, and not just by the ten pound note, smoked salmon, cream cheese and bagels she had managed to purloin.

"Look what my mother gave me," she said. "It's from Riga." And she took off her coat to reveal a magnificent amber necklace with the biggest beads I had ever seen, the colour of dark treacle, the same colour as her eyes. "My mother's had it for years. It's from my father's family."

I remembered the sepia photograph of the large gold and silversmith's Erica's grandfather had owned in the centre of Riga. All thirty of the staff were collected together and smiling for the occasion.

"We must never, ever sell it," I said.

"Of course not. Never."

Not long after that photograph was taken, the Nazis had rounded up the Gordon family and all the Jews of Riga and taken them to the edge of the town. When they had got there they had made them dig a communal grave and then murdered them, one by one, with a bullet to the back of the head.

It was amazing that Erica and I had survived, let alone found each other, considering our family histories. Just before the war my father had received a letter from the rest of his family in Amsterdam, imploring him to take us all back there; they were sure that Holland would stay neutral but that England would be destroyed by the Germans. My father didn't need convincing but it would cost more than a few pounds to take the family back to Amsterdam and he was unemployed and didn't have a pot to piss in. He went around for days trying to beg, borrow or steal the money, exploring every avenue and cul-de-sac, but it was useless. In those days everyone in the East End was broke. I woke up early one morning to find him sobbing, his head on the kitchen table and his tears soaking into the tablecloth. Then when the war ended we learned that all our Dutch family had died in Auschwitz. That's how I didn't go up in smoke, and why, when Erica and I met, we found we were on the same emotional wavelength.

Out of the blue I was commissioned to write a new play for BBC television. *Stray Cats and Empty Bottles* was a picaresque drama about down-and-out dossers sleeping rough, and was inspired by the old East End tale of the White Lady of Wapping. The story goes that the White Lady's fiancé was killed in a car accident on the very day they were due to be married. Stricken with grief, the young bride was unable to accept her fate and took to visiting the crossroads in her wedding dress, with flour on her face.

Stray Cats... took me all of two weeks to write but I held back from delivering it for a few months. If the BBC thought it had been a piece of cake, they wouldn't appreciate its craft; a long labour always makes people more reverential. I told them it had been a sheer bugger to write and they told me that the sheer hard work I had put into it truly showed. We couldn't spend the money soon enough. John Jacobs was assigned as director and telephoned me to announce the cast: Irene Worth, James Booth, Miriam Karlin and Ronnie Fraser.

Colin hadn't been around for several weeks; he'd been too busy chronicling the underbelly of London for the *Sunday Times*. He was concentrating on racism and the corruption of the Metropolitan Police. He was well qualified: he knew more about the Caribbean community than anyone who didn't actually belong to it; and his appreciation of black youths gave him added insight.

Colin never brought these boys back to his pad. When the heat was on him he would leg it to Notting Hill, where he felt more comfortable bingeing on drugs and drink. Back in his room in Hanbury Street he was a sober tenant and followed a rigid discipline.

He must have been calling from there when he rang. It was well after midnight and if it had been anyone else I would have shouted at them, but somehow with Colin I never lost my temper. He never really lived in our time zone. He wanted to know if he could come round immediately and said it was extremely urgent, so we cursed and moaned and prepared coffee. When he arrived he sat down looking like a guilty child about to unload a terrible burden.

"Bernard and Erica, my new novel is out next week, and I hope you won't be offended, but I've taken the liberty of putting you all in it. Bernard, you are Manny the poet, Erica is Miriam your wife, and Adam is Saul your son. I hope you'll agree that I have drawn you with great love." He waited for our response. "Do you forgive me?"

We were delighted. "Colin, it's an honour." I was sure that he would only have written well of us.

He broke into a smile of relief, the sort that could melt an iceberg. "I'll pop an advance copy through your letter box then," he said and left.

Morning came and we were both asleep and entwined as usual when I heard the thump of something coming through the letter box. When I'd managed to connect with my head, I rushed to the door and found Colin's book, *Absolute Beginners*. Erica and I drank coffee and fumbled through the pages we inhabited, taking it in turn to read the bits that particularly moved us. It was a wonderfully warm portrait, if a little starry-eyed. We were Colin's perfect family. These were words of adoration from a man cast out from the tribe. I'm proud to know that we provided him with a little secure corner to take refuge in.

Around three a.m. the next morning, when most human creatures are born and die, there was a tentative tap on our door. I found Colin looking through the crack. "Are you still speaking to me?" he asked nervously.

I laughed but didn't reply, letting him twist on the hook for a few minutes.

He sidled in. "Well?"

"Well what?" Colin as victim was a rare sight indeed.

"What do you think? The book! What did you think of the book?"

"We loved it. We're proud to be in it," I said, and he cuddled us both and we all drank tea.

"Would you mind awfully if I had a little kip?" he asked when we'd talked about the book for a while.

"Our pleasure."

"My black boys gave me a hard night," he said and, laughing wickedly, stumbled towards the divan and went out like a light. He was gone when we got up the next morning.

Years later it was my misfortune to see the appalling film they made of *Absolute Beginners*, after Colin's death. We didn't exist in the screenplay and I was relieved. I don't think Colin would have objected so much to the butchering, though. When it came to films his motto was always "Take the money and run, Bernie."

Irene Worth called to ask if I would show her around the East End as she wanted to familiarise herself with the background to my BBC play. Many of my actors made, and would make, this sort of pilgrimage because so many of my plays use these jagged, derelict landscapes as their setting. And even as late as the early sixties the ravages of war were still there to see, witnesses to madness.

Irene and I traipsed around the bomb-sites and surveyed all the damage caused by the Luftwaffe. The characters in *Stray Cats and Empty Bottles* lived in a derelict house in one such devastated street. Irene was extremely beautiful. There was something so serene about her as she floated beside me against the dereliction. It reminded me of *Orphée* when Jean Marais moves slowly across a wasteland of shattered streets, and a glass seller, carrying enormous sheets of glass on his back, shouts to no one, "*Vitrier! Vitrier!*" Her glamour was so incongruous in the dirty back streets. All my ghosts came out to gawp.

The next evening she came to dinner to talk more about the play and "understand its ethos". We felt a little out of our depth with Irene. It wasn't her grandeur, although she was as grand as a queen, or her fame that disturbed us since she was amazingly down-to-earth. It was just that we came from two different galaxies and we didn't seem to be able to find a common language.

We were in the middle of dinner when the doorbell rang. I knew it had to be Colin and I cursed silently as I went to the door. He looked like Stan Laurel the worse for wear, but I couldn't turn him away so we both stood there, immobilised, until Erica came to the door and took his arm and led him to the table.

"Irene, this is Colin MacInnes! Colin, this is Irene Worth!" I announced.

"Oh!" Irene said, obviously enchanted to meet such exalted company.

Colin salivated. She stood up and he kissed her hand, then pulled her close and stared into her eyes. "Oh, Irene," he whispered, "I adore you." He'd had plenty to drink as usual.

Erica brought an extra plate and Colin sat down, and these two rather supreme artists sat opposite each other, staring each other out. They had nothing else in common, except that they were both colonials. After dinner Colin emptied another bottle of wine and Irene sat back comfortably in an armchair. He couldn't take his eyes off the luminous beauty opposite him. He dredged up an Australian bushwhacking song, "The Road to Gundagai", and then suddenly he shot up, strode over to her and sat on her lap.

"Oh Mummy, please let me suck on your tit."

Erica and I looked at each other aghast but Irene dealt with him with immaculate ease.

"If it pleases you, little boy," she said, not batting an eyelid, and he nuzzled into her, pressing his mouth against the curve of her dress.

When Irene had floated out, Colin asked if we had any brandy.

I shook my head. "We aren't drinkers, really."

"You ridiculous Hebrews. How can you survive without booze?"

"We've somehow managed it for five thousand years."

"As a matter of fact, we do have some brandy," Erica remembered, and Colin jumped up and followed her to the bathroom.

I had forgotten all about the stuff we kept in the medicine chest. "It's for an emergency," I told them.

"With Colin all life is an emergency," Erica replied and handed him the bottle.

He smiled like a six-month-old and cuddled the bottle. "I do love you, Erica. You never stand in judgement."

He finished the bottle and suggested we all play a game. He always wanted to play games. We yawned and yawned, hoping he would take the hint, but he just winked and laughed. "Disgusting! Five years together and still at it." We played along with him and yawned our way suggestively to the bedroom and left him there.

In the morning we found him huddled on the carpet, embracing an empty bottle. A mischievous changeling who never quite belonged anywhere.

18

Summoned to Court

A missive arrived from George Devine. I was invited, along with all the other new writers, to a defining one-day conference at the Royal Court. The subject under discussion was "The Present State of the English Theatre". We were to examine where it was going and the contribution that we, the new playwrights, were making to it. Even if I was utterly sick of the whole gaggle, I was flattered to receive the invitation. Besides, I couldn't simply ignore the Royal Court. This was the beating heart of the new Establishment and if I was welcomed amongst that multitude my path need not be so lonely. "Play the game," I said to myself, "or the game will play you." I knew I'd never get anywhere in theatre if I carried on being so stupidly honest and naive. My future was bleak enough as it was; I'd had one fluke success and two disasters. It was time to conform, attend conferences and bite my tongue.

When we arrived at the theatre, I slipped into the lavatory and searched my pockets for courage. I knew that there was one small, saving speed tablet hiding away somewhere and after some frantic searching I found it in the lining. What I really needed was a regular supply. Then Erica and I took our seats amongst the in-crowd. I knew them all by now, but I might as well have been a stranger. Not one face cracked a smile. *Peter Mann* had turned me into the invisible man. Except for Shelagh Delaney; she waved madly across at me, with an expression which let me know she too was suffering.

"What are we doing here?" Erica asked. She hated obedient gatherings at the best of times.

"I'm trying to be diplomatic for the first time in my life. If you're not in, you're out."

"Maybe it's best to be out," she whispered. "The tortoise and the hare, remember. The bandwagon often ends up in the cul-de-sac."

"I need to learn to compromise," I whispered back.

She looked at me. Compromise wasn't her favourite word.

"Hi, Bernard!" someone called across. "How are things going?" It was Clancy Sigal. I was wrong, not everyone was ignoring me, but then Clancy was New York Jewish, not tight-arsed English socialist. He was Doris Lessing's lover and I liked her too. That made three people amongst this whole glitch of glitterati.

A voice floated across the expanse of expectant faces. "Gosh, everyone who is anyone is here, aren't they? If a bomb dropped on this theatre now, the intellectual life of this country would be wiped out in a flash."

"Erica, a new poem!" I announced. "I've been inspired. Come friendly bombs and drop on Sloane Square. It isn't fit for humans; playwrights are gathered there."

"Thank you, Mr Betjeman."

The proceedings got under way. I was a little child again at school assembly as our benign headmaster, George Devine, delivered his dull introduction. Next John Arden strode on stage and proceeded with a lecture on why the Romans built such straight roads in England. He illustrated his points with chopping hand movements and a straight face. In fact, he was so fanatically serious that I thought it had to be some sort of subtle sketch; I was half expecting Arnold Wesker to walk on the stage and pour a bucket of water over him any minute. In the end I had to push my fist into my mouth to stop myself shticking. Oh for the Marx Brothers! Even the Three Stooges would have been acceptable. Erica was digging me in the ribs but it was a fit of uncontrollable hilarity and soon she had to succumb to it too.

My comrades were furious. Except Shelagh Delaney who looked across and covered her mouth, desperately trying to ward off the affliction – otherwise we'd all be consigned to Outer Darkness. I think she succumbed. I couldn't stop. In the end, Erica and I had to squeeze ourselves along the row and make a very obvious and noisy exodus.

We laughed all the way home. Adam was in his nursery school at Coram Fields and so we jumped into bed and made mad, laughing love. It was only later, dunking chocolate biscuits into coffee, that the consequences of walking out on George Devine dawned on us. I'd isolated myself completely. I certainly wasn't going to be able to play around any more with notions like "should I be in or should I be out?"

In a strange way it felt like liberation. It meant the real work had to begin. I just needed to sort out what I was really trying to say about life, that's all.

★

The Age of Protest was truly upon us. Colin started to write for *Encounter*, an exciting new literary magazine with perfect credentials that appeared out of nowhere but soon acquired a reputation. It was edited by Stephen Spender and Melvin Lasky, and the word got round that they paid their contributors top whack and on the nail. They published the introduction that Colin had written for *The Dream of Peter Mann* and I felt able to claw back a little intellectual respectability: Colin commanded immeasurable respect from the whole literary racket, and if he thought I was talented then I couldn't just be rejected out of hand.

It wasn't long before *Encounter* became THE forum of the New Establishment and everyone was contributing: W. H. Auden, Nigel Dennis, Kingsley Amis, Angus Wilson, David Sylvester, Constantine FitzGibbon. Colin once took me down to their offices in the Haymarket and introduced me to Lasky and Spender, but apparently my face didn't fit.

When we discovered years later that the whole thing had actually been set up by the CIA, we were amazed. *Encounter* was a complex exercise designed to woo the intellectual left away from its obsessional hatred of all things American, and de-romanticise its love affair with the Soviet Union; they were wildly successful, of course. And I have to confess that it was really satisfying to watch those patriarchs of the New Establishment enduring the ridicule that followed.

So it seemed only Colin believed in me, and I reached a full stop. My agent sent letters to producers and theatres suggesting that I go and discuss my new ideas with them, but none of it came to anything. Actors coming towards me on Charing Cross Road would cross over to the other side. I considered going back to selling books at Cambridge Circus but Erica put her foot down.

"Write. If you can't write a word just sit in front of the typewriter and meditate. Why don't you try a novel?"

"Good idea." That way I wouldn't have to put up with all the shit and exposure of theatre. I wouldn't have to deal with the directors who made you rewrite your play until it became something they had wanted to write. The novelist doesn't have to join a company and be part of the fray; his only essential relationship is with his editor. And when a book comes out the reviews are spread over time, and if they're bad it's easier to take it in your stride. A play was either a wild success or an abject failure and I couldn't endure it.

"I'll write best-sellers," I told Erica.

"Just write."

I did. It was gibberish, and I was soon sick of writing novels.

"I'm not writing novels."

"Just write."

But I was all dried up, a tiny comma on the long history of drama; you would need a magnifying glass to see my fading and pathetic contribution.

"I'm a failure," I moaned.

She laughed derisively. "How can you be a failure at thirty-five?"

"I can be a failure any age I choose."

Even my family chided me for my terrible reviews. They complained that I'd let them down.

But the world was far worse off than me. What were my problems compared to the threat of annihilation that hung over all our lives? "William Shakespeare! William Blake! We are marching for your sake!" we chanted. It was Easter and we were marching, pushing Adam in his pram on the Aldermaston march. We went to all of them; Aldermaston was our annual jamboree. I was especially glad of the distraction this year. We were part of a diverse crowd united by a common cause: the survival of the earth. "One! Two! Three! Four! We don't want a nuclear war!" Acquiescence was the greatest threat to the future of humanity. We sang Wobbly songs, "You Can't Get Me, I'm Part of the Union", "Alleluia! I'm a Bum!", "Joe Hill", the songs of the Lincoln Brigade, "The Internationale". The Quakers came too. You could tell they were Quakers because they looked so healthy and they had sensible footwear. Their favourite was, "He who would valiant be, let him come hither, one here will constant be, come wind, come weather..." We worked through the line and walked with old friends, singing "Which side are you on? Which side are you on?" It was all so exhilarating. Aldermaston's how Erica and I saved the world.

Several days before the very first march in 1958, Michael Horovitz, Pete Brown, Adrian Mitchell and myself had got together in Soho and decided to produce a small pamphlet to sell. I contributed "Shalom Bomb", an exuberant poem of family, love and joy that sticks its tongue out at that insane machine of destruction. It only took a morning to write but went on to become my most antholo-gised work. On the day of the march we went backwards and forwards along the line selling our pamphlets like hot cakes for sixpence a copy. I even screwed up my courage and sold one to the director Lindsay Anderson.

"Wait!" he commanded as I began to move away. He read my poem. "This is very good," he said, smiling. "This is excellent." My heart turned over; the great man approved.

When I got back to Erica she noticed the light in my eye and I confessed that I had fallen in love with Lindsay Anderson. He was the most compassionate and intelligent person I had ever met after her.

On the march this time I had the misfortune to fall in line with Leah Wesker, Arnold's mother. The holy monster was obviously in sombre mood.

"When Stalin died, God died," she observed, and sighed. I couldn't think of much to say to that one.

"Bernard," she said a little later, "do you think you would be able to find some acting work in one of your plays for my nephew, Maurice Perlmutter?"

I told her that she should ask Arnold since he was getting more of his work put on than me.

"Oh no," she said, "Maurice is not good enough for Arnold's work."

Disillusioned with the idea of writing novels, I decided to catch Genet's *The Maids* at the Scotch House in Old Compton Street, one of the first fringe theatres in London, and left Erica at home with Adam.

Only when I got to Old Compton I decided I had other fish to fry, and walked right past the theatre and headed for Piccadilly Circus. I knew that addicts clustered around the statue of Eros outside Boots the Chemist, waiting for midnight when the next day's prescription would be dispensed by the night-shift staff. You could get all the dope you desired if you hung around long enough.

I circled round and round a mad circus of gyrating clowns, most of them kids, a few euphoric, but most pacing with their eyes almost closed. There were prostitutes, transvestites, sad little girls from the provinces with lipstick and mascara smudged across their faces. One of them was lifting up her skirt and offering her noonie. "If you don't want the goods, don't maul them," was her only proviso. Eros the god of love was stationed in the ante-room of hell.

At midnight the scene became a frantic saraband; all the fingers rushed into the chemist and emerged again with another supply of oblivion to take into a dark corner and fix themselves with.

There wasn't a copper in sight; they were far too busy collecting their dropsy from the whores.

I clocked a suitable character clocking me. "What's your poison?" he asked me.

"Speed. What've you got?"

"Something much, much better than that." He pulled out a handkerchief and showed me pills of all shapes and sizes and colours. "Try these," he advised. "They're black bombers. They'll give you the greatest high you've ever had."

I gave him five shillings and rushed away.

"Any time! I'm always here," he shouted after me.

As soon as I got away I swallowed two and walked two feet above the ground.

"How was the show?" Erica asked me later.

"Fantastic."

"Coming to bed?"

"Not yet. I feel like working. I'm inspired."

She pondered for a moment, then went to the other room.

I worked like a maniac until dawn. But when I looked at the pages the next day I couldn't read them; I had written reams of indecipherable gibberish.

19

Arnold's Circus

We moved away from our mansion block in Bloomsbury because we couldn't cope with the upkeep any more, and settled in a small, two-room flat in Great Titchfield Street, in the heart of the rag trade just behind Broadcasting House. It was a comedown, but we had each other. And on the very first day we bumped into Doris Lessing who lived just around the corner. We talked about kids and schools and her growing disenchantment with the "left", who she reported were getting more and more hysterical.

I got back home to a telegram. It read, "Assemble Downing Street. Protest." I don't remember the exact time or date now, but the instructions were precise. It was signed by John Arden and his *éminence grise* Margaretta D'Arcy. You have to laugh at the effrontery of it; the assumption that I would blandly follow orders. It was pathetic. I couldn't understand why John Arden was wasting his talent and getting sidelined by all of it. Anyway he should have known that I was beyond the pale and that I didn't jump to commands. I sent a message back telling him that my days with the Protest Posse were over.

By now the Beatles had exploded all over the world and the Days of Hype and Carnaby Cancer were upon us. Even the old Jewish bubbehs and zaydehs in Hackney were humming "Love Me Do". And my father, Joel Kops, alone since the death of my mother twelve years before, found Debbie, twice as blind and four times as fat as him, and married her.

Erica and I and all my brothers and sisters descended on their little flat off Mare Street to celebrate. We toasted the occasion with treacly Palestinian wine and ate bagels, premier-quality smoked salmon and double cream cheese. We were joined by a tribe of their friends and neighbours, survivors of a people that had died out long ago. It was as if I'd given them some of my speed. They talked Yiddish at this hysterical pitch, trying to get all the words in like the world was due to end any second. They were soon well away on the wine and singing sad melodies of the shtetl and the coming of the Cossacks to Kishenev.

At some point my father beckoned my sister Phyllis into the other room. She came out all flushed, and when we left the house she told me what had happened.

"I don't want Debbie to know," he had whispered to her, "but I've taken care of all of you. I've salted away a small fortune over the years."

"What?" I was amazed. My father never had a pot to piss in. The old, conniving dog. "How the hell did he get hold of a fortune?"

Phyllis had tears in her eyes as she continued.

"You all think I've been useless in this life," he'd said, "but bit by bit I've managed to save a healthy sum. When I go, I want all seven of you to share my legacy." And he had pulled her to the wardrobe and shown her the shoe box hidden under a pile of his trousers. "When I pass away one of you must come over and get this as soon as possible. I've taken care of you all."

When he died a couple of years later Phyllis went round and got all his things and collected the shoe box. It contained one hundred pounds. We all laughed like crazy when we gathered for the share-out. There was fourteen pounds and a few shillings for each of us. My poor old daft dad had really believed that this would be enough to take good care of us all.

I remember the few days before he died like a black and white snap. He did his dying at St Joseph's Hospice in Hackney, although he wasn't aware they were his last days. And he couldn't understand why he was being nursed by nuns. He'd never been near a nun in his life.

"They're not bad girls. They smile, talk soft and are kind. They never hit me like they did in Hackney General, but what am I doing here with them? And these horrible crosses on the walls? Me, an old yid from Stepney? What have I done to deserve Jesus girls?"

Just before he finally let go of the world, he demanded to know why there were people at the end of his bed.

"No one's there!" we told him.

"Look!" he insisted. "They're beautiful. Can't you see them?"

Later I told the nuns about what he'd said. "Oh yes, they often see the angels. How nice for him."

I had never particularly taken to Christians but I realised then that some were even good. At St Joseph's they helped you die with some dignity and with as little suffering as possible. Sister Anastasia had a perpetual smile as if she had just been borrowed from heaven.

"We love every one of them. We believe that everyone has a soul and is watched over by Our Lady and the love of our Lord Jesus Christ," she told me.

"Oh yes, Jesus. Nice Jewish boy." Even on that day I couldn't help quipping. "Circumcised and Bar Mitzvah, even. Shame he got in with the wrong crowd."

Those rosy, giggly Jesus girls made a lasting impression upon me. Somehow they had managed to pick up a little Jewish rachmones.

The morning of his death I went down to Hackney with Colin. He loved exploring the grubby back streets and breathing in the filthy air. He swivelled his head around and smiled generously on the dank and depressing factories and goods yards behind the Hackney Road. "Marvellous. Marvellous!" By the huge crucifixion outside the hospice we arranged to meet later and he wandered off.

He was waiting for me when I came out and embraced me. My face said it all. We walked slowly back along Hackney Road towards Shoreditch church and sat in the churchyard. After a few moments he wandered off to explore and called me across. He'd found some tombstones belonging to some of Shakespeare's original band of actors who'd strutted the stage of the Curtain Theatre, just across the road in Curtain Street.

We walked on from there to Brick Lane where I'd spent my dreaming, disturbed youth before going Up West. Queen's Buildings, the tenement we'd moved to after being bombed out of Stepney, was a festering carcass of poverty.

Colin placed both hands tight on my shoulders and fixed me directly with his eyes. "Bernie, you've got to write about all of this. Nobody else can do it. These streets are your memories. Write it down before they all disappear forever. Now. Go home and start today."

I had never seen him so vehement.

I did what I was told. I went straight home and put down the first, bursting words of an unstoppable avalanche, *The World is a Wedding*, my autobiography up to the age of twenty-eight. It took me three months and brought me some of the best reviews I've ever had, although as usual I earned next to nothing, just enough to buy myself a little time to carry on writing. But its reception inspired me. It gave me some pride in myself again and I used it to write a new play, *Enter Solly Gold*, a comedy about a con-man who dresses up as a rabbi, goes to Golders Green and manages to persuade a disillusioned millionaire that he's the Messiah. The Jewish community hated to draw attention to itself in those days, so it was quite a risky venture, but the very religious loved it because it poked fun at those who merely pay lip-service to the faith and like to pretend to be religious. I laughed and laughed as I wrote it. I was a wonderful first audience.

Arnold and I happened to meet again. We had managed to remain almost friendly even though he was part of the Court mob. It helped that I was more my old, optimistic self again. I told him about the new play and his eyes lit up. He was organising a touring festival for the trade union movement; it was going to be called Centre Fortytwo after the 42nd Amendment that advocates taking culture to the masses, so that "all the people have a chance to enjoy the beauty and riches of life in all its forms". He thought my play sounded just right for it.

"Will there be any money in it?" was my first question.

"Absolutely. We're being sponsored by the Movement." I almost baulked at "Movement". It was part of the jargon of those boring, left-wing activists who articulate their farts so endlessly. Still, any port in a storm. I promised to send him a copy.

He telephoned a few days later. He loved the play and wanted me to meet him and a woman called Beba Lavrin in the café of the Greek Cultural Centre in Fitzroy Square.

"Darleng, how vonderful to meet you."

Beba Lavrin sat opposite me wearing dark glasses and smoking from a long cigarette holder. She'd obviously seen too many Garbo films. Her every word was lengthened for maximum sensual effect and she exuded an aura of thick, Paris musk. None of the Greeks could concentrate on their backgammon games. I couldn't help wondering what she was doing with Arnold and what her involvement was with the Movement. Her best sort of movement had to be between the sheets, surely.

"Vhizzy and I love your play, Bernard. Ve think it is just perfect for ze Festival."

Every word was a form of seduction; each carried a subtext of pneumatic bliss. I thought she was great. The quickest way to a playwright's heart is to praise his latest play. I asked her where she came from.

"From Yugoslavia, darleeeng." She sucked on her long cigarette holder. "My father vos Studin. You know Studin?"

"Not offhand."

"He vos ze most talented sculptor in all Yugoslavia, except for my uncle Mestrovitch, who vos ze greatest in ze vorld. You have heard of Mestrovitch?" I had. She continued, "I vas fighting viv Tito in ze Vor. In ze mountains viv ze Partisans. I had pet volf. He vas so beautiful."

She couldn't have been more than about ten years old in 'ze Vor' so Tito obviously needed her badly; Beba's stories had so much colour in them I wondered if taking art to the masses might not be so dreary after all.

So, after rehearsal, I accompanied the circus on the road into the dark provinces of England, first to Nottingham and Leicester and later even deeper into the interior. Christ, how patronising. I knew I wasn't on tour for the Revolution. I was there to get my play on the stage and to get some money to assuage my bank manager. And *Enter Solly Gold* went amazingly well, though what a con-man posing as a rabbi in Golders Green had to do with Arnold's travelling circus, is a mystery to me. At least I provided some exciting, unpretentious entertainment, and proved to myself that my audiences didn't always walk out on me.

I dropped in on Logue one day declaiming his poetry to our masses in a factory canteen: "Do not live out your dreams, but destroy them as vanity. Lose all shame in compromise. Alas, I can do none of these things. It cannot be said that I am wise." You can say that again, Christopher. I also went to see the folk singers who sang with one hand cupped over the ear – that was to be authentic, you see. Jimmy Miller, later known by the more romantic Ewan McColl, was famous for his ear cupping. Michael Kustow was the only person involved in the project I really admired. He had a great sense of humour and it distanced him from the arrogant paternalism of the rest of the do-gooders.

I still remember Beba with fondness, and I laugh; she seemed such a ridiculous commissar along the Leicester high street. Some time after that she was the main character in an amazing sexual scandal that hit all the headlines. And after that she totally disappeared. Years later the poet Trocchi appeared at our door. I respected his work and was horrified to see how drugs had ravaged him. I noted that this could be my future, but then I was sure that I was strong enough to avoid total addiction. Trocchi was a friend of Beba's and was collecting money for her defence. Apparently she was languishing in an Italian prison cell for something or other. I gave him what little I could. He was quiet, and near the end of his days. I never heard from him again nor from Beba.

20

Barricades in West Hampstead

Nineteen sixty-three. Erica and I decided we needed to move away from the centre of town. We wanted more children for one thing. Being parents with just one child is like being a playwright with just one play; too much is riding on it. The Talmud says, "The world exists on the breath of little children." I thought children would save me. More children would mean more need for discipline, more need to do and not just be, watching my days fly away. It would give me less time to think. Erica was going along with whatever I wanted because she could sense my old insecurity coming back, and I almost convinced her that moving away to softer streets would help. Sometimes walking down the road I wondered why I didn't float away. The centre of town was metamorphosing into Kafkaland. It was an enormous beetle, on its back and kicking with its myriad arms and legs at the sky, stabbing out the light. Zombies walked the streets and offices took on skins of glass which displayed their entrails, whirring machines which never stopped working. Even Soho had become a staring place; all the refugees from suburbia who'd once found sanctuary there had returned to their dead, leafy lanes and tourists had appeared in their place; the avant-garde from Japan started to trickle in, softly spoken and smiling. No one sang in the streets any more. All of us were hurtling through time, working to be able to afford to return to a place of sleep, so that tomorrow we could all begin hurtling again.

We bought an A–Z and looked up those areas closest to Soho. Erica had an old compass from her studying days and we marked out an inch radius from the centre of town. West Hampstead lit up so we went there on the tube to have a look. We liked it on first sight. We'd travelled fifteen minutes along the Bakerloo line and found another civilisation, Cosmopolitan Urbania. You could see the actual sun shining in the actual sky, unblocked by threatening orifices. There were no tourists. And as we wandered along the Finchley Road we could hear some survivors of the old world speaking Yiddish. We saw black faces and heard West Indian music. There was such a diversity of smells living side by side. Each flat in every house was singing out with different, sizzling recipes. We saw Jewish restaurants with old ladies inside stuffing themselves like the end of the world. We watched six men almost coming to blows while gently sipping lemon tea. In West Hampstead you could go to your café, greet your neighbour and then try to murder him with a pastry fork.

We tried out Louis' Hungarian Café. The tarts were tart and exactly right and the coffee was bitter-sweet like life so we decided to find a flat in close proximity. These were just the faces we needed. The café across the road, Cosmo, was also crammed with people, some hunched in fur coats even though it was the middle of summer. Through the glass I could see bums, failures, neurotics, even creatures who looked like poets and artists, but not a zombie in sight.

In those days you could find a flat in a few hours and within a week we had signed a short lease, handed over seven hundred pounds and moved in. In theory, things were looking up. I was still taking speed but I reckoned that I'd find things easier to control now I was that much further from the midnight fixers of Piccadilly Circus. I should have been the happiest man alive: I'd found Erica, my anima, and we had Adam, the most intelligent kid in the entire world – he was growing up and could now dance and rhyme and paint and sing and swing his sword. And on top of all that we were not entirely broke. We could even go to a bottle of wine every other night.

Cosmo became my regular. It was ersatz Soho, and it served the most fantastic scrambled eggs on toast in the world. All the writers, directors and actors who lived behind the Finchley Road seemed to go there. At Cosmo I didn't have to face the terror of putting words together. I ate apple strudel with the poets instead. They clutched sheets of manuscripts in their hands and stared upward with soulful expressions. I saw Peter Brent one day; he had a doorstep of scribbled manuscript open conspicuously in front of him. And Elias Canetti often held court in the corner, scattering the crumbs of his amazing intellect to hungry disciples.

Despite its pretensions, Cosmo had none of the desperation of Soho. If any of these inmates dropped down dead on the pavement outside, they would certainly be found wearing clean underwear and there'd be enough cash in their back trouser pocket to pay the undertaker. Their existential posturing made an amusing change from the socialist rants that I had endured over the past few years. Besides, the days of the socialist cliché were over. The extreme left had grown hoarse and no one was listening any more. The truth was cascading out of the Soviet Union: the endemic corruption, the purges, the repression of artists and musicians, the elimination of a whole generation of writers and the pernicious persecution of the Jews, whose only crime was to dream of escaping the secret police.

I was just leaving Cosmo, resolved to return to my machine, when I bumped into the writer Al Alvarez on his way along the main road.

"It's the last time I'm going into that place. It's full of useless bums," I said guiltily.

But Al had something else on his mind. "Look!" he said and handed me a poem by Christopher Logue.

I read, "Six million Jews gassed in shit." The words cried out from the page and I felt sick. It was as if the death of six million took place so that a poet would later be able to exhume them for shocking effect.

Erica announced she was pregnant and although I didn't lift her up and twirl her around with astonishment, Hollywood fashion, "What, pregnant, darling! How come?", we were both delighted. And Colin started to find his way to West Hampstead. We might be in the kitchen, busy preparing tea, when he would push his face against the window and make clowning funny faces, smudging his nose flat against the glass wanting to make mummy and daddy laugh. All joy entered his world when we'd let him in and feed him scones. Then he would join Adam for children's television. It was all part of his preparation for the dark night to come at the Mangrove. When the time came, he would give Adam a final splash in the bath, reach into the medicine cabinet and take a swig of brandy and then be gone. It was as if he had suddenly heard the grey wolves howling in the late evening. He was obeying the call of nature.

Sometimes Colin brought people along to meet us. His friend Michael de Freitas was a charismatic character who soon started coming to see us all by himself. This was a soft-talking guy from the West Indies. Half black and half Jewish, so he said. Later I realised that had I been German, Michael would have been half German, or if my grandmother had been born in Baffinland, Michael would have been half black and half Baffinlander. He also claimed to be a direct descendant of the African revolutionary, Touissaint L'Ouverture, who led the slave uprising in San Domingo. Michael had a soft way of winning you over with his incredible tall stories so that you felt ashamed when you wondered whether to believe him or not. He also had a thing about our spacious living room. "If you ever thought of moving I will bring you the necessary bread on the nail," he often said. "Bread" is such a wonderful way of expressing one of our most basic needs. It was always "dough" in the East End.

Hannah, our first daughter, arrived. When I held her I felt a certain jealousy, a certain inadequacy, and I knew I had to move on and do something. I had to conquer myself and all my fears. I had to learn how to drive for a start. So while Hannah was straining to resemble a human being I dedicated myself to work behind the wheel with the help of a tyrannical driving teacher and, to everyone's astonishment, passed the test first time. I could drive, I could make babies and I could write. I was a fully fledged man.

Colin brought another friend round one evening. He had a familiar face. "Bernie, Erica, meet James Baldwin!"

We tried not to be overwhelmed. The guy must have got sick of sycophants by now. But what do you say when you meet someone you so respect? I had just read *The Fire Next Time* and I was in awe of him. I was about to start reciting the words that had inspired it – "God gave Noah the rainbow sign. No more water. The fire next time" – but Erica gently shook her head and I swallowed the words. I was always trying to impress the people I respected, desperate to prove that I was not just another East End boy.

We sat around the dinner table. Baldwin smiled a lot but his eyes burned with anger. He had a face which said he'd seen it all; that life had thrown at him fifty times the shit it had thrown at me. When we'd finished with small talk he wiped us out with a brilliant speech about racism. I felt it was my turn and I responded by talking about the situation of the Jews in England: about our attempts to become invisible and merge with the crowd; our attempts at being accepted; the polite but obscene racism we experienced and that had recently been diverted away from us and on to another scapegoat, the blacks of Notting Hill. While I spoke Baldwin's fiery eyes were darting all over the place, obviously activated by his unease and impatience. He wasn't interested in my theories, in the similarities of persecution, or in the sociology behind it all. The evening was a bit of a disaster. When he and Colin got up to leave I felt relieved.

Later in bed I told Erica a story I'd heard in Cosmo. "In Cape Town, there was this Jewish woman who was very kind to her servants.

One day she calls her boy, the one who does all the hard jobs around her splendid stockade, and says, 'Joseph, come the Revolution, you won't kill me, will you?' He replies, 'Of course not! Come the Revolution, I kill the woman next door. The boy next door kill you.'"

James Baldwin had disturbed my peace of mind. I didn't think I deserved to be thought the enemy of any black man; until that meeting I had always thought that we were on the same side.

"What a horrible man," I said to Erica. "Brilliant, yes, but burning with hate." She was quietly reading Baldwin's *Giovanni's Room.* "I'm never going to read anything that guy has written ever again," I said.

She laughed and shook her head. "I can understand his anger. I would be as angry if I were black. Anyway, he's brilliant. Now shut up."

But I couldn't stop thinking about it. I'd thought we were safe behind the barricades in West Hampstead, in our leafy garden flat far away from the dangers and temptations of the West End. At night, when my family were all safely tucked away in shuffland, I would go and just watch them gently breathing. I would touch the rose-petal faces of our children, I would look at the Pre-Raphaelite beauty of my sleeping wife, safe in the knowledge that no one would come and drag us away in the early morning, and that the only knock on the door would be the milkman. But in reality, the vermin of fascism, which we thought had been slain when the Jews had fought Mosley's Blackshirts in the Battle of Cable Street, had just scuttled underground; the obscenity was still living, oozing out of the sewers, and had exploded in fire in Notting Hill. The warning of fire next time was a warning to all of us. How long would it be before the poison trickled along the peaceful lanes behind Finchley Road?

A noise woke me in the middle of the night and my hand went out to feel for Erica. I needed to touch her to reassure myself that I was still alive, but she wasn't there. I could hear noises from the other room, so I crept to the corridor. There she was, rummaging through drawers and down the sides of armchairs, seeking out all my hiding places, retrieving the pills that I had so cleverly secreted.

I felt like she was betraying me, just like I'd betrayed her. I crept back to the bedroom to see if I could squeeze a few tears out, but I was too far gone.

She came back holding a small glass tube of my precious blues.

"You bastard," she said.

She didn't seem that surprised; I suppose it had been obvious for a while.

21

Have You Had Your Accident Yet?

"We don't need furniture, we only need us. We are the new Spartans," I said when Erica suddenly noticed how empty the flat was looking. We'd been living off the proceeds of more and more of our possessions.

"Most of those things are my past," she said. We'd sold books, chairs, an elegant Georgian sideboard, an eighteenth-century French mirror, a seventeenth-century English settle, some original nineteenth-century Japanese prints. Everything we had ever acquired was disappearing. And the buyers in the antique shops were good actors; they always managed to hide their excitement and screw me. All our beautiful things went for peanuts and I was too dispirited to argue. One desperate morning I went off to sell a Wedgwood vase edged with silver which had belonged to Erica's grandmother, without asking permission. Erica was furious when I returned with only a few quid. It didn't help matters that I was back on the old speedboat.

"You'll destroy everything just for a few lousy tablets," she said bitterly, when she could bear to speak to me a couple of hours later.

I could only plead with her. "Please! I'm feeling so insecure at the moment."

"Insecure? You? I don't believe it."

I tried to pull her close but she kicked my shin and locked herself in the bedroom.

Speed would never let me sleep. I would sit up all night, and then take more of the stuff. I had an idea for a new play, *David it is Getting Dark,* about a struggling Jewish poet who is taken in by a successful writer. The writer ends up publishing the poet's work as his own. My task was to pull this drowning play out of the deep. I kept dragging it on to the sofa to give it the kiss of life but there was no telling if it would pull through. In the end I gave up and left it there, fighting for its life.

I had other things to worry about. I was obsessing about the energy that speed was giving me: wondering how I would have to pay one day for using what I never really had. I was constantly exhausted but always wired. The days seemed to be getting shorter and shorter and there wasn't enough time left over to write. I thought I'd escaped, but the other me I thought I'd left crawling along the gutter outside Boots had come and found me in Compayne Gardens. You saunter along leafy roads under tall, protecting trees, the neighbours smile without daggers in their eyes and the blackbirds sing. You reach your garden flat and let yourself in, breathe deeply, go to the mirror to see what your journey up the road has done to your face, and there he is, smiling out at you.

I saw Colin outside on the pavement inspecting my spanking new car, a Viva I'd bought on the never-never, so I went out and invited him for a spin. I felt invincible. He came up close and saw that my pupils were enlarged.

"I'm a better driver when I'm high," I assured him. "Everyone is. You drive on automatic pilot."

"So, I get killed," he said and got in. We drove towards Watford Way at speed.

"I must put in for my driving test soon," I said airily and watched him stiffen and grip his seat for dear life. I laughed and he twigged. "I passed first time," I assured him.

"Have you had your accident yet?" he asked me. He sounded serious. "Everyone has a bad accident sooner or later, you know."

"If you're destined to drown, you'll drown in a teaspoon."

He chuckled. "I like that. From the Yiddish?"

"Where else?"

When we got home we had breakfast. Mornings were always a better time. The family in the morning is like theatre. I wondered if Colin had other part-time families like ours to have breakfast with.

Later that day the telephone rang.

"Mr Kops, may I come round and see you? I have good news about your play in Holland," said a breathless voice at the other end.

I turned on my benign writer's tone. "Of course. This afternoon?"

A roly-poly woman beamed at me when I opened the door. "I'm Rosie Pool, your translator."

I had no idea that anyone, anywhere at all was interested in my work, let alone wanted to translate it, and if my agent had told me then I'd forgotten. As far as I was concerned, I was a non-event.

But Rosie was reverential. She told us that *The Hamlet of Stepney Green* was already in production and that everyone in Amsterdam was incredibly excited about it.

Arriving in Amsterdam was mind-blowing. The entire Dutch press was there to greet us and everywhere I went I was received with honour. I asked Rosie if this was because of my Dutch origins.

"A little, yes, but authors here are almost worshipped. They are sacrosanct."

We laughed. We could do with a bit more of that in London.

She took us to the district where my father was born and I spoke to a few literary groups. On entering the room the whole audience would stand to greet me, which was a little unnerving, if good for the ego.

The play opened in Utrecht. The pace was so slow and serious, I could hardly bear it. Erica stroked my hand. Rosie smiled and patted the other one. "They're loving it," she whispered. They were sitting in absolute silence; when the final curtain came they didn't even applaud.

"Why don't they clap? Do they hate it that much?" I asked her.

"This is the best," she said. "This is true. Immediate silence is our way of true appreciation."

Then came the storm of applause. I was in the middle of a kiss with Erica when the entire audience turned round to face me. It lasted a full fifty seconds and was probably the closest I ever got to belonging to a community.

Later, there was a party in a huge medieval house in Prinsengracht a few doors along from where Anne Frank and her family had hidden. Rosie had been part of the Dutch Resistance and had actually tutored Anne at Westerbork, the transit camp Anne was taken to before Auschwitz, after smuggling herself in to organise a break-out.

I was standing by the food, swallowing Dutch herrings whole, when a man approached me and asked about my father's family. I told him that they had all been turned into bars of soap for the Hausfraus of Berlin.

He smiled. "Not all of them, not every single one. I survived. I am your cousin, Joe Kops."

I laughed. I could hardly believe it. Then he embraced me and I burst into tears. I drank some more wine and toasted the extraordinary courage of the Dutch people.

He seemed pained. "Yes, I was hidden, but don't believe the shit propaganda," he told me. "The Dutch were just as bad as the rest of them. In the main they were collaborators, except for a crazy, blessed few."

26. Hermione Baddeley, star of *The Dream of Peter Mann* at the Edinburgh Festival.

27. Irene Worth in my BBC television play, *Stray Cats and Empty Bottles.*

28. *From left to right*: James Booth, Irene Worth, Ronald Fraser and Miriam Karlin.

29. *The Hamlet of Stepney Green* in Utrecht.

30. With the Dutch translator, Rosie Pool.

31. With the literary critic George Steiner, protesting at the Polish embassy.

32. My friend Lindsay Anderson, 1923-1994.

33. The family in Nerja.

Enter Solly Gold
at the Mermaid Theatre.

34. (*above*) The wealthy shoe
magnate, Morry Swartz, played
by David Kossoff, and Joe Melia
as Solly Gold.

35. The wedding breakfast for one of the Swartz daughters.
Stella Moray (*centre*) as Mrs Swartz with Esta Charkham (*left*) and
Pamela Manson as her other daughters and David Lander as her son-in-law.

36. The family in the communal garden.

37. *Playing Sinatra*
at the Warehouse Theatre, Croydon.
Susan Brown as Sandra
and Ian Gelder as Norman.

38. *Who Shall I be Tomorrow?*
at the Greenwich Theatre
Joanna Lumley as Rosalind
and Harry Landis as Gerald.

39. The family growing up.

40. With Lindsay Anderson outside Waitrose in Finchley Road at election time, 1992.

41. With director Vicky Ireland and Glenda Jackson at the reception following the premiere of *Dreams of Anne Frank*.

42. With Quentin at Cooper's Diner, New York, in October 1999, a few weeks before his death.

43. With Erica on Hampstead Heath in 1999.

44. With our grandchildren. *From left to right*: Max, Chloe, Anya and Jessica.

The reviews were sent on to me in London and Rosie came round to translate them. They were all amazingly good, and my pride was somewhat rekindled. *The Hamlet of Stepney Green* went on to be translated into many more languages, and productions followed in Berlin, Warsaw, Copenhagen and Paris. It also opened off-Broadway and did well. A little money even started to trickle through.

Another time I went to Vienna. The Burg Theatre was planning a production of *The Dream of Peter Mann* and wanted me to go over there and discuss the project. I arrived and left within a day. I discovered that I had a problem with the place. Someone I'd met at the theatre in the morning had said that the Austrians were different from the Germans, and I couldn't help thinking they were dead right: you could say Hitler was imposed upon a sleeping German nation, and that for many, when they woke up it was too late, but Vienna went crazy when the Nazis marched in. The murderers were hailed ecstatically and they couldn't wait to round up their Jews. I took a walk round the city, full of animated people enjoying a golden afternoon, and felt I had betrayed all my dead relatives. So I dipped into my jacket lining and brought out a capsule of courage, made my way directly to the railway station and caught the first train back to London. The theatre never went ahead with the production, which was good. The applause would have crucified me.

It was as if Michael de Freitas had been expecting me. He arrived at my flat just as I did and I had no choice but to let him in.

Erica was surprised to see me back so soon. "How did it go?"

"Fantastically," I lied. "Ah, Vienna! Vienna! Beautiful Vienna!" She didn't believe me.

Michael was holding out a wad of notes. He was still after the flat. "I'll buy it now, man, if you give me a price," he said, waving the wad at me.

"I'm not selling at the moment, but when I do, I'll keep you in mind."

He slapped my hand playfully and smiled fiendishly. "I want you both to know I've become a Muslim. Call me Michael X from now on." He laughed as we tried to take in his conversion.

As he went out he slipped a small packet in my hand. "Enjoy!" he said, winking conspiratorially, and whispered, "It's real good shit. My gift to you."

Erica was waiting so I told her about Vienna. Then I went out into our back garden and had a look at my present, hashish. I can

129

only have taken about three puffs of the stuff before it all went badly wrong. It wasn't what was meant to happen, and my instinct told me to get myself back inside. Only the flat was getting smaller and smaller and further away. I was struggling to make my way back towards it, but the other me could see I wasn't making progress. He could hear me screaming, "Help me! Help me!" And I saw his body writhing on the earth like a cartoon in the landscape with the grass heaving around him, until Erica came from the tiny house and pulled him up. There was no feeling in the hands she gripped. He could hear her trying to soothe him as she led him to the door and into a dark room.

She came with tea a long time later.

"Bernard Corpse," she joked. I'd been out of it for three days.

"I'm an artist and therefore I'm fragile. Please understand." I always tried this special pleading but she never let me get away with it. "I promise never to touch drugs again."

She gave a little laugh. "If only I could believe you."

It made me sad. We had believed everything about each other once. Now our lives were descending into banality. "I really do promise," I insisted. "I just need a kick start."

I went round to the doctor, hoping that he'd give me something to calm me down. Even my hands were beginning to frighten me. He was a gentle young man and amazingly understanding. "Your problem, Bernard, is that your machinery is in overdrive. You are naturally high. Most people take drugs to get to where you normally are, but if you take drugs you go over the top. You really can't afford to take any kind of stimulant."

He prescribed me a sedative but I couldn't take it. I'd heard that if you took too many they could end up having the opposite effect.

When I eventually recovered and found my way back entirely into myself, I wanted to get away from England. The sails of winter were scudding across the sky.

I pleaded with Erica to let us go back to Nerja. "We have a little money now, and we can live so much cheaper there."

"That's the pattern," she replied, but she wanted to get away too.

"Come, let's go to Lorca country. Let's go to Andalusia. No more drugs, just that fresh air tinged with the aroma of wild thyme."

"Sounds good," she said.

A few days later we drove away. We sang all the songs. "There were ten in the bed and the little one said roll over, roll over…"

Erica was smiling across at me and I tried to relax; I forced myself to loosen my grip a little on the steering wheel.

22

Bernard, it is Getting Dark

We found Nerja nestling in another century; hard to believe it was actually December 1964. In the distance were the snow-capped mountains, the outstretched arms of the Sierra Nevada holding back the chill of Europe. The spring flowers had already dared to show their faces and were singing. We looked forward to spending winter in the warm and to letting the kids run around without overcoats.

We had only been in the town ten minutes before everyone knew about it. The locals took it in turns to scoop up Hannah, now almost eight months old, and smother her with kisses. Down by the Plaza it was *paseo* time. We found a beautiful, seventeenth-century house to move into. I felt much better already. I planned to get down to *David it is Getting Dark* the next morning, or failing that, certainly the day after.

But I woke in the night to find I'd been crying in my sleep and I knew it had to be an augury.

"Everything with you is the end of the world," Erica said when I woke her up to tell her.

"I came up from a place which felt like death."

"So, what's new?"

"Lorca's words haunt me. They're strumming in my brain. '*Agonía y sueño. Agonía.*'"

She sighed. "Yes, your agony and dream."

"Life!" I said.

"Yes! Let's live it."

Things got better. The peace of Nerja gradually started to rub off on me. I managed to finish a first draft. We celebrated with Black Label Torres Rioja and felt good. A first draft is a secure place to be. When the kids were asleep we stood at the window and watched the amazing storms smashing and splitting the sky above the mountains. Our fire of eucalyptus logs spat and hissed in the dark room.

"Can you believe it? I've almost finished it," I said over and over again.

We bumped into Victor Musgrave in the square. It was a perfect morning. There were just a few tables outside the café for solitary cranks like us who didn't mind the wind. Victor owned Gallery One, the avant-garde art gallery opposite the Ivy restaurant in Soho. He walked straight towards us as if we had an appointment.

"Hello, Bernie, Erica. Lovely morning! How are you?" He sat down. "Marvellous day." He expressed no surprise at seeing us. We might have been at a café in Soho.

I liked Victor; there was no side. He was amongst the first to bring the avant-garde to prominence in London and was responsible for giving some of our best artists, now household names, their first big break. He had an enthusiastic young man working for him back then, busy learning the tricks of the trade. John Kasmin always talked about the "Art beyond Art". I never knew what that was supposed to mean, but the pretension served him well as he went on to become perhaps the most successful art dealer in England. Victor was less ambitious. He was writing a book called *Sitting on a Fortune*. The title came from one brass he'd interviewed who'd been struck by this realisation after a few years of working her guts out in a sweatshop.

Victor looked at me with his beady eye and saw something that worried him. I was chewing a croissant at the time.

"Bernard, if you want to live long, make sure you chew each mouthful of food at least twenty-six times."

"Thank you," I said and slowed my mouth down.

"The answer is in the mastication."

I promised to be a good boy, and he got up to go.

"Be good, Bernie. Erica." And off he strode out of the square.

We never saw Victor again, and he died when he was still a young man.

The unfinished play was on my mind. A play is like mercury: the words that look so alive and perfect when you put them down can seem like utterly useless dreck when you go back to them. In the middle of the night I would creep up to the typewriter and, from a secure distance, arch myself over it to read what I had written a bit earlier. *David it is Getting Dark*. What did that title do, I asked myself.

What did it mean? Could I see that title in lights in Shaftesbury Avenue? Would it magnetise the passers-by so that they would be unable to resist the pull of the box office?

That night I dreamt I was in a bull-ring. The dark bull was snorting. I was poised, my sword ready to thrust into his neck. But he was too close; I could smell his breath. I side-stepped and he charged past me, red lightning in his eyes. Then he turned and came again, thundering towards me. A moment later he thudded into me and I was tossed into the sky. I was hurtling through the air. My blood was seeping into the dust. I was lying on my back, bleeding to death.

I woke up. It was three in the morning.

"We must go home. We must go home."

"Bernard, go back to sleep. Please." She knew I always felt better in the morning.

"We must go home tonight. Now!"

"Why?" She tried to bring me back to my rational self. "Bernard, what's got into you? Did you have a bad dream?"

"What have I done with my life? Nothing!" Boring as it was, my life crisis wouldn't go away. It shadowed me everywhere.

"You've done everything. More than most. Your plays are being done around the world. You've got books of poetry, beautiful kids, and me. What more do you want?"

"I want to go home."

"Come back to bed. It's three in the morning."

"No. London's the only answer."

"But it was you who had to come! You wanted to escape!"

She looked so beautiful in her helplessness. I embraced her, then I got my suitcase. "Start packing." It wasn't like me to command.

"And how the hell are we getting back?"

"We'll drive to Gibraltar and get the boat."

"There are no boats for ages. Anyway, you have to book in advance."

"Then I'll drive home. We do have a car, remember?"

"Do you know how far it is?" She got the map and pointed out the journey.

"I know it's a long way but I'm a good and safe driver. I passed my test first time. As soon as it gets light we're going." I started throwing my things into the case.

"And what happens if I refuse to come with you?"

"You won't. You love me."

She cried with frustration and started packing.

I went to the bathroom and took some speed. I reckoned I would be able to stay awake until Alicante at least.

At the town outskirts I stopped the car and looked back. Old Grandmother Nerja was fast asleep, huddling all her little houses, her sleeping children, towards her. My mood lightened. I sang, "The bear went over the mountain, the bear went over the mountain, the bear went over the mountain to see what he could…" but no one joined in and the rest of the song died in my throat. Erica in the back stared straight ahead not saying a word. Hannah gurgled next to her. Adam beside me was deep in his comics, even at this hour in the morning. The air felt unusually fragrant and balmy for late December.

"It's going to be a piece of cake. Dead easy," I assured them.

Later, as we started our slow ascent into the Sierra Nevada, it was as if the page of a script had been turned and the dramatist had ordered a completely different setting: Winter. A bitterly cold morning. Ice filigreeing the trees. Silence. We skirted past Granada, city of dreams and myth, where the Jews and the gypsies had once gathered in the markets to haggle and chatter.

I played a Segovia tape on the little cassette player. It was my favourite. "Only Segovia can play like this," I enthused, but Erica was still far away, no doubt wondering how she could possibly continue living with me. "Did you know that he's a virulent anti-Semite?" I asked her. I wanted her back on-side.

She shook her head in the mirror. "Really?"

"And Chopin and Ezra Pound and Renoir. Even Voltaire wasn't averse to kicking the odd Jew. And our old anarchist friend, George Orwell. How can such a great man have harboured such obscene ideas?" It was a favourite theme of mine. "And Arnold Toynbee. And Matisse! It doesn't add up."

"Nothing adds up. Why should it?"

"I suppose I have to forgive them their human monstrosity; the way I know you'll forgive me mine."

"Maybe. One day." She smiled a little. She was softening.

Hannah was asleep in the back. Adam was writing a poem about walking around the corner and he read it to me. On either side of us deep ravines yawned. One little lurch of my wrists and it would all be over, I couldn't help thinking.

23

Erica by Lethe

I popped a Drinamyl into my mouth; I needed some tranquillity. Outside the car the snow was falling. We had sailed away from the dream of Andalusia and were soaring up into a Christmassy land of rich pine forests.

"Are you tired?" Erica kept asking.

"No, I'm wide awake."

"When you're tired we must stop. Promise?"

"Promise."

"Even Lorca was an anti-Semite, you know," I reminded her later. We'd just found a town called Lorca further along on our route. "Can you believe it? And I forgot Carlos Williams. He was one too."

"Rumours."

"Tumours! I mean, just read his poem about New York!"

"It was part of the time, Bernard. They didn't mean it like the Nazis." Erica always laughed at me going on like this, but then she hadn't had to endure Mosley ranting hate through the megaphone in the East End every Sunday morning.

"And look at Agatha Christie, Dorothy Sayers, John Buchan."

"They weren't true anti-Semites. Agatha Christie's still alive and she'd be horrified if anyone accused her of that sort of thing." Erica didn't want me excited. She wanted a nice, calm ride.

"Maybe, but they gave comfort to the monster. Every little bit of their hatred helped stoke the fires."

"With most of them it was just a whim. A joke almost."

"Joke ended in smoke."

It was evening and we were on the road to Baza, still climbing steadily upwards, twisting and turning in a silent, white world. We passed some workmen by the side of the road and they stopped what they were doing to watch us, surprised that we were so high up. The weather had closed right in on us and ice was forming on the windscreen. I asked Erica to look out for somewhere where we could stop.

Just past a village which we couldn't identify because its sign was covered with snow we noticed a *fonda*, no doubt a thriving business in the summer season, and the husband and wife said they would give us a meal and a clean bed for the night. The woman took Hannah and nuzzled her with kisses and we all thawed into a happy family again by the open fire.

Our hostess served us plates of steaming rabbit stew in the dining room and asked us where we were from. When we told her she smiled broadly.

"Good, you must be Protestant." She looked around as if she feared she might be arrested before continuing. "I am Protestant, all my family are Protestant. But in this country we are surrounded by Catholics."

"No, we're not Protestant. We're Jewish. Hebrew," I explained, and she recoiled as if she'd received an electric shock. I believe her widening eyes searched our heads for horns. The rest of the meal, and breakfast the next morning, was served in stony silence. Not a word was spoken until she hissed, "This!" and handed us the bill.

The two of them watched us leave from the window. Erica and I opened our hands wide, spat seven times through our fingers and exchanged mad smiles for them to see. "Watch out! You'll turn Jewish before ten o'clock," I shouted as we pulled away, and they scuttled out of view.

Back on the road there was audible quiet. The little Viva swerved so gently and silently as we wound our way around bend after bend above the clouds, the brooding mountains on our left and primeval trees rising out of the swirling mist of the ravine on our right. I was taking a bend and doing my Fred Astaire – "Heaven, I'm in heaven, and my heart beats so that I can hardly speak..." – when a crowd of people, sprawled across the road, appeared straight up ahead of us: men, women, children and donkeys, travelling in our direction. Their colourful clothing and ruddy skins told me they were gypsies, breaking the rules and journeying on the roads rather than by the special tracks provided for them.

My brain went into overdrive, and the scene went into slow motion to compensate. I had three options: if I simply applied the brakes while continuing straight ahead I would certainly skid and kill them all; if I eased myself to my right and drove into the skid there wouldn't be enough time to come to a stop and we would hurtle into the ravine. I took the third option: I jammed on the breaks and swerved to my left. I heard myself shouting "Erica, help me!" as we floated across the road and the astonished faces of the gypsies turned and froze before us. We didn't quite reach the side of the mountain before the car veered back out to our right and then back again, back and forth. My arms and legs tried desperately to stop us from moving until finally the trunk of a huge tree came rushing towards us and solved the problem.

Silence. Then the sound of Adam whimpering. In slow motion, I turned my head and saw him wedged between the side of the raised seat and the door, restrained by one of the belts we'd had put in recently, thank God. That was one of us okay. Next I heard Hannah crying and swivelled round; she was hanging upside down out of the smashed back window. Erica was nowhere to be seen. "Erica!" I screamed but my voice only echoed down the white ravine. I wasn't sure if I was injured or not, even if I was dead or alive, but I managed to reassure Adam, now somehow back in his seat, and got my way out of the crunched metal, just in time to see the gypsies scuttling away around the bend. I couldn't blame them: the Civil Guard were shooting gypsies for lesser offences. I hurried round to the back and released Hannah, crimson in the face from dangling from the straps of her safety seat, and put Adam, dazed and crying, in charge of her.

And then I saw Erica slumped beneath a giant evergreen at the roadside, at least twenty feet from the car. I couldn't work out how she'd managed to get there when she should have been in the car behind me. She looked like a marionette who'd had her strings cut. I could hear Adam crying close behind me as I reached her and Hannah gurgling, joyful at seeing her mother.

Her eyes were closed and she looked peaceful, I thought untouched, until I saw the blood trickling out of her ear. Even I knew that wasn't a good thing, but at least she was breathing. Adam and Hannah pulled at her, and she opened her eyes and stared at me from a place I had never been. "Erica!" I whispered. "Please!" I wanted her to stop playing around and be herself again.

As if sensing the drama, a terrible storm broke open above us. It was thunder and lightning like the end of the world. Sheer Covent Garden. The dying heroine in the arms of her helpless lover.

Erica's eyes flickered open in the rain and she offered the tiniest suggestion of a smile. "Where am I?"

A salt taste engulfed my mouth. "Darling, we're in Spain!"

"Spain? What are we doing in Spain?"

"We're on our way home."

"Home?"

"Who am I?" I asked her.

"You are my Bernard." That was something. She smiled wanly and closed her eyes. A pale Jewish Madonna.

I became aware that other people had gathered around us. It seemed amazing that anyone should come from anywhere in this wilderness, especially in a storm. And I heard the urgent klaxon of an ambulance and forced myself to look at the car: a scrunched tin, a sandwich with a filling of bags, cases, coats, cuddling toys.

I joked with the bystanders, "How could we have got out of that?"

The medics took Erica into the ambulance and the driver indicated that they had to get her urgently to a hospital. Another vehicle would come for us, they explained. They drove away and, operating on auto-pilot, I got Adam and Hannah ready for the journey. Miraculously, they seemed unhurt, if wet and cold.

Two Civil Guards arrived on their metal machines and started to question me from behind their dark glasses.

"Were there gypsies on the road, señor?"

"Gypsies?" I knew what they would do to gypsies given half a chance.

"Yes, we know there were gypsies on that road, people told us."

Then why are you asking me? "Maybe I did see a few gypsies. Yes, I remember now. They were on the side of the road."

"You sure they were on the path?"

"Yes, I'm certain."

They sighed and put away their notebooks and brought me a few things from the wreckage: Erica's handbag and my travel bag containing all our documents. I grabbed some tins of dried milk that were scattered over the roadside. They nodded. It was all a dream. A car approached and the driver opened the door for us. The two guards saluted and I gathered up the kids and trusted that we would be taken to where they had taken Erica.

The hospital at Baza was an amalgam of medical field station and convent. There were crosses all over the place which wasn't a comfort. Worse, though, was the incredible filth of the place. The air was filled with the aroma of shit and urine. And to cap it all, the storm had brought down the power lines in the area and they were relying on the emergency generator for electricity. I felt like we'd arrived in some horror B movie, a charnel-house lit with huge Catholic candles, with nuns scuttling with bedpans towards the urgent cries of yellow apparitions festering in dank corners.

We saw Erica on a stretcher at the end of a corridor but before we could get to her two nuns had wheeled her away, into what looked like a sort of office-cum-theatre. I prayed that the power supply was stable in there at least.

A surgeon came towards us. "What is it? How bad?" I asked him. He looked as if he had just escaped from a Fellini film.

"She has a fractured skull. We cannot be sure how bad it is but we will know soon."

I knew that fractured skulls weren't good. And if Erica didn't die from hers straight away I wondered how she could possibly survive without infection.

"Oh, is that really bad?" I asked him. "She will be alright though, won't she?" More than anything at that moment I wanted the Theatre of Reassurance.

He moved his hand in that universal gesture that indicates it could go either way. "I will do my best," he said in his dark brown voice. I noticed he had hairs growing out of his nostrils.

"Her father is a doctor in London." I figured special pleading couldn't do any harm.

Unfortunately, he misconstrued my meaning and thought I had given him carte blanche to give it to me straight. Again he gently wobbled his hand from side to side. "I am afraid it is very serious. She may not pull through."

Adam listened in silence, clinging on so hard that my neck ached. "Mummy will be alright," I told him. "She just needs looking after."

I retched as I tried to smile reassuringly and cuddled Hannah. She hadn't been changed for hours. I tried to explain this to the top nun, and asked where they had put the few bits of our things that were rescued from the wreckage. She took the reluctant children from me and called for one of her underlings, who led me at a furious pace along corridors and down steep stone stairs.

"*Aqui!*" she announced, leading me into a dark room with her candle.

In the corner on a chair I found all our worldly belongings, including the precious packet of disposable nappies. I grabbed them and turned to run, and caught sight of a dead body on a slab. I was in the morgue; how Spanish.

When I got back the nun brought me some cream and powder and I changed Hannah. Half the population of Baza had arrived by now to take a close look at the crazy Englishman; a rare sight in the mountains in the middle of winter. They gazed in wonder at the strange sight of a man cleaning a baby's bottom, and in truth it was my first time. They were perhaps even more astonished by their first sight of a disposable nappy.

I improvised snakes and ladders with Adam before falling asleep on my chair, and awoke suddenly to see dawn through the window, poking its fingers into the sky. There was a familiar sound: it was the refrigerator humming, so the electricity was flowing again. I could see Erica lying on a bed in the ward. I was too afraid to talk to anyone first and went straight to her. She smiled.

"It's all very well for you," I croaked, so unbelievably thankful she wasn't dead. "All you have to do is lie there. But what about me? I have to try and manage without you." I wanted her to know that nothing changes, that I could always be relied upon to be a selfish bastard. I was rewarded with a faint strand of laughter.

"Do you have insurance?" the surgeon asked when I was back with the children.

At first I couldn't connect but then I recalled the last conversation I had with my accountant Aubrey, who had rung me minutes before we left the house to insist I send a cheque so he could organise insurance. I thanked him in my head. "Yes, yes, I am insured."

The surgeon grinned and opened his hands in that Latin gesture of thankfulness.

"Incidentally, thank you for bringing my wife back from the shores of Lethe. She was ready to cross." All this in terrible, painfully slow Spanish, scooped up word for word from the tiny but thick Spanish/ English dictionary I called my Sancho Panza.

"Your wife is seriously ill. She has a very bad fracture to the skull," he explained. "She has pulled through so far but we are afraid of infection."

Looking around it was obvious that avoiding infection would be nothing short of a miracle.

"Señor, you have a choice…"

It was up to me. He could get us an ambulance and send us all to Granada where they had all the latest facilities, and where Erica would stand a far better chance of survival; or she could stay in Baza and we could pray. There was nothing more they could do for her; they lacked every sort of facility and modern equipment.

"But the journey to Granada will take hours. Such terrible mountain roads, such terrible weather." I gestured helplessly.

He nodded gravely. "Yes, the slightest jolt and a piece of broken bone could pierce the brain. It is up to you. She needs specialist care. They have everything in Granada."

I looked around at the squalor. "She will probably die if she stays here."

He nodded again. "I agree."

Adam tugged at my coat. "Dad, what's happening? Is Mummy going to die?"

"Never! She's not the dying sort," I told him, as firmly as I could. I'd made my decision. "We're going to Granada."

24

Slippery Slope

While we waited for the ambulance, one of the nuns signed that someone was on the line for me and took me through to the telephone in the operating theatre, next to the knives and hammers. As I lifted the receiver the cast from the Baza *Oresteia* gathered round to gawp.

My agent's urgent voice was calling to me. "Bernard! Bernard! What's wrong? What is it? Is that you, Bernard?"

"Dina! Dina!" But the words got strangled in my throat. My mind was busy collecting the sounds but my mouth wouldn't obey the orders. I was a drowning fish, gasping for air. The crowd were nudging each other, happily observing Agamemnon at the mercy of the Fates.

"Bernard, are you there?"

I wasn't, so I gave up and walked out of the theatre and out of the stinking hospital, just as they were placing Erica into the ambulance, a nun standing by in attendance with the kids. I wondered how Dina knew what had happened and how she had managed to find me. Later I discovered that the accident was reported on Spanish television and had been picked up by the British press.

Erica was carefully strapped into place and the driver told me that we would be proceeding at the slowest possible pace. I thanked the doctor and the Jesus girls and climbed into the ambulance and cuddled the kids. Erica was out of it.

We were all ready to go when the Civil Guards appeared on their bikes. They informed me that I was at that moment being tried in my absence in Alicante.

"I am being tried? Why?"

"For nearly killing your wife. All people in Spain involved in accidents are tried. Don't worry, they might even find you innocent."

I laughed. The moustaches didn't see the joke. They told me that witnesses had come forward to say that gypsies had been on the road at the time of the accident, and they wanted me to revise my statement.

The suggestion was that it would help me no end with the final judgement. I thanked them, said nothing, and told the driver to start his engine.

With Hannah and Adam asleep, head to toe on a stretcher, I sat with Erica all through that night and watched her breathing.

In snow-covered Granada, Erica was gently unloaded. The hospital, the work of some modern architect, could not have been more different from Baza. Franco's deal with John Foster Dulles after the Second World War – American money in exchange for atomic weapon bases in Spain – was obviously paying off. At reception I was asked to prove we had insurance to cover the mountainous charges and then whisked to a suite of rooms lifted straight out of a thirties Hollywood set. Soft musak came out of nowhere and two Spanish dollies fussed around us. These weren't nurses, but sexy waitresses who attended to our every need. They were able to tell me that the trial had taken place and I had been found not guilty; and despite my efforts, the authorities were actively searching for the gypsy gang who had been ruled responsible.

Later that day, to my surprise and delight, Dina's assistant Rae Ellison arrived, all four feet nine of her. Her fear of flying was no less intense than my own, but to help us she had dared the journey. She passed on a note from Arnold, asking if he could help in any way, and then set herself up in the next room with her little portable and attended to all the forms and business paraphernalia of Erica's medical care. The insurance company assured her they would pay for the wrecked car, the hospital, the nuns, injections, operations, the food, everything. She also arranged over the phone for Adam to stay with neighbours in Compayne Gardens who had twin boys his own age, and she took him back home the next day. I was so relieved and so sorry waving goodbye to him.

You could buy as much speed as you wanted over the counter in Spanish pharmacies back then, so I upped my daily ration, which had fallen off somewhat since leaving England, to three a day. There's not much you can do for a fractured skull except hold on until the fracture heals, and I needed a crutch to help me smile and keep Erica's spirits high in the meantime. We were told that she would either get better or she wouldn't. She was attended by a charming young doctor who seemed intent on wooing his patients back to health. I don't know whether he was a good surgeon but he was certainly an excellent shmoozer. Either way, we were lucky; after a few weeks Erica started making her way back down the river. I explained to her that she had been haggling with the boatman for quite some time, as if she wasn't quite sure what she wanted to do, knowing that I might give her an even rougher ride if she returned to us.

While Erica's skull began slowly knitting itself together I was left to look after Hannah. We explored Granada together while the crowds looked on in astonishment at the sight of a man pushing a pram. We went for long walks every day through the slums, trying to sniff out the past, when the Moors came with their religion, their poetry, music and art and brought with them their Jewish doctors, poets, lawyers and advisers, and the two peoples shared a thousand golden years of peace and prosperity together. Most of the time I was as high as a kite zigzagging in the azure winter sky above us. I sat by the fountains and read the poetry of Judah Ha-Levi, written so many years before. "My love washes her clothes in the water/ Of my tears, and her brilliance makes them dry,/ Having my two eyes, she does not need/ Well water. Her beauty contains the sun."

Every afternoon we would go to the Generalife, the magic garden of the Sultans, where the noise of the fountains mingled with the laughter of ghost children hiding amongst the cypresses. The voice of Lorca came from the mouths of stone lizards. "Enjoy! Enjoy!" he said. "Life is fleeting." I would sit on an ornate stone seat, rocking Hannah in her pram until she fell asleep and just watch the visiting hoards, the Americans doing Europe. Their purpose was not to actually see and enjoy the fountains, but rather to take photographs of them, just to prove they'd visited, I suppose.

When Erica was almost herself again, I apologised. "I'm sorry. The sudden need to go home, the panic. Forgive me."

"You can't expect to be a good dramatist unless you serve your apprenticeship."

"Oh God! This has been the longest apprenticeship of all time."

Soon after that Erica was strong enough to fly home with Hannah and it was arranged for her to be met by her parents at Heathrow. I took the land and sea route and arrived home three days later. Erica's father reassured us that she would return to absolute normality over the course of time. For now her body, her arms and her legs were covered with enormous bruises. When she tried to stand and take a few steps her vision started to slip. She also began suffering from vertigo and her father insisted she see a top neurologist in Harley Street. We were flat broke so he paid. We were told that the organ of balance in Erica's ear had been impaired and would need a long time to correct itself, if it ever did. There was no medicine available for the condition but he prescribed Dexedrine for the depression.

The thought of Erica carrying a whole bottle of uppers in her handbag sent shockwaves of fear through me. Up until now the only thing that had held me back from total addiction was the difficulty of getting a long-term regular supply and here was one only fingertips away. A wonderfully full bottle. I couldn't think about anything else. I kept on having the same dream: I'd be driving a great house on wheels through the night and my family would be up ahead, signalling to me to slow down, but as I hurtled towards them I could not or would not apply the brakes. I'd wake up in a sweat, wondering how I could stop myself from dipping into her prescription.

It wasn't long before I began to reason that Erica would understand what I was going through. She'd realise that I needed this kick to finish my play, and she certainly wouldn't want me to risk my luck again at Piccadilly Circus. Surely she would grant me this one thing and forgive me my trespasses into her handbag? So I started. At first one, twice a day. Then perhaps two in the morning and one in the late afternoon. I thought she wouldn't notice. Poor, beautiful Erica, I decided she had enough on her plate. Why should she have to take on board something so trivial when I could just as easily deal with it on my own, instead of always running to her for confession? I had to take more and more pills to handle the hypocrisy.

One morning, not long after my first foray, she stood before me holding a small bottle, now almost empty. She was crying.

"These were meant to get me better," she said and ran from the room.

I followed. She slammed the door in my face. I pleaded and cried. I needed another chance. And God, I needed a tab of speed. My bones were starting to cry out for the stuff. The pills! The pills! My Kinkdom for some pills!

My father-in-law Max telephoned. He must have got the hint from Erica. He told me he wanted to check my health, especially my blood pressure, and so I went over to Blackfriars Road where Erica was born.

He sounded my heart. "Perfect!" he purred. Took my pulse. "Normal!"

Then he took my blood pressure. "Beautiful," he said. "Slightly low, which is also good." Then he knocked my knees. He was all smiles. "Reflexes good." The caning I was giving my body didn't seem to be doing me much harm.

Then someone tapped on the door and Max went out to investigate. I quickly grabbed a prescription pad from the table and stuffed it inside my shirt. If I hadn't been a writer I definitely would have made it as a criminal. It was serious, I knew, but I figured that Erica's father was such an honest and honourable man he could never believe that his son-in-law would stoop to such a despicable act. And even if his suspicion did come round to me surely he would want to shield his beloved daughter from the truth. You didn't need to be a dramatist to imagine the headlines. "Doctor's Son-in-Law Sentenced for Forgery and Drug Addiction." In any case, I told myself on the bus home, it wasn't entirely my fault. Max should never have left his prescription pad lying around. It was far too tempting for a creative and fragile spirit.

When I got back I locked myself in the lavatory. I had read somewhere that the best method of forging a signature was to turn the original upside down so that you can concentrate on copying the graphic rather than something you recognise as a name. I sat on the throne, took a book from the shelf and set to work. I copied the upside-down ink shapes before me and there it was, Doctor Gordon's signature. All I needed now was to forge the correct prescription. This would take further research. I had to get it dead right so that I could secure an endless supply. But it could wait until the morning; I had secreted away six tablets, the remains of Erica's little bottle, and that would be more than enough to tide me over. I hid the pad inside my pillow and went to the kitchen to get on with *David it is Getting Dark*. The characters were frozen there and very glad to see me.

As I sat down at the typewriter I at last admitted something important to myself: drugs were my reality; I was an addict. Then I popped a few pills and began to write. I was still trying to do this and failing miserably when Erica stormed in. She had taken the pillow slips to wash and discovered the prescription pad, the pen, and her father's forged half-finished signature.

"What can I say?" I asked pathetically.

"Say nothing. You're not only a thief but a forger."

"I'm sorry." It seemed so inadequate. "Please forgive me."

She started to tear up the pad. It was like she was tearing me apart.

"Don't!" I begged but she ignored my pleading.

She chucked all the little pieces up in the air and they sprinkled down around us.

"Tell me, what can I do?"

"Get help. Or go to hell."

"I'm lost," I cried.

She laughed darkly and left the room.

25

O'Flaherty Will Get You Nowhere

I've heard somewhere that the withdrawal from speed can be even worse than from heroin. I hadn't made a conscious decision to stop taking, but I needed more and more and I was getting less and less; and in the end nothing. Every bone in my body seemed to be cracking open, crying out for chemicals.

Adam and Hannah watched, scared and not understanding, as I screamed out in pain, fell backwards from my typing chair, and writhed and crawled along the floor. Erica told them I had caught a virus and that I would soon get better. I didn't know how I could continue to live with such a strong woman. She looked after me, bathed me, gently massaged me, encouraged me, and I began to see why men often get their partners hooked on the same shit that they're on. It's to bring them down, so that they can both be in the same place and descend to the lowest level together. When you're desperately sick it's hard to live up close to someone outside the experience. You begin to despise the virtue of your partner and their normal life because it's something you can't have.

When I'd come through the worst of it, Erica told me she was pregnant, several months gone. She had been in no state to tell me earlier and I had been in no state to receive the news. The joy of another child coming lifted me for a few weeks. I hoped, as I'd done before, that it would provide me with some foundation that would fix me to sanity and that would make me see sense.

I was only fooling myself. The emotional craving was still rooted within me, even if the physical craving, the urgent need for a fix, had left me. I wasn't operating as a playwright and without that I felt I had no identity. Calling myself a writer covered an enormous amount of question marks for me. It papered over the void. There was absolutely no doubt in my mind: if I was going to be able to get back to writing again, then I had to get hold of some speed.

My next-door neighbour was an actor, Leo McGuire, a clever sod from Glasgow. He knew about needs and his sort never stood in judgement. We exercised a common bond in sarcastic exchanges about the people who lived in our pishposh street, Compayne Gardens, somehow a respectable English enclave in amongst the Cosmopolitania of West Hampstead. Leo told me about a doctor he knew, Tim O'Flaherty, who loved artists, and especially writers. He supplied generous amounts of uppers and downers to most of the in-crowd.

Praying that I still counted as one of the in-crowd, I ran practically all the way to O'Flaherty's surgery, situated somewhere between Kilburn and St John's Wood. He said he was charmed to see me and put me on his temporary list, no problem. He'd read my work and we talked drama. He was delighted that I knew so much about the Irish and their literature. We talked about Finn MacCumhaill, Cathleen Nihoulihan and Kevin Barry. I quoted O'Casey, and talked about The Troubles. I marvelled at the miracle of *Ulysses*, the greatness of Joyce. We took turns to quote Yeats and Beckett. We talked about the affinity the Irish have with the Jews and our obsessional need of the family. I quoted Yeats's epitaph, "Cast a cold eye on life, on death. Horseman ride by," and he loved me for that. I told him that the Irish and the Jews loved life and the beauty of the world and the whole dancing thing of existence but that they also liked to wallow in the depths of gloom and listen to the music and the moans of their ancestors. In short, I worked bloody hard for my speed, and after half an hour I began to feel sorry for his other patients in the waiting room, so I cut to the chase and told him I needed a little something to finalise my new play.

"We all have our own poison, our own crutch," he said and wrote me out a prescription. I clutched it like a Dead Sea scroll. Then he added, "Do be careful and take as prescribed. These can make you psychotic."

"Life is psychotic. In this world you need a little bit of it to survive."

We shook hands and I rushed to Lionel Stein, the chemist. Later, I bumped into Leo on his way back from the pub. He could see that the cloud had lifted from my eyes. "Be careful, Bernie," he said, "O'Flaherty will get you nowhere in the end."

Abigail was born. We gave each of our children a substantial biblical name, a talisman from the bedrock of our romantic union, and something to hold me to the earth. Abigail had dark treacly eyes, as if Erica's long-gone amber, the stuff we vowed we'd never sell but which I did, had been returned to us. You could just eat her up, she was so beautiful. Days were burnt gold; the wonderful sound of our new baby's cry blended perfectly with the early morning Mozart.

I was grabbed by the desire to write a novel and I put my play aside for a while; the theme and the characters must have read my mind because they immediately burst in though the door. "We're here! So, what's for dinner?" *The Dissent of Dominick Shapiro* wrote itself in two months. I loved my Jewish adolescent and his sexual fantasies, and his family he loved and hated; the tasteless home opposite the Heath extension near Golders Green that he needed but couldn't wait to get away from; his escape to Cornwall and discovery of Daffodil, a sexy young English blonde, six inches taller. Then his initiation into the Joys of Sex, and finally his return to the heaving bosom of his mother and his neurotic loving father. The book received universally favourable reviews and it was good to get congratulatory phone calls from friends. It proved I was still operating as a writer.

Then Hannah, three years old, was struck down and became seriously ill with gastroenteritis. I was overwhelmed by a sense of sin, the first time that I had experienced such a Christian sensation, and blamed myself before anyone else could do it for me. Meanwhile Hannah was hallucinating and turning blue and was rushed into hospital in an advanced state of dehydration. She lay there for hours, crying about the bees that were attacking her; we were frantic. The young doctor explained that she needed liquid urgently but that the veins of young children are notoriously difficult to find and open. She was turning more and more blue.

In the end I screamed at the Sister. "Where the hell is the bloody consultant?"

She responded in her best home-county patois. "How dare you speak to me like that."

I shouted. "I dare! I dare! She's my daughter and she's going to die. Get that bloody consultant or your head will roll!"

She went crimson and turned on her heels, and within half an hour the consultant, Leonard Sinclair, arrived in evening dress, straight from a Bar Mitzvah. He went to Hannah and immediately found the vein in her arm, and the drip was inserted.

"It was touch and go," he confided later. He had heard of my work, and had actually read *The World is a Wedding*. It helped.

★

Hannah recovered and returned to us in a few days and became her beautiful, translucent self again. And Leonard Sinclair and his wife Anne became good and lasting friends. But the relief of it all left me thinking that I deserved a reward. I was losing weight dramatically but I wasn't dead yet.

I went back to Tim and he wrote me a prescription. I downed two as soon as I came out of the chemist, and when I got home I hid the bottle in an old pair of my shoes under the bed.

There must have been something in my mood, the way the words rattled constantly from my mouth, which gave me away and let Erica know I'd refreshed my supplies. The next morning I reached under the bed for the shoes but the bottle was gone.

"Here!" she said when she found me. "I give up. Kill yourself."

Erica always found my hiding places. It was like hide and seek. I would find the most perfect locations: the top of the wardrobe, deep in the upholstery of the armchair, between the books on the bookshelf, but she always winkled them out.

Later that morning, she said she was going shopping and went out. When she returned she informed me that she had gone round to my Irish doctor and ordered him to stop supplying me with speed. "We all have our weaknesses," he had said. There was a half-full bottle of whisky on his desk. So she'd threatened him with the Medical Council, the BMA, *The Ham and High*, everything, and made sure he got the message. "It's no use going there any more," she told me triumphantly.

"Thank you!" I cried, and meant it. Another avenue of supply had been closed to me. That meant respite. Just for now I had come to my senses.

"If only we could move," I said later. If we could move I thought I'd have a better chance of a new beginning. And no one could deny that the five of us were outgrowing the flat.

"But can you move away from you?"

"Sometimes moving does the trick. New home, new life."

"More money."

"Why am I doing this to myself, Erica? Most men would settle for far less than I've got and be happy."

"You are not most men, unfortunately."

★

Drug taking is the loneliest place there is. I thought that if I could only share its terrible landscape I could somehow halve the desperation and possibly survive; that if I tried the weed again then perhaps I wouldn't have to pop pills and mix with those lost zombies at the Circus. So I went out to Westbourne Grove, hung around with a happier sort of addict for a while, and scored. Then I hurried home and begged Erica to share a high with me. I had the dubious idea that we could do drugs as a family.

We dragged and dragged on the holy weed, mixing the smoke with the air and pulling it deep into our lungs. Erica didn't really enjoy it but she put on a brave face. It seemed to work, for a couple of hours at least. Later it was a different story. But for the moment everything was floating and high.

We put on a hilarious but oddly beautiful record, Hillel and Aviva on the banks of the Jordan, with him playing a flute plucked from the reeds and her singing a deep-throated, incredibly sexy, early Hebrew rendering of the Song of Solomon. Erica danced in her nightdress and I pulled her close. I wasn't able to do much more but she didn't rebuke me for it. Her anger had subsided and I was her fourth child. It would take a long time, and many drafts, before I would emerge as the full and finished husband she deserved.

I always had time for Mrs Quirk, our Irish neighbour. She amused me. Only a few days before, she had stopped me in the street and pronounced in her broadest Dublin brogue, "The trouble with this country, Mr Kops, is that they let too many Irish people in." And she was always a gossip. "There's an enormous flat going round in Canfield Gardens. Too bad it's been vandalised," she informed me that morning.

I ran home to tell Erica and we rushed round to see it. Canfield Gardens was just around the corner, but whereas Compayne was stuck up its own arse, Canfield was busier and the houses were closer and more mixed. It was perfect for us. There were these vast, empty Victorian dwellings in West Hampstead in those days, very often occupied by squatters and crying out for families to love them and bring them back to life. The squatters had gone from this one but they'd left their slogans behind. "Psychiatry kills!" and "If politics changed anything they would have abolished it years ago." Sentiments close to my heart, but it was getting near to the end of the sixties, I was forty, and I really couldn't put off growing up any longer. This was just the sort of place we could live in for the rest of our lives. We loved the area; we even loved the people we hated. You need your monsters to avoid each day, as well as the neighbours you like. And we knew we could make it beautiful. Four bedrooms, two huge reception rooms, two bathrooms. "We could even afford to have another child," I said in my excitement.

Erica sighed. "Live beyond your means. That is the whole of the law."

Behind the flat was a vast communal garden: three acres of grass and trees. Kids of all ages were playing together. Tiny wrens flitted and chattered in the trees. We could grow roots and flowers and eat porridge for breakfast and maybe I would calm down at last. I could write here. The incredibly high ceilings would provide me with lofty thoughts and epic plays. It was exactly what we were really looking for. When you come face to face with it, you know.

On the way home we bumped into Mrs Quirk. She knew everything. She told us that the landlord wanted three and a half thousand pounds for a short lease but they would consider extending to a longer lease or even a freehold. We quickly came back down to Compayne Gardens and reality.

"It was so full of promise," I said sadly.

"Just like our lives," Erica replied, smiling wistfully. Three and a half lousy thousand pounds. There was no way we could ever dream of getting hold of that kind of money.

26

Take the Money and Run

Friday night. I still felt a lingering nostalgia for the chala, the plaited Sabbath bread. Friday nights were always overcrowded with vivid memories. As a child, Friday night was the oasis at the far end of a terrible week of struggle and hunger because on Friday afternoons the Jewish Board of Guardians delivered a food parcel and tickets we could take to the butcher. They always left us a big chicken. I remember my mother singing in the kitchen, stirring the soup, and me hiding under the table as usual, savouring the wonderful aroma. The whole family used to spruce themselves up for the feast.

On this Friday night in West Hampstead it was spaghetti and tomato sauce. We were totally skint.

"Would you like me to sell out?" I asked Erica.

"Never! Anyway, you are what you are."

There was a knock on the door. It was Michael de Freitas, or Michael X as he preferred to be known.

"I've brought the bread," he said, and opened a tin which contained a roll of crisp twenty-pound notes. "Seven hundred smackeroos, my friends." He counted them out. It was the exact amount of money we had paid for the flat three years before.

"Michael, I told you, we're not moving!"

He smiled, a happy and knowing cobra. "I hear different. I think I hear you found a beautiful new place."

"If only."

"Here! It's yours. Bread on the nose. I must have this flat. I hear my voices deep in the walls."

We told him how much money we would need to move. "Good. Good," he said, placing the notes back in his tin. "I'll be back soon. It will happen for you, I know it will."

In a way he was right. God, the old gunof, moves in mysterious ways. The next morning there was an early telephone call.

It was Dina. She purred with elation. "Bernard, are you listening? I think I've just sold the film rights of *The Dissent of Dominick Shapiro* to an American producer."

Erica was watching my face. "Good news?"

I nodded. "I think so."

"Here we go again. The helter-skelter." But hope springs eternal and she hugged me as I listened.

Dina assured me it was a genuine offer. "The director Michael Powell wants to do it."

"Michael Powell? The great dictator?" I joked. I had worked as an extra on his film *The Red Shoes* years before. I spoke an aside to Erica in funereal tones. "Guess what, I'm going to meet Michael Powell."

"Dina, are you sure? Are you sure? Have you signed the contract?"

"Not quite. I'm negotiating."

"How much?"

"Twenty grand."

"Are you sure? How much down?"

"At least five thousand."

"Will you confirm that with my bank manager?"

"Absolutely." She was so happy for me. How could someone so optimistic be such a successful agent? Plus, she always smelt nice. Whenever you sat close Chanel No. 5 lifted you.

When I put the phone down we all danced to an old Yiddish record in time-honoured tradition. Abigail gurgled as we twirled around. Good news was just as infectious as bad news and this time I knew it was going to work. What's more, now we'd be able to move to our flat around the corner; we'd even have the money to make it really beautiful.

I met up with Michael Powell at the Savoy the next morning. He strode into the room, smiled broadly, and shook my hand firmly.

"It's a lovely book," he said. "Congratulations. I want to do this very much. We are talking to your agent." Then he asked if I had any time spare to write the screenplay – I told him that I would probably be able to revise my schedule to fit it in – and that was it.

Along Old Compton I bumped into Colin.

"Where's your usual Kafka expression?" he asked.

"Even Kafka must have had one moment of joy, surely?" I told him the good news.

Colin shook his head sagely. "Careful, Bernie, you can't beat them.

Just take the money and run. Failing that, just sell out and be happy."

"I want to sell out, Colin!" To sell out and lots of other things: to throw away my blasted German Olympia because the bitch wouldn't ever go wrong; to rush to a florist's and buy a taxi-load of orchids for the living room and go back to that shop in the Burlington Arcade and buy back Erica's priceless amber necklace if they still had it. I wanted to go to Fortnum and Mason and buy five sides of their best quality smoked salmon and fifty little glass jars of beluga caviar.

I headed for Dina's office off Regent Street. It was late afternoon and she was on the phone to New York. She waved frantically at me to stay shtoom. The conversation was all about me. Then she handed me the phone.

It was my husky American agent. "BerNARD," she whispered in silky black tones. It was as if she was lying beside me in bed. "BerNARD, my darling, you've just had a rave review on the book page of *The New York Times*, and tomorrow morning *Time Magazine* are going to devote a whole, raving, smash page on you and your masterpiece and Michael Powell is hot for it."

"Are you sure?" I piped.

"Am I sure? Listen baby, on the strength of these notices those Hollywood tom-toms have been beating through the night. You're IT, BABY and your price is going up! We've got them by the balls, BerNARD! It's going to cost them fifty grand at least."

I sat down. I was stunned. If only I had some speed on me. With that kind of money we could not only afford the new flat in Canfield Gardens, we could buy a flat in Soho and a house in Nerja too.

"Buy *Time Magazine* tomorrow morning, BerNARD. It's published all over the world," she cooed as if she was licking my ear.

The next day I went to see my bank manager, seeking an immediate advance. I spieled out my wonderful news.

"Are you sure about this, Mr Kops?"

"I can assure you it's all happening. My agent is now in negotiation. She's Herbert Lom's wife. Please telephone her."

"Really! Herbert Lom's wife?" That seemed to impress him more than anything. He said he would give me an answer before closing time. I hurried home.

Later that afternoon he was as good as his word. "Okay, go ahead. I'll loan you the money." They just don't make bank managers like that any more.

We went round to Nam Ting's to celebrate and stuffed ourselves on exotic monosodium glutamate. We even splashed out on a baby-sitter to stay the night. We wanted to creep out on a special mission very early the next morning.

It was just a little past dawn when we got to Piccadilly Circus. Eros stood alone. No lovers. No tourists. It was too late for the drug addicts and too early for the news vendors; we went to Lyon's Corner House in Leicester Square and had eggs and bacon. When it was light we tripped back to the Circus, my heart pounding. The news stall was open, with all the latest disasters screaming out for feasting eyes. And there it was, my future, the very new edition of *Time*. We bought a copy and searched frantically for the review. The book page seemed unusually truncated and my review didn't seem to be in it. There had to be some mistake.

"Did she say *Time Magazine* or *Newsweek*?" Erica asked nervously.

"TIME BLOODY MAGAZINE!"

I went back to the stall and politely asked the man if some pages might have dropped out, but he shook his head as if I was mad. I walked around and around in a small circle, holding my head until Erica told me to stop making a spectacle of myself. There was no rave review. In fact, there were no reviews at all. "I never should have koshered that bacon," I said, and laughed maniacally. "Just my luck!"

Erica took a look at the front cover. "Christ! Look!"

The headlines screamed that some astronauts had burned up in space. It had all happened overnight and practically the whole magazine was devoted to the grotesque story of those brave, American pioneers. I wanted to be sick.

"Bloody astronauts. How dare they get burned up in space. Just my bloody luck. Just my luck!" I said again and again all the way home. I tried to tell myself that they might hold the reviews over to the next week, but even as I sounded this one, thin bugle call of hope, I knew the score. The review would never appear.

When we got home all the papers and news bulletins were crammed with reports of the burned-up spaceship and the gallant astronauts. I went to bed and pulled the bedclothes over my head.

In the evening Dina called. "You heard the bad news?"

"Yes. Does my other rave review count for anything? What about the film deal?"

"It's not looking good," she said sadly.

"You mean to say the whole deal depended upon the *Time Magazine* review?"

"Let's just hope it's in next week's edition." She sighed and put the phone down. It was all over. There was a nodding, gently smiling silence from Erica.

"Say it!" I said.

"Say what?"

"Say that I should never have fallen for all that crap and pinned all my hopes on the film world."

"You never should have fallen for all that crap and pinned all OUR hopes on the film world!"

"Never! Never again!"

A few days later, when I had stopped fuming and cursing, I summoned up what little courage I had left and called my bank manager. He thanked me for being so up front but said he had already initiated the loan of three and a half thousand. He asked whether there would be any chance of my being able to make the monthly repayments now my circumstances had changed.

"There's not a shadow of a doubt." I replied. "Anyway, the book's got such wonderful reviews, it's bound to be snapped up eventually."

"Right, I'll let it go through." He sounded relieved. I was just elated that we could go ahead and buy our dream flat.

"Not to worry," I reassured Erica, sounding like my mother. "Something will turn up. We live in hope."

Michael appeared magically at the door, as if he had sniffed the blood of a transaction waiting to be finalised. "Here's the bread, Bernie." Those immaculate, virgin notes again; each one seemed to light up and sizzle in my open palms. He hugged me. I hugged him back, but shivered. Then he slapped his open hand against mine, as if to say the deed was done, and went to make a telephone call.

Colin dropped by and it all turned into a party. A black guy with a beard arrived with drums and brought in a white girl he'd found loitering outside. She looked Jewish and sad. "Look what I found," he said.

"Where've you been, you stupid cunt?" Michael screamed, his Caribbean lilt drowned out by his rage. Then his contorted face softened and he pulled her close and whispered suggestive endearments into her ear. I was surprised that Michael X, self-styled leader of the black community of Great Britain, had a white girlfriend. I couldn't think that it would help his ambition.

When we moved, Horace Ove, a lovely, Trinidadian film director, moved in with his family. Michael was a friend of his and had sold him the lease. He made more than two hundred per cent profit on the deal. Still, it was good to know that Horace and his lovely wife Mary would be living there with their kids Zack and Indira after us.

Michael X left London not long after. It turned out that he was involved in shady deals all over London, and he fled to Trinidad to avoid a financial scandal. His girlfriend was later found hacked to death. Michael managed to get away before being charged with her murder and hid in the Guyanan jungle. But he was caught, brought back to Trinidad and put on trial. He was hanged in Port of Spain in 1975.

In Canfield Gardens, Erica and I decided to cancel out the problems of the future and just indulge in the joy of finding a place where we could spend the rest of our lives. We sat in our almost empty flat, furnished just the way we liked: a carpet and a few modern, comfy chairs, and mattresses on the floor in the bedrooms, and were content simply enjoying the space and the peace, with Adam and Hannah playing in the garden and Abigail, four months old, gurgling in her cot.

My brother Jack came round for tea. "Lovely flat. When are you getting the furniture delivered?"

When he left, Erica said, "How am I going to manage? I've only got a lap big enough for two."

At first it didn't sink in. "What are you trying to say?"

"I'm pregnant."

"Whoopee!" We could just about afford champagne. I kissed her. "Anyway, you've got a lap big enough for the whole world."

"How will we survive?" I asked her later as we snuggled together in bed. I should have been reassuring her, but it always seemed to be the other way around.

"We'll survive by looking back on all this and laughing."

"Please don't let me ever take drugs again."

"You can't now. There's too much at stake."

"Yes," I replied. "Absolutely. Why should I want to throw all this away?" I was feeling clean and virtuous. Once an addict always an addict, but sometimes the craving idled in neutral. Five cups of coffee a day were keeping me sane and ticking over for the time being. "And please don't let me ever get involved in the film racket again."

"You always pass the onus on to me, have you noticed?"

"Why are you giving me more problems?"

I was resolute. It was plays and only plays from now on. That is, until two days later when a nice man called Otto Plaschkes telephoned me. He had a film project in mind and thought I would be the perfect person to do the screenplay. I arranged to go and see him in St John's Wood the next morning.

27

Lindsay

As it turned out, Otto Plaschkes was a good angel, a Jewish boy who had not only survived the war but also Wardour Street. At the time I didn't realise just how rare his decency was in the film game. He was fresh from producing *Georgie Girl*, a palpable hit, and had just acquired the rights of a book by Yael Dayan, the daughter of the one-eyed Israeli general. We got on immediately. I always judged people by wondering what Erica would make of them and in this case I was sure she would approve.

Otto thought I was just the right person to do the screenplay but, after reading the book, I felt it wasn't for me. There we were, trying desperately to keep up with the new loan, and I was sitting on my high horse. Why couldn't I just climb down once in a while and do something quite good for the money? I told Otto it would be better if he got himself a woman screenwriter – after all the main protagonist was a young girl in the Israeli army – and suggested Shelagh Delaney.

"I would still like us to work together," he said. "I do good crap, whereas they all do bad crap. Why not do some crap for me?"

I had been toying with an idea for a novel based around the death of my father. It was hardly the basis for a rip-roaring comedy but I told Otto about it anyway and he got quite excited. He agreed to give me a small option on a first treatment and said we could see how things worked out from there.

We all whooped with delight in our great echoing new empty flat, even if an advance of a few hundred would go nowhere near to solving all our financial problems. It was the beginning of a happy time. I was able to take a break from speed, and Erica's belly was growing apace. She seemed to have thrown all her usual cares out the window and decided that the best thing to do was live for the day and enjoy each moment.

We always did our shopping in John Barnes, the local general store. It was just opposite Finchley Road underground station, at the junction that brings all the multi-cultural flotsam from Europe and suburbia together from the streets around it. John Barnes was the sort of place where you could buy all your food in the basement, and your socks and darning thread on the next floor up. Its café and restaurant on the first floor soaked up the overspill from Cosmo down the road.

I knew that Lindsay Anderson lived somewhere nearby and I often saw him slowly negotiating the food aisles, as if making a life or death decision. He had been very nice to me at Aldermaston, and I was eager to remake his acquaintance, even if his kindness turned out to have been only public school politeness. One brave morning I contrived to double back and go once again around by the jams and marmalades where I had seen him lingering.

The stooping figure looked up at me. "My dear boy!" His welcome seemed genuine enough. He sighed. "Do you remember, Bernard, the days of the great conserves?" He sighed again. "Where are the conserves of yesteryear? The fig? The quince? The mulberry?" He sighed better than any other non-Jew I had ever known.

I ventured an opinion. "Any man who can sigh like that cannot be a true Englishman."

"Never forget that I am a Scot," he said. "If I were an Englishman I would cut my throat and die of shame."

Proximity is a very important cement in making a friendship. Our quick chat revealed that we lived two streets away from each other and he seemed to like me. He even told me that he admired my work. We retreated from the jams and went upstairs for coffee and toast and marmalade. He was very polite to the waitress, and carefully insistent that it had to be Frank Coopers thick cut marmalade, and none other. I sat watching him, hardly able to believe that I was taking coffee with the great Lindsay Anderson. Yet he was a man totally without pretension, happy to talk about the price of herrings one minute and the greatness of Eisenstein the next.

We were almost ready to go when he asked me what I was working on. I told him about Otto Plaschkes and the idea I had about my father: a story based around an old Jewish man dying in a Catholic hospice, questioning his life, while his children look on, disparate and yet joined together. Lindsay's eyes lit up as I told him and that gave me the courage to ask him if he would consider directing it if it ever came to fruition. He said he would be delighted to talk further on the subject. I danced all the way home. By the time I got there I really believed Lindsay had committed himself to the project. Otto was thrilled and immediately called my agent to discuss terms for an option. He also phoned Lindsay, who very kindly protected my bursting bonfire of vanity and didn't dismiss the notion.

Lindsay and I started to work together on getting the story line of *Yes from No-Man's Land* into some kind of viable shape. For a few months I went round to his house in Greencroft Gardens every morning. He would greet me in his incredibly threadbare dressing gown, we would discuss the best way to make coffee and the best brands, and then he would prepare two mugs of instant and we would get down to work. He would quiz me on my deepest intentions: what I thought my story was about and what it really was about. I loved it when the phone rang and it would be someone like John Gielgud, Rachel Roberts, Malcolm McDowell or Richard Harris. The way he kept faith with all his actors was what I admired most about Lindsay; the ones who worked for him in his early days were still working for him at the end.

We soon put together what he and I thought was an excellent story line. Unfortunately, however, the money ran out and I never got to write the first draft.

"So what's new?" Erica observed drily.

I groaned. "Never again."

Colin laughed. "Take the money and run."

"Fuck the theatre and fuck films."

Rebekah, my third daughter, was born and we had three sisters. That meant there were six of us now in the Kops family. "Enough already," I could hear my dead mother say. "How are you going to provide for them?" In an attempt to answer her, I went to Secker and Warburg to see if they would publish me. I hit it off with both of them and set about writing some novels.

Lindsay moved into the block of flats opposite. Our work rooms almost faced each other, so I got to watch him work. I would sometimes get to my typewriter at six in the morning and find Lindsay already there. I started popping over to his place for breakfast. He would fulminate about the pernicious Establishment and the tyranny of their public schools, all the while surrounded by walls adorned with pictures of the smiling Queen Mother and Big Ears. He would lean forward to peruse their faces and smile. In amongst the royals were glum columns of public school boys, row upon row, staring out at us, the inspiration for his 1968 film *If.* Songbooks from Harrow and Eton were piled on the sideboard.

I also bumped into him in the street at least once a day. He was nearly always on his way to John Barnes or Sketchley's with shirts or a suit to be dry cleaned. He told me that he always used Sketchley's because he had shares in the company. An anarchist with shares!

I found him in John Barnes one morning looking so angry I suspected another film deal had fallen through, but it turned out he'd just sacked his new secretary and was desperately trying to find another one. "And I don't mean any smart little English bitch who sits prim and upright at the typewriter," he said. I recommended Cathy Burke, a volatile woman who had once done some work for me and laughed a lot. She lived in the council flats just around the corner and her daughter Jackie and Hannah were best friends at their primary school.

"Burke? Could she be Irish?" He seemed much brighter already.

"Yes, probably London Irish from way back."

"She sounds quite perfect. Get her to call me."

They hit it off from the very first moment and she became indispensable. I was glad to be of some help to the great man.

Back at the flat, I was still attempting to finalise my maverick play *David it is Getting Dark.* Sometimes you can go so far with a text and then you get bogged down. You put it away in a drawer with the vague hope that maybe one day you will take it out and see how to resolve all its problems. So I was astonished when Dina rang while I was working on it and announced that she had sent an earlier draft to Paris and it was now in production. The first night was just two weeks away.

"They want you there for the opening," she told me. "Will you go to Paris?"

In France the play was called *David le Nuit Tombe,* which immediately made it sound most important. I watched the final rehearsals in the incredible, early Georgian Theatre du Plaisance. The director informed me how lucky we all were to get Laurent Terzief, one of the leading actors in France. Laurent was tall and concave and had a beautiful, melancholic face. He carried a small bag of dried fruit around with him which he nibbled at every so often.

The night before we opened he invited me out for a drink, just the two of us. We got very drunk in a café close to the theatre in Montmartre and didn't emerge until well into the early hours, both singing merrily. I was John and he was Paul. "I wanna hold your haaaand, I wanna hold your haaannnnnnd..."

We were zigzagging along the deserted boulevard with our arms linked when two policemen came up and blocked our path, their hands clutching their truncheons. I saw their van close by and the doors were open, ready to receive customers. They were about to beat us up for sure when one of them suddenly stopped in his tracks. His mouth dropped open. "*Monsieur Terzief! Pardon, Monsieur Terzief!*" he exclaimed, and said something about famous actors having a special licence. Whatever it was, we certainly weren't in trouble any more. They joked with delight and Laurent joked back and they apologised again and waved us on like arse-licking courtiers, indicating that the boulevard was ours to dance or shit in as we wished. I wondered how many English policemen on night patrol would recognise Laurence Olivier on the prowl and treat him with such ceremony.

The play opened and it seemed to work. Terzief was fantastic and I began to think that the play was not at all bad. The reaction at the curtain was warm, the applause intense and sustained. Although one can never tell. I knew that appreciation could easily dwindle into damning invective if the reviews were bad.

The actors emerged, high and excited, and took turns to kiss me. We were all going to a restaurant for the customary feast on food and words; their usual custom after every performance. They said they would wait while I had a quick shower, and I went backstage into the small apartment the theatre had let me stay in.

I never did get to the restaurant. I was about to step into the shower room when a huge Alsatian dog hurtled towards me and gave me the shock of my life. I only just managed to dash inside before it got to me with its fangs, and it hurled itself against the door in a fury of disappointment. Unfortunately, the theatre people had forgotten to tell me that each night the night-watchman would sit in his cubby hole at the stage door, letting his Cerberus roam freely. And they had also forgotten to tell the night-watchman that they had a guest staying there. Every time I ventured to open the door of the shower the dog dashed towards me, gnashing its teeth and crashing against the wood. In the end I became desperate to relieve myself and there was nothing to do but piss and shit in the shower and wash all the stuff away with water, helping it go down with one hand and holding my nose with the other. I spent my night of triumph shitting in the shower and sleeping on the floor.

After I was able to break out the next morning, I was told that the cast had been disappointed but understood that artists were often overcome by the enormity of a first night.

That trip away set something off in me. When I got back to Victoria the craving I'd kept suppressed came right to the surface and I needed speed badly. I went straight to Piccadilly and picked up a reward of at least fifty tabs before heading for home.

The children were happy enough to see me and get their boxes of chocolate sardines and all those other wonderful confections that the French are so good at creating. But Erica took one look at my dilated pupils and knew. She didn't say a word.

"Welcome home!" said my nodding image in the shaving mirror.

David it is Getting Dark was never to see life in the country of its conception. It was born, lived and died in Paris. It had no afterlife except to be published in French by Gallimard in France.

28

The Big Time Beckons

In many ways money was the cause of my continuing emotional breakdown. Poverty was always hovering just outside the door. Final demands were beginning to pile up and if we couldn't meet the monthly repayments of our bank loan we were going to have to leave our home.

The phone rang. It was a soft, American voice and I was on my guard immediately.

"Hello, BerNARD Kops? Cubby Broccoli."

I had heard the name before. When Broccoli asked me if I would go to Mayfair to meet him and his partner Harry Saltzman the penny dropped: these were the producers of the James Bond movies. What could they be wanting from me? I soared. I plummeted. It's funny how you fall into the same trap over and over again. You want so much to believe that things can change. I had a double addiction. One was speed and the other was hope.

The soft voice was waiting for my reply. "BerNARD? Are you there?"

"Yes, good morning, Mr Broccoli. Sorry. Yes, of course I will come. When?"

Erica was standing behind me when I put the phone down, looking underwhelmed. "Darling, this is kosher. This could be big!"

She groaned. "Not again, please not again."

This time I knew I was about to prove her wrong. These guys, Harry and Cubby, were the big time.

Next Dina rang. She duplicated almost exactly the news I had already received. "Bernard, good news! How would you like to go to Mayfair to meet Cubby Broccoli and Harry Saltzman?"

I played the innocent. "Are they important?"

"Bernard, these are only two of the most important producers in the industry."

"Great!" I pretended I didn't already know. I didn't want to deflate her excitement. "When do they want to see me?"

"Next Monday morning. Eleven o'clock."

"Why do they want to see me?"

"Why? They want you to lead an expedition to the North Pole."

"What?"

She laughed. "Why do you think they want to see you? To write a film, of course! They have a project in mind and they think you are just the right person."

"Will it be good money if it happens?"

"Bernard, how many times have I had to come to your place and plead with the broker's men not to remove your furniture?"

"I meant how much can I expect?"

"Lots. Thousands." She sounded so happy for me.

"We're going to be rich," I told Erica.

"Here we go again," she said, but not too cynically this time.

"To bend your principles just once for a bit of security is not a shame. It's Talmudic. It's for the sake of the family."

She sighed. "Darling, I just want you to write a great play."

"Yes, I know, but I've got to get some peace of mind and buy some time first."

That week I bought an old black taxi-cab on the strength of it all. I'd seen an advertisement in the classified second-hand car section of the *Evening Standard* and I rushed round to a mews in Cricklewood Lane and there she was. I bought her for a hundred and fifty pounds, the last bit of money we could conjure up. It was falling to pieces, obviously saved from the knacker's yard and given the kiss of life, but it had such elegance. The smell of the leather took me back to days of serenity that I had only ever dreamed about. And it drove like a dream. In my state I shouldn't have been driving at all, but if I were to have a collision in this, I figured I'd be okay, if very sorry for the other driver. It was built like a tank on a chassis. On my way home along Kilburn High Road I wondered why so many people were waving at me, until I realised they were trying to hail me. I waved back.

And so I found myself in a mews in Mayfair taking tea with these big-time producers. I had made a special effort to make myself look respectable. I had even polished my shoes.

Harry Saltzman was a cliché, the perfect image of every little film producer rolled into one. He was my uncle Hymie: a dealer, a spieler, an operator with the guntz. He could have been selling anything.

"BerNARD, we want you to write the screenplay of this fabulous stage play we recently acquired."

Cubby Broccoli played the nice, quiet one. He just smiled and nodded. I liked him.

Before we got down to it I went to the loo and swallowed some speed. Chemical assistance was invaluable at times like this. Then I ate slabs of cherry cake while the producers ate out of my hands. It was obvious they wanted me. As far as they were concerned, I was a very successful author. I had books and plays to my credit, I had good reviews, and they'd been told by my agent that I was perfect for the enterprise.

"We think you've written a great book." Cubby got a rare word in.

"Which one?"

"The one about being on the bum. About Soho, the East End. *The World is My Oyster.*"

"Oh, you mean my autobiography, *The World is a Wedding.*"

"That's the one."

Harry chimed in. "It's a beautiful book, BerNARD. That's why we know you can handle this fabulous work."

I sat there with almost calm indifference while they did their spiel. Harry was selling tablecloths down Petticoat Lane. Surely he could read the Jewish runes and see that I didn't need to be convinced, that I was entirely in his lap already?

"Hang on." I was bold that afternoon; speed had given me poise. "What's the name of the work? Is it a play? Is it a book? Is it Superman?"

"It's *Fings Ain't Wot They Used T'Be* by Frank Norman."

I nearly choked on my cherry cake. "Do you know Frank?" Cubby asked.

Did I know him? Frank was my old Soho protector. The day after I'd met Erica we had shared a boiled egg with Frank for our Christmas dinner, the best Christmas feast I ever had. And a year later when he had just come out of the nick, I'd given him an old portable I had lying around so he could start writing. He had gone back to his pad and written an article about his life in and out of the Scrubs and brought it back to me. I'd sent it to Kingsley Martin, the editor of the *New Statesman* and *Misquotation* and Frank was launched. It kept him busy and out of crime, and he became happy and successful.

"Frank's one of my best friends."

"Of course, that's why we wanted you," Harry lied. "You have the talent and the knowledge that's needed to give this wonderful work true authenticity."

They told me how they wanted me to approach the subject. It had to be Funny. Serious. Sexy. Evocative. Light. Scary. Gentle/ Tender. Harsh. Revealing. Loving. Hating. Fresh. Familiar. Different. Sweet. Funny. It had to be a family film of corruption. Seamy but Moral. They wanted blackmail, true love, frightening criminals, but Hearts of Gold.

"Above all, BerNARD, it has to be about Redemption."

I nodded. "Sounds easy." I wondered what Frank would say when he found out I was being offered the job. There was a terrible idea going round in those days that the creator of the work should never be allowed anywhere near the screenplay.

We stood up, shook hands and they beamed. "We know you'll do a great job. We'll be in touch with your agent."

I floated home, half expecting flags to be flying on top of our roof.

"Darling, we've hit the big time at last!"

"Big? That'll make a change!" That loving glance. When Erica joked like this, fings were like they used to be. That night I even managed to perform. Speed is a cunning bastard. It raises the desire but inhibits the performance; I somehow got under its radar and the bedroom was happy.

Dina negotiated a wonderful deal. It worked out at roughly five hundred pounds per week while I was working on the script and five thousand pounds on the day they started shooting. In those days it was a veritable fortune, and it's not to be sneezed at even forty years on. We were going to be rich. The news got around. My bank manager took me to lunch. My grasping uncles hid their daggers behind their backs and rang late at night to wish me luck. My brothers and sisters hooted. Adam and Hannah danced.

Cubby and Harry wanted me to work at Pinewood, I suppose to keep their eyes on me and see that I was actually doing a full week's work. I would be provided with an office and a secretary. I told them I hated travelling as journeys always sapped my creativity, so on Monday morning an immaculate chauffeur-driven Austin Princess glided up to my front door. I strode out of the flat and sank into the upholstery.

Cubby and Harry beamed as they ushered me into my office.

The table was bare except for a telephone, a ream of virgin paper, and a dozen highly sharpened pencils.

"First, we'd like a story line. Something a bit more up to date. Naughty, even salacious, but clean," they instructed.

Then I was on my own. My secretary sat with her knees close together in the other room, ready to obey my commands. The birds of Pinewood sang outside the window.

As soon as I sat down I missed the wonderful trivia of family life. In the next office two boa constrictors were waiting for my story line. Speed might have helped but I knew drugs were out for the duration.

I rang home. "How can I possibly work in these pasteurised conditions?"

But the thought of that first five hundred soon inspired me. My pencil raced across the paper. I crammed ten pages with ideas. It wasn't even noon and I had finished. This would never do.

At lunch I met them in the restaurant.

"How's it going, Bernie?" Cubby asked.

"It's coming, but it's very hard." I sighed.

He patted me on the shoulder. "We have every faith in you."

On the Friday morning I gave my secretary Sandra her first job: I handed her my story line to type up. Then I sat back in the armchair, meditating upon my first pay cheque, and waited for my producers to come and disturb my reverie and shower me with kisses.

Sydney J. Furie, a young director, came in and introduced himself. He laughed when he saw the scrunched-up sheets of paper.

I asked him why he found it all so funny. "It's Harry with his cigar and his feet up on the table. And Cubby, playing the good guy. It's as if they have seen a movie on how real producers are meant to behave," he explained, still laughing. He told me about the baptism of *Doctor No*. Apparently Cubby and Harry had taken the book completely seriously, and had no idea that Ian Fleming wrote the whole thing tongue in cheek. When the audience at the first screening laughed, and applauded the impossible antics of the hero, they had been horrified. But they quickly cottoned on, joined in the jollity and said it was exactly as they had intended.

"Kafka! Sheer Kafka," I said, eager as ever to demonstrate my broad knowledge of world literature. "If the leopard enters the temple and drinks the sacrificial wine often enough, it soon becomes part of the ceremony." He nodded sagely. He didn't have the faintest idea what I was on about.

Sandra returned from lunch. "Harry wants to see you," she said.

I went to his office. Harry hurled my pages at me. "Call this a story line? This is crap, utter crap!" I was speechless. Red in the face, he puffed furiously on his cigar. "This film is for people who read the *Daily Mirror*. We don't want your *Manchester Guardian* crap. You've made this significant. Significance is the last thing we need."

"I get it. You want a beautiful story about a bunch of nice villains in romantic Soho."

"Exactly! We don't want corruption and porn shops, this sordid world of pathetic losers and the things that are really going on."

I was on the verge of tears. "I wanted to write the truth."

"THE TRUTH?" It was almost apoplexy time. "Who asked you for truth? Go back to your office and start again." It was a command and I could do without it. "Try to recapture the fun of the stage play. Okay?" He smiled like a cheap, lacquered Buddha. "You are a consummate wordsmith, BerNARD, and we just love having you around. Now go!"

If only I could order my conscience to take a month off, I could feed my kids on fillet steak and buy myself a nice new pair of shoes and an amber necklace for Erica. I took one last shot at it. "But Harry, you know what I am capable of doing and not doing. You read my book. You said it was beautiful."

"Book? What book?"

"My autobiography. You loved it."

"Did I? Did I? No, I didn't actually read it. But I did read the reviews." He took my arm and gently led me to the door. "BerNARD, be a good chap. Come down to earth and live a nice comfortable life."

When I got back to my office I called Erica. "I'm getting out. I'm not writing this crap."

She sighed. "I wondered how long you would last."

"But the money, Erica. The money!"

"Oh, to hell with the money. If we wanted security I could have become a doctor and you could be a rich, fat bookseller. Come home."

I had to tell my agent. Dina was away so I spoke to Rae. "Rae, I'm withdrawing from the project. I want out."

"But you're only just in."

"I've decided. Fuck them."

"But Bernard," she cried, "this is such a wonderful opportunity." Then she actually did cry. Whoever heard of an agent crying?

I strode back into Harry's office. "Harry, you can stick your fings back up your toches. Goodbye!"

"Wait! You can't do that. You're under contract."

"Sue me!" I knew they never did. Besides, you can't get blood out of a stone, and I was one.

He slumped backwards in his chair and that was the last I saw of Mr Harry Saltzman. I don't think he had ever come across such a high-minded shmock in all his days.

On the way out of the building I passed the sweet Broccoli. I told him I was off to dry clean my soul. He looked mystified.

"I'm genuinely sorry," he said when he understood.

On the way home I wondered how we were going to cope. If I wasn't a writer I was nothing, but I did have a family to support. "Take the money and run," Colin had said. I was running alright but I was leaving out the most important part of the equation. Now we were back to stony broke. My books were getting wonderful reviews but earning me nothing. They never even quite reached break-even point; I couldn't earn more than the advance, and the advance was always swallowed by final demands.

That night in bed I swore to Erica that I would never fall for the crap of the film world ever again. Or take drugs. She raised her eyebrows.

"How will we survive?" I asked. I was like a little child seeking reassurance.

"We'll survive by looking back on this one day and laughing," she said.

It all seemed strangely familiar.

29

One Door Closes, Another Door Closes

I seemed to have blown a filter somewhere in my brain; work now started at five in the morning. Writing during the evenings or at night was too fraught. In the dark, the demons came. Sometimes my mother would call my name from her grave over in Plaistow. So I tried to get in at least two hours writing before breakfast. When the words wouldn't come, I would just sit there before the typewriter cursing my ridiculous need to spew out words day after day, this crazy pounding out of people. When the words did come and they were good, I was all the more scared. My characters were so dark, so full of anger and bitterness. It was only the laughter of my children bouncing to breakfast that brought me back to the restraining world of light again. Then we would push Abigail and Rebekah in their huge green pram and take Hannah to her primary school. The daily ritual helped to keep me sane. "Why can't they stay as they are? Why do they have to grow up?" was my usual morning cry as Hannah skipped giggling ahead of us to hide in doorways.

Those two hours of work each morning became the bedrock of my existence. Secker and Warburg did me proud. David Secker was a fantastic editor and he gave me encouragement and helped me lick the work into shape. I managed to produce five dark and funny novels for them. I wrote through it all: winter or summer, happy, or black despair, Erica furious or Erica benign, the ever growing pile of final demands. It was all grist to the mill. I stayed behind my barricades and the world forgot me. No one sought out my views on the latest cultural or political situation, and I was glad.

Late one night, when all the kids were asleep, and Erica lay in the darkened bedroom listening to Mozart, I went silently to the bathroom. I thought I could wash away the morbidity that had got hold of me with the speed I had hidden away in there, the remains of the last lot I had bought at the Circus. I climbed up to the high cubby hole, got on all fours, and used my fingers to search into the corners under

175

the heater in the airing cupboard. Nothing, so I ran a bath to help me remember. Even my memory was slipping away from me.

As I undressed I caught sight of myself in the mirror. It was a horrible and unexpected glimpse of what I was doing to myself. I made sure not to undress in front of Erica in those days. My on-off speed habit had turned me into skin and bone and there I was, ready for the furnace. I actually made myself stand on the scales, something Erica always wanted me to do but which I had avoided. I looked down my skeleton and saw that I was less than eight stone; the shock helped me remember my hiding place – the communal garden beneath a pile of last year's dead leaves under the willow tree.

The jangling phone made me jump.

It was Dina. "How are you, Bernard?"

"I'm wonderful."

"Good, because I have some marvellous news."

"Oh God, not again," I muttered to myself. When she told me that *Enter Solly Gold* was going to be performed at the Mermaid Theatre I almost burst out crying. I was forty-three, and I didn't think that I could survive another bout of hope.

I lunched with Bernard Miles and his statuesque wife Josephine in the theatre restaurant overlooking the Thames and we discussed things. Bernard was my kind of person, a loveable rogue, a jovial rascal whose assumed rustic accent masked a sharp operator. His veins coursed with chutzpah. Our meeting made me realise how much I missed being a playwright. The Mermaid was then at the zenith of its fame. It had certainly come a long way since Bernard and Josephine first brought their dream to life in a tent in the back garden of their house in St John's Wood.

When I got home the old excitement entered the door with me.

"This time it *has* to work out, doesn't it, Erica?"

"If it doesn't, the law of averages doesn't exist." We splashed out on champagne and guzzled the whole bottle between us.

Within a few weeks it was down to business. Ron Pember was the director, Larry Adler the composer, and David Kossoff and Joe Melia were playing the leads. Ron Pember had directness, energy and enthusiasm, and no bullshit. And Larry Adler's music was hummable and clever. He was so famous yet so unassuming, I had to wonder where he had buried his ego. David Kossoff was a professional to the tips of his fingers, and so generous to work with. Joe Melia was so clever, so talented, so technically accomplished, and so cold.

"If this fails I'm giving it all up," I whispered to Erica on the opening night. I was in a speed stupor, locked in a cotton wool prison all through the performance. I wanted to be home with Erica in bed, drinking hot cocoa and watching something banal on television. I was going through the motions but I wasn't feeling the thrills. The fawning adulation I received for something I had written a few years before was meaningless. My only concern was whether the production would transfer to the West End and give us some security at last.

All the reviews were great. Even Milton Shulman, who usually hated my work, was in favour. And sure enough, a West End management decided that they wanted the play and we were offered a transfer to the Duchess Theatre, providing we moved immediately. All this was perfectly, wonderfully acceptable. Dina and I rubbed our palms together with glee. Until Joe Melia announced that he wasn't interested in parading his talents before a West End audience and would be unable to transfer. I screamed. I stamped. I cried. I howled with anger. I laughed and laughed. My mind was too drugged up to try and fathom out his real reasons; I could only think he'd caught an unexpected dose of acute socialism. It's just as well I haven't seen him since.

So the play did its run at the Mermaid and closed and we realised we were never going to be rich and afford a house like Shelagh Delaney's, and that was that. I did, at least, get to earn some money for a change, my percentage of the gross. It wasn't exactly a fortune but it was enough to keep us from becoming homeless vagrants for a while.

The playwright David Mercer lived just around the corner and we would often meet in the street and chat about nothing in particular. I was leaving the flat one morning when I saw him walking up the road towards me. His face was buried in an open newspaper. As he got nearer he lowered it as if he knew I was there. Tears were running down his cheeks.

"What's wrong, David?" I wondered if his wife and kids were alright. "David! What's happened?"

He seemed surprised. "Haven't you seen the papers? Don't you know what those Russian bastards are doing?"

It was 1968 and Eastern Europe was in turmoil. The Soviet army had sent hundreds of tanks into Prague where a crowd of fifty thousand were chanting "Russians, go home!" and pounding their fists against the Soviet monolith.

I asked him why he was so shocked. We all knew deep down what the Russians were capable of, whatever our rhetoric.

He nodded and wiped away his tears and we dawdled towards Cosmo. "We are men without faith. We have lost all our gods," he said.

I nodded agreement and was ashamed of the elation I felt. There's nothing like a crisis to exorcise the ghosts within.

30

You'll Never Get Out of Life Alive

"Bernard! Wonderful news. Jackie Mason is going to play Solly Gold on Broadway." It was six o'clock in the morning and Dina's excited voice seeped through my deep sleep.

"Oh no."

"Bernard? Are you there?"

"No, Dina, I am never all there."

She repeated her amazing news.

I was less than ecstatic but I feigned interest. "I'm awake now. Are you sure?"

"Bernard, this is our big chance. The Big Time at last." We had somehow reversed roles. She was the naive, young writer and I was the hard-bitten agent.

"Dina, I'm ignorant. Who is Jackie Mason?"

She told me that Mason was an ex-rabbi who was starting to make it big as a comedian. "Bernard, he's perfect for the role." Dina got around a lot; she had seen him in some cramped New York cellar. "He's a genius. We can't fail."

"Bless you, Dina. You're always so optimistic."

By this time Erica was awake and searching my face for a sign. I sighed and nodded. Here we go again.

"This time, Bernard, we've hit the bull's-eye," Dina assured me.

It was useless fighting against hope. I had done my best to immunise myself. I had developed a skin of cynicism, a protective armour of knowing the score, I had erected defences to hold off the virus and here I was being infected again.

I put the phone down and did some mental arithmetic to calculate a seven and half per cent box-office cut of a typical New York hit.

"Fantastic! We're going to be rich!" I told Erica when I'd arrived at some outlandish figure. "This time for sure." I told her all about the fabulous Jackie Mason, his unique skill and dark delivery.

"I've never heard of him. Have you?"

"Have I? You kidding? Who hasn't heard of Jackie Mason?"

179

"Bernard, how many near misses have there been?"

I made coffee. I danced. The children laughed all the way to school. Erica shook her head at the impossibility of it all but even she enjoyed the injection of hope. After all, the misfortune of many another playwright had been dramatically turned around on unpredictable Broadway. Why not me?

"Darling, when we're rich what's the very first thing I'm going to do?"

She smiled bravely and shook her head. "I can't imagine."

"I'm going to buy you the most enormous amber necklace in the world."

The play was to go into rehearsal almost immediately, then it would tour the usual places before opening on the Great White Way. We were all going over for the Broadway opening. I was even prepared to face my fear head on and fly for the first time in my life. They insisted on the whole happy family; it meant great coverage. I could see the banner headlines: "Impoverished Playwright and Starving Family Experience Fame, Wealth and Apple Strudel at Opening of Hit Play."

We hurried down to the American Embassy in Grosvenor Square and got our visa application forms.

There was just a niggling doubt in my mind. "Will the Americans let me in, do you think?"

"What?"

"Remember? I joined the Communist Party in August 1945."

"Yes, but you resigned from the Communist Party in September 1945!"

"Yes, but I did sell twenty-five copies of the *Daily Worker* outside Whitechapel station as a Communist Party member."

"Yes, but you also sold the anarchist pamphlet *Never Again!* outside Whitechapel station as an anarchist!"

"Absolutely, that's even worse." In a way I was quite pleased. It meant I didn't have to face yet another debacle, or risk travel by air.

Erica wasn't going to let me get away with it that easily. "Darling, that was all years ago! Do you think the FBI will have photos of little Bernie Kops standing in the pissing rain in the East End of London twenty-five years ago?"

I pointed out one particular question on the visa application form. "Do you want to overthrow the Government of the United States of America?" I scribbled "Yes" and tore up the form.

"The show must go on, with or without you," Dina said and advised me to seek an interview with an Embassy official. "You're probably far more of an anti-Communist than he could ever be."

I went to the American Embassy and was interrogated by the counsellor, a young Jewish guy with an Ivy League tie.

"Tell me, Mr Kops, why exactly did you join the Communist Party in the first place?" he asked me.

I quoted Bernard Shaw. "If you are not a Communist at eighteen you have no heart. If you are still a Communist at twenty-eight you have no brain." But he wasn't amused so I tried a different tack. "Listen, every Jewish kid in the East End joined the Communist Party in those days," I told him. "It was the natural thing to do; our bulwark against the resurgence of fascism. You're a Jewish boy. Didn't you ever sign up and join the comrades?"

His reaction was somewhere between anger and embarrassment. "Absolutely not."

"How strange," I replied.

He went out of the room and swiftly returned. "We cannot grant you a visa, Mr Kops, but under the circumstances we are prepared to extend you a waiver."

"If it lets me into God's Own Country to see my play open on Broadway, I don't care what you call it," I said, and thanked him.

We had already started to pack for the journey when the telegram arrived. "Stop. Don't travel. Play cancelled. Explanation follows."

They were as bad as their word. A few days later a letter arrived from the producers, filling in the details. Somewhere in New Jersey and in the middle of his performance, Jackie Mason had had some kind of brainstorm, walked to the front of the stage and told the audience that he couldn't continue in the play because as an ex-rabbi he identified too closely with the leading role. At least, that was the story I was given. The play died on the spot.

"Let's go to Spain," I said when it was confirmed. "Let's get away from it all."

"Okay," Erica replied. I was taken aback. This wasn't typical. "We may as well," she added. "We're almost packed."

I started to backtrack. "Are you sure?"

"Yes, let's go."

"But where in Spain?

"Where else?"

"Nerja? Are you mad? We almost died there. Twice." It was the very last place on earth I had thought of going.

"Third time lucky," she replied. "It will lay the ghost."

The children were just as happy to be going to Nerja as New York. We arrived in late February. And we found that the Nerja we knew was a thing of the past. The cobbled streets were gone. Hamburger joints glared at each other across the narrow streets. You could buy sliced bread. Nerja had entered the modern world. There were builders all over the place. The cement mixers whirred and chugged all day, and high-rises were appearing before our eyes.

Only the people were the same. They were so pleased to see us alive. They told us that our accident had been on the television news, and that the village had sent a small group over the mountains to the hospital in Baza, but when they arrived we had already departed for Granada. They had been told that Erica might not make it.

Adam couldn't understand our gloom. He was fourteen and happy at not having to go to school. People back home called us irresponsible, but as far as we were concerned, education wiped the joy out of kids, squeezed them until they squeaked and hung them out to dry. Erica was doing a better job. Hannah was seven, Abigail five and our baby Rebekah was now three. Erica was teaching them all.

We were a few nights into our sojourn and went to bed with Segovia playing Albéniz and Granados on the tape machine as usual. Listening to a solitary guitar was our way of slipping into the dark.

At some point much later I was disturbed. I could hear someone crying far away. A child. Through half-opened eyes I could vaguely make out dawn breaking on the other side of the window. Somehow I knew I had to get up but I just couldn't gather myself together. My head was so far away, I couldn't attach it to me. I was floating out of the window and into the sky. The child cried and cried and then I was scuttling above the floor of an ocean. It wasn't unpleasant. I knew I would soon sink into the dark silt beneath me. The child kept crying.

"Quick! Quick!" Erica was calling. "Quick! The window."

I remembered that I had to get back up to the surface. I found I could move, but I couldn't think. I saw Abigail. She was the child whimpering at the door. She never could sleep well.

Erica was screaming and I could see myself spread-eagled on the bed. "Quick! Quick!" she was gurgling.

Strange! I thought. This is where it ends. I heard my voice from far away. "Erica, help me!"

"The window! The window!" she shouted. Funny, I thought. I can move but cannot think. She can think but cannot move.

"The window! The window!" she kept shouting. I held her. She slumped in my arms.

"Bathroom! Bathroom!" she commanded in gasps. I saw myself, the monster carrying a child through the fog.

"Window!" she insisted. Her terrified eyes looked straight into mine and I finally understood.

I laid her on the floor, crawled to the window, grabbed a chair and hurled it at the glass. The air gushed in. I crawled back, dragged Erica close to the smashed window and we both took quick, deep gasps of air before rushing to the children's room. Adam, Hannah and Rebekah were in deepest sleep. We shook them and shouted their names until they stirred. Then we threw open all the windows. They were in the far room. The gas escaping in the kitchen had not yet entirely overpowered them. We started searching frantically for Abigail and found her whimpering behind our bedroom door. She was hiding, worried that she had been naughty. I grabbed her and smothered her with kisses. Thank God she suffered from a weak stomach and had detected the gas early and been sick. If she had not cried we all would have died.

In the morning we learned that the old man with his scythe had gathered quite a harvest along the coast by the same means. Another English family had died in the next village because the multi-point water heater was faulty or hadn't been fitted properly.

We went back home. I looked in the mirror in the bathroom but my reflection had beaten me to it and was already there, smiling at me. Erica came to find me. "That was a near miss," she said. "Bernard, please tell me you won't take any drugs now we're back."

"We live and learn."

"Well, we live. Please promise."

"I promise. I promise. I promise."

"One promise is enough," she said. She should have known better.

31

Can Anyone Direct Me to Where I Am?

Even three promises weren't enough, and that was on top of all the promises I'd made before. My body could no longer operate at any level without chemicals. Every day I told myself to take it easy and then took more of the little beauties. It wasn't long before ten a day began to have no effect so I upped it to fifteen. If I'd taken that many a year before I would have dropped dead. Now I measured life and time by the intervals between doses. Soon I was swallowing twenty-five a day just to stoke the fires and speed the blood to my bones, twenty-five just to be able to open my brain and go to the typewriter to prove that I could continue as a human. I was staring down a loaded barrel into oblivion.

Hannah sat on my lap and combed my hair. "Do you still love me?" I'd ask her. It's risky asking a child such a direct question. Often she would laugh and run away. Abigail would stare at me from a distance with her sad, luminous eyes. Why was Cordelia such a self-righteous bitch, I wondered. Why couldn't she just humour the old bastard? Why couldn't she just say she loved him with all her heart and soul, even if she didn't feel it? I rewrote *King Lear* to suit me better.

"Nothing will come of nothing. Speak again," says the King to Cordelia.

"Forgive me. My sisters distract my true intent. You are my adored father and I love Your Majesty with all of my heart." The end.

I couldn't write, but satisfied the creative urge still twitching within me by slapping paint all over the walls, day and night, creating huge, frightening images of Modigliani people amidst swirls of crimson fire, and always a talisman of Erica, my Hebrew princess, at the centre.

Three in the morning and someone was knocking at the door.

"Who is it?" I called, my heart pounding.

"Mr Kops? Mrs Kops? It's the police."

They had come for me at last. Who was I to think I could escape the law?

Erica opened the door to a middle-aged copper in uniform.

He spoke in a soft, sad voice. "Mrs Kops? I'm very sorry to inform you that your mother Mrs Gordon has passed away."

The juxtaposition of compassion and uniform surprised me even more than the news.

Gertie Gordon's unexpected death and her cremation at Golders Green pulled me up a degree. Although she hadn't taken to me in the very early days, she had softened towards me when she realised how close Erica and I were together, and we'd become good friends. There is nothing more sobering than the death of someone close.

We only found out after her death that she had been born in Odessa. She had been brought to Scotland as a baby by her parents, fleeing the pogroms. With her distinctive Scots brogue we always imagined she had been born in Dundee, and she had never said a word to contradict that.

Gertie had a brain as sharp as a cut-throat razor, and a wicked sense of humour. She was a surgeon with words and conversation. In her and Max's flat in Blackfriars there were bookshelves all around the rooms filled with books I yearned to possess. First editions, read again and again, of all the authors I most admired: Sartre, Malraux, Proust, Joyce, Orwell, Koestler, Schnitzler, Chekhov. Gertie had absorbed every one of them.

In her last days she was bedridden and looked after by Erica's father. She often complained that she had no money of her own, so when she died we were astonished to discover that she had left several thousand pounds to each of her three children: David, Gillian and Erica, her youngest. It soon came out that Gertie had been playing the stock market from her sick bed. Her small salary as secretary to her husband's practice was no more than a few hundred pounds per year but she had cleverly invested this and turned it into small fortune.

Gertie had no actual money in the bank. It was all in stocks and shares at her brokers. All this went to Max, Erica's father, for him to look after in trust. A few weeks after she died he showed us his will. It stated that Erica would receive a third of this money on his death. We photocopied this and presented the evidence to our bank manager. It was the first time I had seen him smile. All the shares were blue chip and were bound to rise and rise in value. In his eyes, we had finally made it. Naturally, we immediately took out a loan on the strength of our great expectations. We felt we had money to burn and it gave us a new lease on life. For a while Selfridges food hall became a daily safari. And we got toys and books for the kids; records and clothes and furniture; perfume; a new bathroom; a gigantic new television set; carpets; cushions; dressing gowns; actual pyjamas; shoes; kimonos; paintings; African masks. "Save it for a rainy day," friends and relatives sang in chorus, not noticing that outside the window it was pissing down. The money Gertie had earned was not real money. It seemed right and proper that it should help get us out of our perpetual mess.

We did manage to be just a little bit practical and extended the lease on our flat and paid off most of our debts. It postponed complete financial crisis for at least a few years. Then we went on holidays to Bournemouth and Viareggio and Lake Garda. We both knew that life was slipping through our fingers.

I still hadn't forgiven myself for selling the amber necklace that Erica had brought back from her parents that day. I couldn't forget that family outside the jewellery shop in Riga; little flies trapped in sepia time. I knew nothing could compensate Erica for the loss of a people and their memories but, with Gertie's help, I realised I could finally afford to buy a replacement, a necklace with rich, red amber beads as big as apples. So I searched through the jewellery shops in Portobello, Cutler Street, the Cut, Bermondsey and Hatton Garden, but I found nothing to match the memory of the necklace I'd sold, nothing to assuage the guilt and the sense of betrayal I still felt.

I was grabbed by a crazy notion that it might still be there, in the shop in the Burlington Arcade, and that I might be able to buy it back. I had made the transaction years before, but stranger things had happened, so I was hopeful.

The man thought I was mad. "I'm afraid I can't remember the particular piece, sir."

"It wasn't a piece, it was a miracle of rare device."

"Amber you want? I got plenty."

Several strands were laid out before me. Various hues from light yellow corn to dark treacle, graduating into deepest sunset red and then to black. How many dreams did these strands contain? What hands had offered these? What hands had clasped them round their neck? How many thousands of years were locked in these beads? How much laughter? How many tears? How many screams? How many stories could each strand tell of joy, suffering and unbelieving departures?

When I got home Erica was worried about me, and I confessed.

"Leave it," she said. "Nothing can replace it. It's gone forever."

I knew she was right, and I reluctantly untied the quest and let it drift away. But I still think of amber as a metaphor for loss. Someone, somewhere is wearing that necklace. And I remember those people, Erica's family on their knees in the dirt, being shot through the skull by the Latvian SS guards.

Nineteen seventy-three came and went in a blink of my eyes. We were flat broke again and I started falling apart again, only this time much more slowly; if riches had fallen upon us once more, I'm sure I would have vaporised in a flash. All my life force had been sucked out of my bones, and all my thoughts and dreams had been hoovered out of my head. The blues that had once prompted an endless torrent of words and a bubbling flow of Superman energy no longer had any effect.

Erica and I slept facing different directions, she to the south and me to the north.

"Goodnight, darling. I love you."

"Goodnight, darling. I love you."

My soul was in intensive care but no angels came to the foot of my bed to soothe me.

In the day my occupation was keeping myself topped up on enough speed to get me through. I mainly operated at night, when I would freefall into nothingness and hang out where the murderers and suicides reside. I was back with Eros at the Circus again, that grunting, stinking watering hole for addicts. I never knew how I got there. No one could tell me where I was, or why or how. Despair led me on automatic pilot all the way back to West Hampstead. I would try to control the steering wheel and hold my face at the same time, to keep my head together and my brain from exploding all over the windscreen.

At four in the morning I fell against the door. Erica opened it and I collapsed on to the floor.

"You stink!" she shouted at me. "You're worse than Paul Potts." And she forcibly marched me to the bathroom. I was skin and bone; a child could have lifted me.

She ordered me to undress and cried when she saw my wasted body. Then she lifted me into the bath. I had chucked everything away for the blue tablet I was even now clutching in my fist. It melted away in the warm water.

In the bath I fell into the motherly embrace of sleep, and Erica lifted me out of the water and guided me into bed. She never argued with me now, or begged me to see sense. I was too far gone to know how far gone I was. Will you take this man for better or for worse or for something even more terrible?

Most nights I would try to put some words together but I was like an old man crouching alone in the wilderness obsessed only with his next bowel movement. Erica would find me in the morning, on my back on the floor, catatonic, my paws poised and ready to attack, like something delivered from the Egyptian Room of the British Museum.

When I returned to the world later on in the day I would beg her to throw me out before I could descend again. Then moments or days or weeks down the line I would be struggling up to the world of light once more to plead with her never to leave my side. And always the need, the craving to feed the emptiness, the icy cold sweating, the searing pain that racked throughout the day when the levels in my bloodstream started falling.

On the rack of yet another bout of withdrawal, my body cried out for more. "I must have more!" the slave inside me cried. Chronology jumped out the window. I saw myself disappearing round the corner long ago. Only jagged shards of events floated back to me, an impossible jigsaw stretched across my skeleton.

One night in particular I try hard to forget. I had parked my taxi and I needed speed. I found some speed, but lost my taxi, although I couldn't be certain if the loss had been yesterday or earlier on that same day. I never could remember where I parked it.

I'd sold another piece of Gertie and had some crisp notes in my pocket and a craving to feed. There was a wonderful firework display over the Circus. The clowns were spewing black outside Boots, and all the Japanese tourists were grouped together, grinning and watching me scoring under the god of love. I was selling the past and betraying all the Jews who had ever lived and died and I didn't care. I swallowed down the sweet poison and my body was slowly brought back to life. Shadows were busy making transactions all around me, moving around in slow motion, buying and selling, crying and giggling, and shooting up in corners.

Later, a week or a day, I found my taxi in a cul-de-sac. "Bernie boy, congratulations. You're doing a wonderful job. Keep up the good work." I climbed in the back and slept all day until I heard the sound of the tumbrels and felt the unbelievable pain of withdrawal: my shoulders being broken again and again; the excruciating fury of my exploding bones; my flayed flesh being torn away from my cheeks; my hysterical skull. I knew that if I couldn't score that night there would be no point in facing my children and torturing them for yet another day. How could I walk them to school feeling like this? How could I possibly tell them to be good? How could I even face the lollipop man? I parked my taxi again, and when I turned around it had gone. I must have parked it in another street.

Only a lonely deal could sustain me and this was my reality. All the crap was gone. There would be no resurrection. This was the price I had to pay for rejecting the world of my family, for reaching out and escaping. I should have died like the rest of them and poked a little girl from Stamford Hill and made her pregnant, and settled down in Leytonstone with a settee and two armchairs covered in uncut moquette.

I paced the pavement, anxious to use up time until the witching hour would start off the trading. I spotted a young man pissing in a corner off Haymarket. He was my main supplier and I needed to remind him that I was still alive, so I went up and tapped him on the shoulder.

He turned round and it wasn't him. The stranger smashed me in the face. "You fucking pervert!"

I apologised. I could feel the blood trickling down my face. "Sorry, thought you were someone else." I laughed.

He handed me a pristine, white linen handkerchief. That was always the way: sometimes you scored; sometimes a silver chiv would flash in your face; sometimes you were kissed and fumbled with before you fell over and someone was shoving you a packet of your heart's desire.

I had just got home when I was already creeping out of the bed. Time was gobbling itself up.

Erica moaned deep from sleep. "Please, don't, Bernard! Please don't go out."

"I won't be long, darling," I said, sounding just like a regular husband. "You go back to sleep." I knew there was further to fall. If I could reach the bottom I could have something solid to kick against, and maybe that way I could come up again. How could I explain that to Erica?

I was home again and getting dressed, just about to leave to get back to where I came from. Erica was fully awake now, and looking at me and wincing.

"You're wasting away."

"Erica, am I just going out or have I just come in?" Tears were her answer.

I left the room. She ran after me to pull me back.

"I'm going to the doctor tomorrow. I promise, I really promise."

"You pathetic, weak bastard!"

A child cried. I left the house.

She shouted after me. "Go to hell!"

"I'm there already!" I shouted back.

I climbed into the back of my cab, and breathed in that womblike smell, the lives of all the people who had polished that old leather; the scent of clandestine meetings and fumbled relationships; journeys and dreams.

Then I went round to the driving seat and started the engine. I could see Erica looking at me from out of the window. Her Etruscan eyes were staring into me. My own eyes flooded with tears as I drove away.

32

All the Way Down

Everything was running together through the windscreen. The red, morning sky was dripping down all over the gasometers behind King's Cross station. I brought my taxi to a stop, with consummate ease considering the circumstances – people like me should not be allowed – and I went round into the back and out like a light.

When I woke I wasn't sure what time it was. Night and day had coalesced into one unfocused time space where there was no future and no past. I got out the back and saw a little girl leaning against the long, desolate wall. She came slowly towards me, smiling and trying pathetically to roll the hips she hadn't got. I quickly climbed in behind the wheel and drove away. It was tomorrow. Everything had fallen into place again.

It was far too late to score at the Circus; they would all have dossed down in their little holes by now, so I headed for home and for another inevitable bout of withdrawal.

The playwright in the taxi mirror shook his head sadly. "Look at you, you pitiful fool. How could you have done this to yourself? How could you have fallen so far?"

"Piss off!" I told him. "You're just a stupid, fucking playwright. How dare you stand in judgement. What do you know of the world?" He was always there, smirking.

I took a detour to my favourite chemist, Gerald Aarons, who plied his pharmaceuticals in Belsize Park. I was no ordinary customer and Gerald was always pleased to see me. He followed my career so closely that when I walked in I would always ask the same thing: "Gerald, what's happening in my life?" He even kept a scrapbook full of little cuttings just about me and my career. It was spooky but his vicarious interest served me well. Sometimes he would do me little favours and advance me a few tablets when he knew I would be popping into my doctor's in a few days for a prescription.

I was really desperate this time but we cracked the old jokes, same as usual. He didn't seem to notice my dramatic weight loss but told me that I had let him down by not being in the news lately. He loved to boast to his neighbours in Kingsbury that I was a personal friend.

"What have you got on the stocks, Bernie?"

"Only myself," I replied. "I'm getting a script tomorrow from my GP. Can you loan me a few amphetamines until then? Please?"

He wasn't keen but he counted out half a dozen. "Careful, Bernie, time runs out if you only run on these."

"You've always got time for your funeral," I cracked and we both laughed.

Six tablets were practically useless but it would keep the searing pain away for the night.

I awoke in another universe. Dawn. Tiny wrens were arguing furiously in the treetops. I was lying on a slab. There were no ostentatious gravestones, just the flat stones and Hebrew lettering. Evidently, on my way home the night before I had somehow managed not to kill anyone and stumbled on the Sephardic cemetery near Golders Green.

I found a telephone box and rang home.

"How are you? Where are you?" I was surprised she wasn't angry.

"I'm on my way home."

I bought some hot bagels at a shop in Golders Green and offered them to her when she opened the door. She didn't say a word and she didn't take the bagels.

I glanced in at the kids. They were fast asleep with that wonderful bloom on their cheeks. I knew the best gift I could give them all was the taking of my life, but I was always a terrible coward, and I had an ego to match.

Erica took me to bed and I cuddled right into her and felt the beautiful warmth of her belly. It was five o'clock in the morning. I vowed I was finished with drugs. I would never go out again.

The kids had to go to school. I could hear them pillow fighting in the corridor.

"Where were you?" she asked quietly.

"I don't know."

"What did you do?"

"Nothing. I just slipped out for a few hours."

"Bernard, you've been away for days. What did you do?"

"I don't know." I cried. She cuddled me more. Surely by now she had used up all her compassion. Personally, I had run out of the commodity too long ago to even recall.

★

That night I sat in my workroom, trying to tap out a sentence that made sense. One page of dialogue would suffice. I had been a playwright once. But I had used up all my words. There was no plot, no story. My characters had no character; they were without faces or agendas. There was no purpose, no through line, no denouement and no play. And who the fucking hell cared? Certainly not me.

Erica looked in on me before turning in.

"I love you forever," I said.

"Huh!" she replied, then offered a small smile. "And I love you."

I listened to some Chopin on Radio Three and then pulled the carpet back and brought out a packet of black bombers, an emergency supply I had secreted months before under a small floorboard. For once, Erica hadn't got there first.

Gulping them down, I slipped out of the window, into my taxi, and made straight for Kingsbury. I knew exactly where my chemist Gerald Aarons lived; the obsequious bastard had invited me and Erica so many times for dinner. We'd gone once and he had brought the neighbours in to show off his trophies. I also knew that when he locked up his shop in Belsize Park he always put his keys into his deep overcoat pocket, and I had once casually enquired if he locked up his keys when he got home, to be on the safe side. "No, no, they're safe in here," he had said, and patted his pocket. "They're safe in Kingsbury. Everyone and everything is safe in Kingsbury."

So tonight I wasn't going to Piccadilly. I couldn't face that hell any more. If I could get those keys I could unlock the door to his shop and feast upon a sweet supper of oblivion. My only problem would be getting into his house.

It was three in the morning. My whole life seemed to revolve around three in the morning. The roads were deserted. I clocked a police car waiting in a side road by the traffic lights, but to them I was just another black cab passing by. It was a cold and howling sort of night. The lone wolf, Bernard Kops, was on the prowl.

Kingsbury was fast asleep. Its good and respectable Jews, who had slaved their kishkes out all their young lives and had finally made it from Stamford Hill across the North-West passage, were all dreaming on their Slumberlands.

I found Gerald's pebble-dashed house. There were no lights on. There were no lights burning all along the street. No one suffered from insomnia in Kingsbury; no one was yentzing his wife on the new shagpile carpet.

My plan was to get behind the house and somehow get in by the back door. That way I would be less exposed. It would mean crossing gardens, climbing over fences and skirting walls, but my sense of event seemed to have charged me with extra energy. I ran silently in slow motion until I reached the end of the road and then slipped behind the row of houses, my body tingling with fear and excitement. I was heading for the tenth house along, and I was the greatest Olympic high jumper in the world as I leapt over walls and fences. I soared in slow motion. The silence of the imagined crowd hovered in the air as I vaulted and sailed. My tolerance had taken a holiday and the two black bombers surged through my blood and soaked my brain with joy. It was a cinch. I hadn't felt alive like this for ages; I had enough euphoria to write a dozen plays. There was nothing I couldn't do. I could break into Kenneth Tynan's flat and hold a dagger to his jugular and make him dance a fandango. I could take down a whip from his wall and make him beg for mercy and forgiveness. "Now pray, you loathsome toad!" No wonder the Nazi airmen, high as kites on amphetamines, had thought they were invincible as they rained bombs down on the East End. I could truly fly. I was Superman and Flash Gordon rolled into one. Golden euphoria was washing all over me and I felt immortal.

I was just two houses away when I kicked over an empty dustbin and a terrible clatter shattered the whole of Kingsbury. The bin rolled on and on along the concrete ground, the clashing climax to a symphony. I was willing the bin to stop and considering my options when a dog came from nowhere and leapt towards me. I froze as the great, black, slobbering hound hurtled upwards, aiming straight at my throat, and I clenched my eyes closed, waiting for the end. It didn't come. The stupid mutt just barked and barked. When I finally dared to open my eyes the bastard was hovering in front of me, inches from my face and straining to get nearer, saliva dripping from its fangs. He was tethered to a tree on a long leash and was in a canine fury because he couldn't get any nearer.

By now all the lights of Kingsbury had come on and all back doors were opening. I stumbled back the way I had come, remembering that my mother used to call me Ruach, the Hebrew for spirit or wind. I ripped my trousers and jacket on barbed wire. My knee was wet and I guessed it was blood but it wasn't hurting. Someone had switched the moon full on and I could hear men shouting behind me.

I had done many things in my forty-odd years but I had never yet been bludgeoned to death by a posse of Jews in nightshirts. Their shouts were shattering the quiet. "There he is! Get him! GET HIM! THIEF!"

My mother had also called me The Snake because I slithered and darted here and there. I was always fast and never still. I would scoot everywhere, always impatient and never waiting for others, berating them for their snailpace. I would rush downstairs from the top flight of our building four steps at a time. In those days a whippet could take lessons from me. And that night, even at my age, I found I was able to recapture some of that lost, hurtling boy of my youth. I made my way across the gardens, running the film backwards until I got to the street. My cab was parked along the road and I sprinted towards it picturing the headlines in the *Daily Mirror*: "Downfall and Shame of Playwright." And the *Daily Mail*: "Peeping Tom Playwright Cornered in Kingsbury." What was I doing here? What had I done with my brain, my life, my dreams? I would certainly make the *Willesden and Kingsbury Gazette* and the *Jewish Chronicle*. The shame of it turned my blood to ice and I was shaking uncontrollably by the time I reached my cab.

I had the sense to realise that I didn't have enough time to climb into the driving seat and switch on the engine. That way my pursuers would nab me easily or would certainly be able to get my registration number. So I dived into the back and lay curled up in a corner on the floor, just as they came into the road, shouting and blowing whistles. "Stop, thief! Stop, thief!" They rushed right past me and down to the main road.

I gave it a minute and then started the engine and was away, driving straight ahead, hoping to find another way out of that maze of streets. They heard me and came rushing, shouting and hollering. But by then I'd slipped into third gear. I could see them brandishing their fists in the rear mirror.

I felt elated until I came to the huge industrial estate near Staples Corner, and then I plunged down into total depression. Life felt empty and meaningless. I prayed that I would meet a police car that would lead me towards some sort of solution, but all I got was a swaying man hopping about at some traffic lights and clinging to a smudged, laughing secretary bird. They hailed me hopefully and I waved back and sped on through the dead suburbs to West Hampstead.

I went straight through the passage and on to the dark, deserted communal garden and sat beneath a willow tree. Nothing stirred as I communed with my ghosts. "Mother, what am I doing to myself?" She had no answers for me. She just cried with the voice of the wind, "What are you doing to yourself?" Jews always answer a question with a question.

When I got up to go in it must have been around five. I fumbled for my key at the street door but Erica had got there before me and opened it.

"What's wrong? Why are you up?" I asked.

She cried. I put my arm around her and took her inside. Abigail was peeping from her room.

"When I heard you at the door I thought it was the police come to tell me you were dead," Erica said.

"I'm not the dying sort."

We slowly swayed together. "I'm very sick. I must see the doctor."

"I'll take you there first thing tomorrow."

I felt unusually content when she undressed me. She was my strong lady; the spirit of my mother and all those amazons of Zion had been poured into her. I had come to the end of the road and she wasn't going to allow me to go any further.

"Are you there? Are you really there?" I kept asking her.

"I'm here."

She stroked my forehead until I fell asleep.

33

Exit Downstage

The young doctor knew us well, and greeted us warmly as friends. I hoped he could save me, if only for the sake of the kids. He was Greek Cypriot and had a young family of his own. They smiled out at us from a photograph on his desk.

He whistled through his teeth as he gently worked over my limbs, my groin, hands and feet, mouth and fingers. It took just a few minutes to go over my pitiful skeleton. Then he listened to my heart and took my blood pressure.

"Get dressed," he told me quietly. It was laborious and painful. "Mr Kops, what have you done to yourself?"

It was too late to tell him anything other than the truth.

"How much are you using?"

"Twenty to thirty uppers a day, either speed or black bombers. And whatever else can lift me."

"And do they do the trick?"

"No, nothing lifts me any more."

"Of course, your body has built up tolerance." He looked at Erica, commiserating, shaking his head in puzzlement. "Why? You've got everything: a wonderful wife, a lovely family, you're successful in your trade. You're respected. Why?" The Greek was appealing to the Jew. This sort of behaviour was unimaginable. Greeks and Jews never did this sort of thing to their families. "No wonder your teeth are rotting – it's like you've been subjected to radiation."

"How bad am I?"

He sighed dramatically. "If you carry on like this, I give you no more than six weeks. Every speed addict has his boundary. You could down thirty-nine tablets every day and still survive, but just one more tablet could kill you. I think you have reached that boundary. I give you six weeks at the most." He really rubbed it in.

I told him about the pain – he knew it all already but I told him anyway – and the inertia that took hold of me, when I could barely

197

open my eyes and didn't dare move a muscle, but just lay there petrified, locked in a place where all morality, all compassion, all logic and love has gone. "I'm on another planet," I told him. "Nothing moves me. Nothing makes sense." Then the dam burst and my head fell on to his desk and I sobbed. All my pride had gone and I was overwhelmed with grief and relief.

The doctor turned to Erica, and repeated his diagnosis. "If Bernard doesn't stop taking these drugs I give him six weeks at the most."

My repeated death sentence was a sort of music, a kiss of life. It told me I had gone as far down as I could go.

Erica somehow managed to retain her usual calm, at least on the surface. "And if he can get off the drugs, what then? Has he done any lasting damage?"

"That's in the lap of the gods. Speed is one of the most harmful of drugs. It destroys the blood vessels, the capillary system; the body as well as the mind."

"If only I could replace it with something less deadly," I said lamely. I knew that the only cure was complete abstention.

We were moving to the door when the doctor mentioned Holloway Sanatorium. "It's a place of sanctuary, a retreat in magnificent grounds. I've sent other people and it helped. They may be able to help you."

We grabbed at the lifeline. What did we have to lose?

Then he brought us down again. "It's private and the fees are quite stiff. Can you afford it?"

"We're flat broke," Erica told him. The young doctor just couldn't understand how a successful writer could be without means.

He took us to the door. "Phone me if you can find a way of raising the money."

That afternoon I telephoned Dina. Up until now I had managed to hide the enormity of my sickness from her and the rest of the world, but over the phone I let it all unravel, the whole story of my pathetic, ignominious weakness.

Later my publisher Freddie Warburg called. Dina had told him I was in a bad way and he offered to pay for my treatment. "One day, when you're over this bad patch, we'll get it back from your royalties," he said.

"Let's hope we live that long," I replied, and we laughed.

Sadly Freddie died not long after, as did the old school of English publishing when Tom Maschler came back from America with the rights to *Catch 22* and changed the face of the 'gentleman's profession' forever.

Freddie was one such gentleman. A book to him was not just a commodity: it was a living, luminous expression of the human heart and soul. He nurtured his authors. He didn't need to discover a new, saleable genius every other week. Bless his bones.

The next morning we travelled by train into deepest Surrey and hailed a real and functioning taxi outside the station to drive us to the gates of Holloway Sanatorium. I felt good as we entered the grounds and the gates clanked behind us. It felt like the beginning of a new life, a real chance to save myself.

I felt less sure when we entered the sumptuous, warm reception. The staff spoke softly and politely and wore perpetual smiles that put the shits up me. I wouldn't have been surprised if they planned to drug my cocoa and suspend me in deep narcosis, or amputate my brain and swap it with a computer. Still, I knew I desperately needed help and I went quietly as they guided me along the highly polished corridors.

Erica waited until after I was examined and weighed. Then she left me there in Surrey. It was the worst day of my life. I went into my little room and a nice young man accompanied me. He searched my case, then frisked the clothes I was wearing.

"Hang on," I protested. "I'm not in prison. I'm a voluntary, paying patient. I can discharge myself at any time."

"Sorry, sir. Orders." All my strength had drained away so I just let him get on with it.

"We never take chances, sir, for your own sake." He undid my shoes and took away the laces. Then my belt. "Just procedure, sir. Sorry." He left the room.

I lay on the bed and felt depleted. The overhead light had no flex. The bulb seemed fixed to the ceiling and I couldn't see the switch to turn it off. The door had one small square of glass in it at the top and every half an hour an eye would ogle in at me.

Later, the beddybyes woman came to see me with two tablets. I swallowed them and fell into deep sleep for a while but kept bobbing up to the surface and hovering there. Drums rolled and bugles blared. People screamed and cackled. It was the laughter of torture victims, hysterical at the madness of it all.

In the morning my young man came to help me wash and to announce that breakfast was being served in the refectory. I shooed him away so he just watched me give five licks to my face and then took me down the corridors to the huge hall.

"How did you sleep, sir?"

"Terribly."

"Oh dear, poor you. Perhaps we didn't give you enough Oblivion to go deep enough. We'll increase your dose tonight."

Gargoyles grinned down on us from all around the ceiling, red and gold grotesques with tongues hanging out of lascivious mouths and horns poking from their foreheads. It all seemed so familiar somehow.

"I've been here before," I said.

"Yes, you might well recognise this place. It's used for those Hammer Horror films, you know, with Christopher Lee."

"Of course. How appropriate."

Other somnambulists were floating in for breakfast, all doing their slow-motion moonwalking, their arms stiff beside them, doped up to the eyebrows on phenothiazines. My nurse sat me down at a table for two, opposite a man contemplating the egg in the eggcup before him. His eyes darted across to me, surreptitiously taking me in, a new patient who dared to share his table and intrude on his eggy meditation.

His eyes fell upon my hands. "Dirty hands, dirty hands, dirty hands," he mumbled. "Jewboy!" He had a posh accent. "You killed Christ. You killed Christ with your dirty hands."

"Yes, I did, in fact. Behind the gasworks at King's Cross."

He began cracking his boiled egg with suburban finesse.

"Remember, no crucifixion no resurrection," I added.

"Thank you." He was digging out the yolk, nodding with satisfaction. His attention had shifted elsewhere.

"I'll get you breakfast," my young man said. "Porridge?"

"Yes, please."

But I pulled him back. "What were those noises I heard in the night? Like drums and screaming."

"Oh, that would be the ghosts. This was a real madhouse once, in Victorian times, for the slightly better-off. The patients often had to be restrained, and lots of them died screaming in their straitjackets."

That was it. "Forget the porridge," I told him. "I'm skipping breakfast."

I went straight to my cell, packed my small case and walked out of the building, scrunching my toes so my shoes wouldn't fall off.

The man at the gate politely asked me where I was going and took up the telephone. "Hello, gate here. There's a man wanting to leave."

"I'm a paying guest. I can do what I like," I told him.

"Yes, sir. Sorry, sir. Just checking."

A car arrived and needed to be let in. The gate man couldn't handle doing two things at once so he put down the receiver to open the gate. I was out and away in a flash.

Down the lane I telephoned Erica.

"Come home, darling," she said. "Be careful."

When I got back to London it was time for lunch.

Erica, shaking her head, smiled across the table. She seemed very tired. "What are we going to do with you, you ridiculous man?"

"You hold everything together," I said. "Once we floated across starry skies. We will again."

"I hope so."

"I'm so bored with my breakdown. I have to find a way to prove I love you all."

"First find a way to love yourself."

She started getting busy on the phone working out what to do with me. I felt relieved that my fate was out of my hands and lay on the couch in the kitchen for the next two days, listening to music. All the while Erica was on the phone, nodding and quietly talking, negotiating a garage where I could take my clapped-out body and mind for a refit.

"You're very strong," I called to her.

"I'm sick of being strong. I don't need another son, I want a lover," she shouted back.

If only I could have obliged. When the kids were safely at school or far away in dreamland it often crossed my mind to take her to bed. But I knew it would be useless. Better not even to try than face the ignominy.

A few days of phone calls later she came and told me the deal. She and Dina had found a halfway house in Oxford run by the Brothers of the Resurrection, aimed at helping the ever increasing number of undergraduates who, under great strain, were living on the edge and dicing with death. The suicide rate in recent years had climbed to frightening new heights and the Brothers had decided that all this was more important than growing parsley and praying.

"We're stony broke," I reminded her. "I can't go to Oxford."

"Your publishers have agreed to give us two hundred a month to pay for the treatment."

There seemed to be no way out.

"Why do they bother? Why do they have such faith in me?"

"Why indeed? We have no other choice."

I felt like a decrepit character in a play who has just arrived at the moment of truth. This was my last chance. If I didn't take it, a relentless narrative would lead me straight to Bushey cemetery.

"We're going to make it," Erica said. "We're survivors." She kissed me and left the train and I woke up in Oxford. On the platform I looked around for the Christian resurrectionists, and wondered how I'd be able to cope with them.

"Are you Bernard Kops? The playwright?" A man with a ruddy face greeted me. "I'm here to collect you." He wore country clothes: a cap, pullover and cords. "I'm Peter." He took my case and guided me out of the station.

"Do you work at the house?" He laughed. "What are you?"

"Anything you want me to be: dogsbody, gardener, chauffeur, cook, bottlewasher, you name it."

"You're not a priest, are you?"

"For my sins." He seemed a very jolly person. He obviously didn't read the morning papers.

"Where's your dog collar?"

"Oh, I often forget to wear it."

"I've never met a Christian before. Well, not a proper one."

"I understand that. Sometimes I wonder what Christianity is all about." This sounded promising. I was beginning to like him.

"Do you consider yourself a true Christian?"

"Good Lord, no!"

"What sort of a priest are you?"

"Not a terribly good one. Actually, I'm really supposed to be a monk. The Brothers of the Resurrection are a rather radical, Anglican order. We're based in Yorkshire."

"Resurrection? I wish I could have a second coming. Come to think of it, even one would be nice."

I fully expected him to tell me off but instead he bellowed. "That's very, very funny. I really appreciate that." He guffawed like mad all the way into the city.

"Our boss, of course, is God, but underneath him we have Father Trevor Huddleston. Have you heard of him?"

"I certainly have." I relaxed. I didn't need to hate this Christian. His order was kosher. Trevor Huddleston had been the Anglican bishop in South Africa and I'd read his book, *Naught for Your Comfort.*

"Here we are," Peter said when we arrived at Woodstock Road and its hugely beautiful Victorian and Edwardian houses.

"Why do you call it a halfway house?" I asked as I followed him towards the door.

"Because we're all halfway between heaven and hell."

"You can say that again," I joked, and we went inside.

Funny, my career had been launched in Oxford. I often counted meeting Erica and writing my first play as my true beginning. And now I'd fallen all the way down and full circle.

Peter took me upstairs and showed me my room.

"Hi, skelly!" I greeted myself in the mirror. He was always there, waiting to say hello. I wondered if I'd die here, amongst Christians, the same ironic way my father had.

34

Fire in My Head

I hadn't used for days; I hadn't brought anything with me, and I couldn't see a way of scoring. Proximity was always my enemy. Peter had said, "Look, we cannot stop you taking drugs. No one can stop you but you. We will not search you and you can do what you like in this room. All we can do is give you some distance."

My body screamed for chemical nourishment. "Fucking Christians!" I cried under the bedclothes. "What have you done to me?"

Then one morning, after I'd been there a few days, a miracle at breakfast: I experienced the first pangs of hunger I'd had in years. I munched on half a slice of toast. Soon I was devouring eggs and bacon. Within a week I gained several pounds.

"Good," said Peter. "We're building you up for the real battle, the one you will face when you leave here."

They always talked so softly those Christians, and they always smiled benignly. Where was their subtext? Where had they hidden their anger? Was all this lark actually Erica's revenge for the years of pain and anguish I had given her? My paranoia was rampant.

"You're not secretly trying to convert me, are you, Peter?"

"I wouldn't presume. Your people gave us the Ten Commandments, and the day of rest, one of the greatest leaps in the history of civilisation. By separating last week from next week you, Bernard, brought order out of chaos."

"Not guilty. All I've ever done is bring chaos out of order."

They laughed. These people were too good, it was most confusing.

There were a few others around the table. Munching, pimply adolescents, monosyllabic for the most part. After breakfast we all did the washing-up together and the Beatles sang an accompaniment on the radio. It was all so English.

Later Peter took me down to the river where he introduced me to his little motorboat and gave me some simple lessons in rivercraft. Day after whispering day, I swished alongside the green, up and down the murmuring river. I slept and read and listened to Mozart, shoved food into my body and let the river nurse my soul.

After I'd been at the retreat a while, Erica came on the train to visit with the children. My daughters smiled shyly on seeing me but hung back, and their eyes told me that I had deserted them. Abigail looked terrified. I knew I didn't deserve them; I had thrown away such precious time, missed their priceless infancies and so much of the gradual unfolding of character and uniqueness.

Later, when I took them down to the river and on to the boat, they whooped with delight and, forgetting themselves, hugged and kissed me. I struggled to hold back a flood of tears.

I took them down to the station and waved goodbye to all the small, waving arms and then sat down on a bench and let myself cry. Peter stood well back, whistling and pretending not to notice.

In the car on the way back, I attempted to change the mood with an ancient Jewish joke.

"Peter! What is green, hangs on the wall and whistles?"

"I dunno!"

"A red herring."

"But a red herring isn't green!"

"So, you can paint it green."

"But a red herring doesn't hang on the wall!"

"So, you can hang it on the wall."

"But a red herring doesn't whistle!"

"So, it doesn't whistle."

He couldn't stop himself giggling.

"It's about the nature of survival; how to turn things around."

He stopped laughing then. He knew I was really saying that I was as ready to leave as I would ever be.

That same weekend his wife hugged me at the door and Peter drove me to the station. I never saw him again.

"You look so well!" all the neighbours said.

Outwardly there was a mood of joy and hilarity in the house. Erica was happy just to have me physically well again. Colin came round and was delighted to see me as my old self. As far as I was aware, he had only ever smoked dope. Alcohol was his poison.

"You seem fine," he said.

"Thank you. It's been a long struggle."

"You're back. You're cured."

"Yes, I'm back! I'm cured."

"You must be amazingly strong to kick speed."

"Yes, Colin, I am amazingly strong."

Erica laughed. She was never fooled by craptalk. She just watched and listened, and didn't allow herself to be taken in by false hope. She knew the score.

And sure enough, within a month, I was back on the tablets, telling myself that it was impossible to achieve the necessary "otherness" otherwise. I got up at five every morning and tried to work on *Golem*, a play about that mythical creature created out of mud which was brought forth by a rabbi to save the persecuted Jewish community of medieval Prague. *Golem* had been evading me for years. The dream of salvation that goes so horribly wrong; the theme was close to my heart and burning in my head. There I was trying to create the golem and I was it.

It wasn't long before I was completely out of control again. 1974 was apparently happening outside and I was slumped before my Olympia with rejected drafts of *Golem* littered on the floor all around me. I came to see that I'd never had a chance, that writing had merely been a good excuse for using up a life. I couldn't even pretend to be a writer any more.

In the early morning I paced the communal garden to consider the answer but couldn't find one, so I went back inside to peep at my sleeping children. As I looked at them, it became glaringly obvious. There was just one thing that I could do that would give these four people the chance to survive, without having to witness the gradual disintegration of their father and the end of everything. My exit was the only gift I had left to give. These characters would manage much better in another play without me.

I went to our bedroom and watched Erica sleeping. I always knew she deserved someone nicer and more stable than I could ever be, someone to cherish her unique beauty and intelligence. She would really appreciate a comfortable, quiet life post-Kops. With a loving accountant, maybe. I laughed out loud at the thought as I looked down on her. Erica would never settle for a quiet life. I hoped that she would have several passionate love affairs on the side, and remember me, a fucking playwright who couldn't fuck.

I kissed her gently goodbye and she smiled from sleep. "I'm sorry," I whispered and then took one last look at my kids, these little people of incredible beauty. Their skin was like pale-pink tulip petals. It was clear they had been lumbered with me long enough; it was high time another man entered their lives, a quiet, gentle influence who would love them all and tuck them up in bed and make them all cocoa. Children need that security.

I heard Erica stirring and rushed to the door.

"Christ!" It wouldn't open. Erica had gone and locked it from the inside and hidden the key, the clever cow. Well fuck that then, I thought, I'll just get out through the window.

I was almost out when she came and grabbed my legs with both her arms and tried to pull me back inside. All at once we were featuring in a cheap getaway farce.

"Don't go. Please don't go!" she pleaded. I'd never heard her beg like this before.

I tried kicking her away with my free foot, and I kicked and kicked and carried on kicking while she struggled to hold on. It wasn't real. I was kicking out behind me, fighting a force which was trying to hold me back, not my wife, please God, not Erica. "Would Bernard Kops, the playwright and loving family man, please come up on to the stage to receive his award for outstanding hypocrisy?"

We carried on dancing; I was halfway out and halfway in. I screamed and kicked until at last I was kicking space. Then I was out of the window and on to the pavement. I had just kicked away the most precious thing in my life.

Her face appeared in the space. It was wet and looking at me with infinite sadness. I could hear sobbing as I ran triumphantly down the street, still kicking with all the force I had left in me.

Lindsay was on the telephone in the mansion block in his dressing gown. It was the only flat in the road with the light on. I ran by his window and fast forwarded to where my taxi was parked. Then I got in behind the wheel and made my escape.

Erica would be wide awake, reassuring the children back at the flat, but I exorcised all that from my mind. Where I was headed was no place to take family. I already knew my exit, a vast, solid Victorian wall made out of dark grey bricks, just behind the main road where Kilburn High Road becomes Maida Vale; the back of a sweatshop, possibly. It was as good a place as any.

I drove with utmost care. Police cars often lurked in side roads in the very early morning.

The wall of dirty bricks was straight ahead. I gave myself a good run at it so I could build up speed and pushed my foot down.

I think I knew almost at once that I wasn't going to be allowed to get away with it. That man in the taxi mirror was watching me with a beady eye.

He sighed heavily. "Is this ant pissing in the Atlantic contemplating suicide?" he asked. "Or are you God, do you think?"

I just kept my foot on the pedal and tried not to hear.

It got louder. "So, why not ask yourself who it is you're really trying to hurt here."

"Only me!"

His eyebrows were raised very high in the mirror. "Go on! Let the shit pour out of your ears!"

"Please," I whimpered. I wanted to go as a victim, not a coward.

"You arrogant bastard."

Bastard yourself, I thought with bad grace as I slammed on the brakes. My cab screeched to a stop a few feet away from the wall.

I was definitely not dead; I was lumbered with living. I closed my eyes and could hear the birds singing, the beginning of a morning I wasn't supposed to be in.

I turned the cab around and drove to Vallance Road in Whitechapel to buy some piping-hot bagels at the All Night Bagel Shop, for the family.

35

Has Anyone Seen an Old Black Cab?

The bagels were just coming out of the oven and the steam of life was rising from them. The night cabbies were gossiping at the counter, each demanding to be served first so that they could get off home to Hendon and their steaming-hot, sleeping wives, now one quarter awake and ready to be stirred with a nice little bit of conjugaling.

I was on my way home too, with a bag of hot bagels for the family. I drove my taxi most of the way, but parked the old girl around St John's Wood and walked the rest. I felt a rush of exhilaration as I walked into the wind. I had finally got rid of the crazy guy on my shoulder. The early morning sky was liquid gold. I gulped it down and hurried home.

When I turned the key and opened the door Erica was standing there waiting for me. Her face was long and drawn.

"I've bought some bagels for breakfast," I said and kissed her. "And I want you to know that I'm never taking drugs again." She smiled.

I never have either. For the last twenty-five years aspirin has been my outer limit.

Later that morning, after taking the kids to school, Erica and I returned to the back streets behind Kilburn to look for our taxi. I thought I knew where I had left her but, as had happened so often before, I turned out to be mistaken. She was nowhere to be seen. We searched for more than an hour but got nowhere.

"Maybe tomorrow you'll remember," Erica comforted me as we made our way home.

For the rest of that week we combed the streets between Kilburn and Maida Vale but we never did find it. My taxi must have found some other madman to fly her crazily through the sky. It seemed appropriate somehow that I should lose her on the same day that I rediscovered my sanity. These days, whenever I do something a little mad and outrageous, which is often, my son-in-law Mark teases me and says, "Where's your taxi, Bernard? Shall we go and look for it?"

★

One night in bed, sometime in the mid-seventies, I awoke with a start to find Erica wide awake and staring at the ceiling.

"What's wrong?" I asked her. I could see she was thinking hard. "Tell me what you're thinking and take the weight off your brain."

"I'm scared, Bernard. There's no money coming in."

I was earning practically nothing. I couldn't figure out what the hell I wanted to write about. I hadn't yet started to capitalise on my darkest days or even got them into proper perspective.

Soon after that, Erica surprised me one morning. She quietly put on her overcoat and went to the door. "Goodbye," she said, and left.

I rushed out after her. After all, days of relative tranquillity were upon us and we went everywhere together. "Where you going?" I shouted.

"Somewhere!"

That didn't sound so good. "Where?"

"I want to be on my own." She walked briskly away. "See you later."

It wasn't at all characteristic. I lay on the bed and listened to music all afternoon and wondered.

She returned after a few hours, smiling all over. "I've done it."

"Done what?"

"I've found a job," she said. "People need money, you know. We do need to eat."

Later she told me she had gone to the Royal Free Hospital and asked for work. They had welcomed her at once and given her a white coat. What with her father being a doctor and all her uncles in the medical game, hospitals were her entire background. She was starting the following Monday, identifying viruses in the virology lab.

I grabbed the plump cheeks of her bottom. "Thank God," I said. "At last we'll have a bit of money coming in to pay the bank. And I'll do the cooking and get the kids from school."

"And of course you'll make a fortune by writing the play of your dreams," she added, and screwed up her face into a wry smile. We both knew I lived in dreamland.

I was relieved someone at least was going to be earning, even if I also felt guilty. Poor Erica, she could have had a fabulous career in medicine, gone in any direction she chose, but she had thrown everything away to be with me. She had been made to watch from the sidelines as younger, strident women started to rise and rise to impossible heights. "We have four wonderful children," I always reminded her in my defence, knowing that this was the one thing she could never feel bitter about.

My slow climb back up the slopes to health and sanity was beginning and it was all so wonderfully banal. I was making my way to the secure plateau of ordinariness. I was re-entering my family, and getting back to the typewriter, back to the endless, five-draft grind again.

Erica and I started walking every day over Hampstead Heath. We did at least one hour of brisk walking and talking, and gradually brought everything back to our sort of normal. Funny, we had lived in the area for over ten years and only just discovered the Heath.

It was about then that I happened to bump into Ron Pember. Ron had directed *Enter Solly Gold* at the Mermaid Theatre and had always respected my writing. I felt that I could trust him. We got talking, and we got excited. Some people stay faithful till the end of the world. He took me to a greasy spoon along Tottenham Court Road so we could talk more. The place was crammed with working men; builders, plumbers and lorry drivers, stuffing their mouths with fried bread and eggs and bacon and sausages and baked beans. When they looked up and saw Ron they broke into smiles and jocular banter. As well as being a director, Ron is a wonderfully energetic actor and his face was well known from countless television appearances.

He insisted on treating me to breakfast, my second of the morning, and told me about CV4, a small touring company he was running which was subsidised by the Arts Council. He asked me to write a play for them. If I was inspired, he said, it would be an immediate commission. Naturally, I said that I was bursting with ideas, although it was just a little too early to discuss them, and that I had a wonderful idea for a play that CV4 would be proud to produce.

I panicked all the way home and agonised until about four in the morning. I didn't have a single dramatic idea in my head.

Two days later it was Sunday and I went to our newsagents to buy the posh papers, only my attention was grabbed by a headline on one of the popular tabloids instead. I bought the paper and sat down on a doorstep and read.

The full story took up two pages. It described how, in response to a recent white paper on the need to rehabilitate the mentally ill, various mental institutions were disgorging their patients and dumping them at seaside resorts in Kent. The idea was to get these people back into society so that the poor buggers could start to come to terms with the real world.

Unfortunately, it wasn't turning out as planned. The article revealed that these unfortunate men and women were being dumped in little bed and breakfasts. They weren't allowed to stay there during the day, but had to fill their time hanging about the town or around the esplanade doing nothing, at the mercy of the elements and the local louts. When they were finally allowed back into their digs at night they faced tyrannical and unscrupulous landladies and landlords. I had experienced something like it in my mad days before Erica.

Serendipity! Here was an issue that had to be written about.

36

Mr Love and Justice

The smell of coffee permeated the flat and the children were laughing. It was good to see my old friends again, especially Colin. He had stayed away for most of all my season in hell, and I couldn't blame him. Now I was back to my slightly less impossible old self, he was back to dropping in almost every evening. He was still writing about the "scene" and was still very much the lone loper of the night streets. In many ways, he seemed more alone than ever.

We now called him Mr Love and Justice. It was the title of his novel about a freewheeling black guy and a corrupt copper who somehow do a swap over. He meant it cynically but our epithet was quite the opposite. Colin was absolutely a Mr Love and Justice. He certainly believed in love, of all kinds, and the need for justice burned out with his every breath and every word. Colin had missionary zeal.

He was hunched on the floor one evening, leaning back against the wall, glass in hand, and asked me if I'd been inspired to start writing again. "Bernie, it's the only life we have. Words." He'd had a few swigs of whisky and was almost in tears at the sentiment.

I gave him the newspaper article about the poor bastards in Margate. "I'm compelled to write about all this stuff," I told him. "These tragic creatures slouching around in out-of-season Margate, waiting to be born." I was trying to be clever as usual, misquoting Yeats.

"On Margate sands I can connect nothing with nothing," he rejoined.

I couldn't place it straight away.

"Old Possum! *The Waste Land.* He wrote that about his stay in Margate, also convalescing after a breakdown."

Well, that settled it. "I'm going to Margate, although not for a breakdown; I've done all that."

I called Ron Pember and told him I had the perfect new play for his company, and that same day I went down to Margate. What I saw sickened me.

★

As soon as I came out of the station I started being followed by a crazy scarecrow. I went to a telephone box to ring home and he hung about outside, trying hard to look inconspicuous. When I had finished he came right up to me, laughing and nodding, no doubt recognising a kindred spirit, and offered to show me the sights. The sights of Margate? He had to be mad, I told him. I explained my mission and he took me down to the front. There they all were, the dispossessed; some just standing there in the slanting rain, drugged up to the eyeballs, their hands stiff down beside them; others shuffling along in slow motion, moonwalkers on their way to nowhere.

Peter the scarecrow asked me for a quid to buy some chips and returned with a great bag of them. All the silent others surrounded him and dipped in, eager for a little warmth on that unfriendly front in rather unseasonable May. Later they found their voices and told me about the wicked landlady who ran their bed and breakfast and how nice she pretended to be to everyone else; about her smiling face and her homely Birmingham accent which disguised a tyrant who beat them black and blue and tyrannised them.

"She can teach the louts and coppers a thing or two," my scarecrow said. "We've nuffin to do all day. She half-inches our money and our allowance books, then turfs us out after breakfast so we hang about all day in all wevvers. You're lucky if you die."

I stood around a whole day with them, freezing, nodding and listening. At the end of it I bunged my scarecrow a fiver. He didn't show it to the others but hid it down his trousers and danced, as if I had given him a hundred. Then I found a bed and breakfast of my own for the night. The landlady's smile seemed real enough but I was a nice paying guest in full possession of my marbles.

The next morning I watched from my window as they all took their places. They huddled together on the esplanade, with nothing to do but pass the time and watch it passing.

I completed a first draft of *On Margate Sands* within a week, and discovered that my writing had undergone a sea change. It was much better. My adolescent verve had always needed a touch of the dark and the fearsome, some twist of acid. Like me, my writing had grown another layer of skin. It had paid its dues.

Dina Lom, my lovely agent, decided it was time to get herself a bit of living and retired from the game. And so John Rush came into my life, a tall, organised fellow, ex boxing and rowing blue from Cambridge. It seemed an unlikely match but it worked from the start, and has lasted for more than twenty-five years.

I talk to John every day, very often about nothing. It's cheaper than therapy. I kid myself that I am his only client. He's one of the three essential people in my writing life. Most important is Erica, of course, the one who gives me all my problems by telling me the truth. Then John, who helps to find me work and reads and understands the small print on the contracts; and lastly there's my accountant, Aubrey Sheena, who guides me across the minefields of my bank statements and sorts out that most emotional subject of all.

On Margate Sands opened in Nottingham. The critics were favourable and I hoped that Colin would call round to congratulate me the day the reviews were out. We hadn't heard from him for several weeks, but then I had been busy getting the play on, and he usually turned up whenever things were terrible or marvellous; I even opened a bottle of wine so it could breathe, in anticipation.

He didn't make it, though, and we never got to drink the wine together, because the next morning when I was reading the obituaries in the paper to make sure I was still alive, I turned the page and found Colin staring out at me. It didn't register immediately. When I actually realised he was dead I shivered from the base of my spine to the top of my head. I read the words in disbelief. Colin MacInnes had had cancer of the oesophagus and was gone. We would never see him again. Who would I gossip with now? I couldn't take in that he'd just died like that, with no warning, and without Erica and I saying goodbye.

I wandered Soho that afternoon in the ridiculous hope that I would see him loping about somewhere. I needed to unearth some of the old blaggers that were still hanging on so that we could talk about him and share commiserations. I found Dirty Charles, the First Acolyte of Ironfoot Jack who had preceded Colin to the isles of dust aeons before. He was able to tell me about Colin's last days. He had died joking and bravely, he said, and I confess I felt a little relieved that I hadn't been a witness. Colin on his deathbed seemed like a contradiction in terms.

I only wish that he had found more peace for himself. Colin MacInnes was one of the most irascible and generous humans I ever met. He gave me a broader vision of the world and helped me open my mind to all it is. He could be impossible, but he was always my friend. He was either totally thoughtless or incredibly thoughtful, sometimes mean and often generous. But he never found real love, only passion fruit. Mr Love and Justice died more alone and more unloved than anyone ever should. Without him, my world is a less friendly place.

37

Ezra

Five minutes to 1981 and I was fifty-five years old. Most of my life was now in the past and it had all happened so quickly. I turned round three times and that old geezer with his grasscutter caught my eye, smiled and nodded.

Bad times are easy to write about, everyone wants to know. But who really wants to hear that things are going well for you, that nothing is really happening except you are dancing around the living room with a laughing child on your shoulder? It's perhaps unbearably sentimental for outsiders looking in through the window.

I was far from finished. I still had a string of unborn plays queuing up inside me and one of them, *Ezra*, was about to announce itself. Writing and Erica were the two things in the world that stopped me from losing it. All I could do to keep myself together was write and expiate and exorcise my angels and monsters. "Dear Colin, I miss you. Dear Paul Potts, the world is a colder and lonelier place without you, my Don Quixote of Soho. Quentin Crisp, pioneer of precious Camp and Coming Out, hanging on in there at Cooper's Diner in New York, I have need of thee, my monster. Ironfoot Jack, come back, come back!" I missed all my monsters; even my uncle Hymie.

I was asked at the BBC if I had any new ideas in my head. In those days, just nineteen years ago, they were still in love with writers. You were doing them a favour, and there were no commissioning editors still in their nappies. There was just Jack Emery sitting at the other side of the table with fire and humour in his eyes.

"Yes, Jack, there is one play I would love to write for you," I said and did my pitch. At the time I knew next to nothing about Ezra Pound except for his poetry, most of it unintelligible to me, and most of it unquotable, but something about the terrible man kept nagging at me.

I was scared out of my smiling wits when Jack commissioned me on the spot. It was a double commission. *Ezra* would also be produced at the Half Moon Theatre in the East End.

★

So there I was stuck with my monster, just him and me. I weighed up what information I had on him. Firstly, I knew he had greatly influenced Eliot, and that Eliot acknowledged Ezra as the greater talent. Two other things I knew about the man: towards the end of the Second World War he was flung into a gorilla cage on the shores of Italy near Pisa, where in the throes of madness he had worked on his life work, the *Cantos*; secondly, he had been indicted for treason by the United States government.

Clearly, I had some reading to do, and I spent four weeks in the reference library at Swiss Cottage. The librarian could hardly keep up with me. Ezra came towards me from his dark cell, took his clothes off, opened his forehead, ripped open his mind, and tore open his chest to reveal his dark and crazy heart.

Ezra, grizzled genius and traitor, giant of poetry and virulent anti-Semite. How could such a great poet end up despised and imprisoned in a gorilla cage? How could a man of such talent have ended up spewing out the obscenities of a shithouse? What was this madness of anti-Semitism that still persists after the evidence of the incinerators? How could anyone be a great poet and set down words of such memorable beauty and at the same time proclaim Hitler as a prophet and martyr, and give comfort and assistance to those intent on wiping out an entire people?

After being incarcerated in that cage at Pisa, Ezra was shipped back to the USA and placed in a criminal asylum. Most of the world's great writers petitioned the American president for his release. Only Robert Graves refused to sign that petition. Years later, an old man, Ezra stumbled back to Venice to live out his remaining years. He was shocked to discover that the Sephardic Jews of Rome were no longer around; like the rest of their brethren they had gone up in smoke.

Allen Ginsberg, who had been one of the prime movers for Ezra's release, later visited Pound in Venice.

"How could I have been anti-Semite?" Ezra asked him. "Danny Kaye is a Jew."

And at his end, just before he cloaked himself in total silence, he remarked, "The worst mistake I ever made was that stupid suburban prejudice of anti-Semitism."

It made for powerful drama.

Ezra proved to be one my most successful plays and I had the great fortune to have both Ian Holm and Ian McDiarmid play my marvellous old monster; Holm on radio, and McDiarmid on stage, directed by the immensely creative Rob Walker.

The run wasn't without its problems, though. I suppose it must have been well known that the play running at the Half Moon was written by a Jew and that the core of the play was about the evils of prejudice – Kops the yid playwright who was born not two hundred yards from the theatre was delving into the entrails of fascism. It ignited a backlash. I received scurrilous letters, telling me that my days were numbered, along with all the other yids, and in the middle of the night, the second week into the run, some local louts tried to burn the theatre down. They were not completely successful but the offices were destroyed.

It wasn't long after the arson attack on the Half Moon that I saw a youngish woman blithely allowing her dog to drop its coil on the path. Our communal garden had minimal rules. Number one rule: no dog shit.

I politely pointed out to the woman that children played around the area and reminded her of the rule.

She smiled. "Hitler obviously didn't finish the job properly."

What can you do with people like that? I laughed and left her with her turd and went inside to shake my head at the white reflection in the mirror.

A couple of days later I went for morning coffee at Cosmo as usual. It was crammed with the usual bums and a gaggle of psychoanalysts who practised nearby. The chat was so rarefied you could smell it.

"Hello, Bernie!" Old Monty, an emigré from Russia, came through the door. Monty was over seventy and working on his twentieth novel, although he was yet to be published.

He sat down beside me, looking grave. "I read in the *Standard* about your play and the fire in the theatre. Those momzers, Bernie! You've got to take great care."

His seriousness scared me and I got up quickly to make my getaway.

"Wait!" he said. "You could be in danger. You're in the front line." And he scrawled a telephone number on a paper serviette. "Ring these people. They can help you with certain safety precautions."

That afternoon I dialled the number. A man with a gruff Israeli accent answered and I told him who I was. There was a pause and then he asked me if I had time to call on him.

"When?" I asked.

"Where are you?"

I told him. "We are very close. Come now," he said, and gave me the address. It was a modern block along the Finchley Road, not even five minutes' walk away.

Two men sat opposite me and listened impassively as I recounted all the events at the Half Moon and showed them some of the letters that I had received. Then they smiled and became human, and offered me coffee. As they hovered over the kettle and spoke quietly in Hebrew, I realised with a shock that these two guys were Mossad. They could be nothing else.

They told me that other Jews were receiving similar threats, and that only a few days before two youths had approached a woman pushing a pram in Stamford Hill and slashed her child with an open razor before running away, laughing.

"We Jews no longer acquiesce to our own execution," the ginger one said. "We can give you a few simple precautions."

I was amazed, and comforted, that these two Israelis should be here, operating along the Finchley Road, advising me on how to protect myself.

They told me that I should vary my movements when leaving the house. One day I should go out of the front door, the next day out of the back door. I should always look carefully before fully emerging; and one day I should walk to the right and the next day turn to the left. I should always check the underneath of my car to make sure there were no strange attachments.

"But surely no one would go to such lengths to blow up a mere playwright?" I asked.

"We hope not. Unless you write terrible plays."

We all laughed and I said I would keep in touch. When I left the block of flats I looked both ways before walking quickly home.

Ezra's mistress Olga Rudge, now well into her nineties, came to England. Somehow she had managed to get hold of a copy of my play and wanted to see me. Erica and I met up with her at an exhibition at a small art gallery behind Regent Street which was showing the famous head of Ezra by Gaudier-Brzeska.

Olga was a wiry battleaxe, but there was a Colin MacInnes twinkle in her eye. She thanked me. "You have been the most compassionate to my Ezra. And you are a Jew. Funny."

It was the sort of compliment I cared for. Not surprisingly, Ezra was not well liked amongst Jewish writers. I had been criticised by friends and by a few of the minion of regular worshippers at the little synagogue at the end of the street for daring to write about him with any sympathy. I found it harder to stand in judgement. Only a few years before I had also been a monster. I had almost destroyed my entire family, everything I loved. I did the most despicable things. I crawled into sewers and wallowed in the stench and witnessed base deeds of human creatures without speaking out.

Olga Rudge rambled over her life with Ezra; how she and Ezra and his wife, Dorothy Shakespeare, all lived together in the good days. She also mentioned that she was a musicologist.

"Then it was you and not Ezra who rediscovered Vivaldi?" Erica asked her.

She giggled. "How clever of you. How did you know? Men always seem to get the credit, don't they?"

After *Ezra* I was back in the thick of things. People began to talk about me again, and even the critics began to reappraise my work. I sometimes bump into one of the creatures who damned me; one does in this small, tight world of the stage. Face to face they often say that they have always enjoyed my work; you could have fooled me.

38

The World is a Wedding

So suddenly it was 1991 and despite all those years of trying to destroy myself, it looked as if I had every possibility of living deep into old age, which was convenient as I felt I had at least ten or twelve more plays within me. Everything seemed to spark drama.

We were invited to a neighbour's house to dinner. Derek lived in what was considered a posh modern flat along the Finchley Road, although in reality it was more like a box of bricks, and a smell like boiled cabbages permeated the corridors. As soon as we got there I yearned for the security of our own untidy space and tall ceilings.

Derek lived with his sister, and they were both obsessed with Frank Sinatra. The two of them seemed completely oblivious to the fact that we were there that night. Old Blue Eyes sang right through the meal, and stared down at us from posters all over the walls while brother and sister asked each other questions about him. Questions, answers, quips, anecdotes, both of them vying for ascendancy and trying to catch the other out. They'd built themselves a Sinatra cocoon in their little flat to shelter them from life.

When we prepared to leave, Derek seemed to notice us for the first time. "Do you like Sinatra?" he asked.

"Of course. Love him. Goodnight."

Playing Sinatra was produced at the Warehouse Theatre in Croydon. Ted Craig, the artistic director, did an excellent job, directing it to perfection. The reviews were good and Eddie Kulukundis tried hard to transfer it to the West End but it never happened, although it did transfer successfully to Greenwich.

Needless to say, it wasn't enough to solve our on-going financial crisis. We had borrowed so much against the value of the flat over the years that our mortgage had risen sky high. If it wasn't for Darren McDonnell, our young bank manager, we would certainly have had to sell up. He afforded us some breathing space and gave us understanding, time and advice, and I thank him for it.

★

About then I started work on *Who Shall I be Tomorrow?*, a play about an impoverished actress who is forever searching for her giro and going to auditions which she never gets. After three drafts it was ready to be licked into final shape and was crying out for a friendly critical eye.

I bumped into Lindsay in Waitrose. He was studying the various marmalades, agonising over which one to choose. I tried pulling him out of his deliberations by assuring him that Cooper's Original Oxford was the best.

"But are you sure?" he asked me.

"Marmalade is a subjective business, but that is the one to go for, I am absolutely certain."

"In that case I have no choice," he said, and put the jar into his trolley.

We met like this three or four times a week and always had the same sort of conversation.

"You seem unusually happy on such a miserable day," he remarked.

"That's because I've just finished a new play."

"A play is never finished. May I see it?"

"Yes, please! Shall I pop it over later?"

"It would be a pleasure." He was always so polite.

I dropped the manuscript through his door that afternoon and waited nervously for his reaction. Experiencing Lindsay and his eagle eye was never what you would call a pleasure. He wasn't one to waste words and I knew that he could easily tell me that it was a bloody awful waste of my time and his.

Two days later he telephoned and said that he had read it and asked me to call on him that evening. He didn't say whether he liked it, loved it or hated it.

I was eager for his immediate response but first he made me watch a video of John Ford's *Stagecoach*. We went into his living room and he brought tea and cake. I was too much on edge to enjoy the masterpiece. Lindsay was totally absorbed, even though he must have seen it dozens of times.

When it was over he turned to me. "Bernie, I like the play, but there's work to do on it."

There was always work to do, but I felt a great sense of elation. "Does that mean you would be prepared to direct it?" I asked.

He smiled and nodded his head.

And so for a few weeks we worked together, whenever he could find an oasis of time, just as we had for the Otto Plaschkes film treatment years before. After a while Lindsay's mood lightened. He started smiling more and being openly affectionate.

"It's good," he said one evening. "It's almost there."

We talked about theatres where he might stage it. Unfortunately, a lot of managements were scared of Lindsay; he had argued with most of them.

"Who do you think would be right for the actress?" I asked.

"I think Rachel Roberts would be perfect."

"That's a very good idea." We would often make obnoxious quips like this. Rachel Roberts was long since dead and I knew just how much he loved and missed her. He had brought her to prominence in *This Sporting Life*, one of the most outstanding films of all time. Later she killed herself in California, and Lindsay had never quite got over the shock.

"So, you would like Rachel for your play. Well, why not?" He creaked and stumbled to his feet and went into another room. He returned with an urn and plonked it down on the coffee table between us. "Here she is."

The incident was as stark as a scene in one of his films.

Actually I wanted Susannah York for the part and I contacted her and sent the script. She said she was very interested. Lindsay thought she might be right too, so we both went to the French Institute to see her performing in a classical French play. I forget the title but she was excellent and we were both completely sold on the idea of having her for *Who Shall I be Tomorrow?*

Sadly, Lindsay never did direct the play in the end. My agent sent it to the Greenwich Theatre and they replied swiftly, saying they wanted to produce it. I had a meeting with Francis Matthews, the artistic director, and he enthused and said that he wanted to direct the play himself. Lindsay was away at the time, planning or filming *The Whales of August* so I couldn't consult him and agreed. Francis also told me that he had shown the play to Joanna Lumley and that she very much wanted to play Rosalind, the lead.

"I hope Lindsay will approve of Miss Lumley," he said while my heart sank. I had promised the play to Susannah York.

I rang her and she was cold but magnanimous. She said she understood. She had every right to loathe me and I felt rotten.

I also had to face Lindsay, now back in London. I wanted to telephone him, but Erica insisted I go round and see him face to face.

He came to the door in his dressing gown as usual and I blurted out the news on the doorstep.

He asked me inside for coffee. "Dear boy, I quite understand. We all have to make a living."

There was something essentially magnificent about Lindsay Anderson. I still felt I had betrayed him.

Hard to believe I was approaching my mid-sixties. Inside I was still a school boy and I couldn't believe the evidence in the mirror. All my teeth had fallen out, and my hair was white and my dome was bare.

"Darling, is it too late for me to learn how to use a computer?" I asked Erica one night.

I fell asleep one afternoon soon after and when I awoke there was the machine on the coffee table before me. A young friend Paul, a creative writing student of mine at the City Lit, had furnished me with a box of tricks.

That night I crept out with my old mistress, my decrepit but still terribly efficient Olympia typewriter, and, with all the vestiges of my fading might, I chucked it out with the rubbish. "Goodbye, you old Teutonic bitch." At last I had vanquished those incredibly efficient Germans. Now I am told I must learn to forgive them.

Vicky Ireland at the Polka Theatre in Wimbledon commissioned me to write a play about Anne Frank. The original dramatised staging of the diary was a tired old thing and beginning to look threadbare. Some students in Amsterdam had even laughed derisively during a recent production.

Anne Frank has become one of the greatest icons of all time. I wanted to take a journey into her dreams and fantasies. She was a normal thirteen-year-old girl, she had to be stirring with erotic thoughts. I wanted to allow her to be real, passionate, intelligent, beautiful. She cried out for it. She was an ordinary girl in an extraordinary situation. In *Dreams of Anne Frank* I try to deal with the darker side of humanity, the knowledge of what we also are, and I follow Anne to her desperate end. Most people revere Anne and the way she affirmed life. In her diary she proclaimed that the goodness of people would prevail. But in truth she died alone with all joy and all hope gone. Her faith in human goodness preceded a terrible death. My play is for young people. I think they can face the truth, and have a right to know.

Dreams of Anne Frank and *Playing Sinatra* both received broad critical acclaim; the critics were universal in their praise.

"What clever, discerning fellows they are. How dare they give me such good reviews," I said. Our laughter was tinged with relief.

"At last you're getting the recognition you deserve," Erica rejoined. "Better late than never."

Lindsay Anderson died in 1994. He was in France and had a heart attack in an old friend's swimming pool. He will never offer me another ginger biscuit. I shall never see him again around the corner conversing with the girl in the dry cleaners. Lindsay was a person who changed lives, and I have so much to thank him for. He swept away all the crap. You just got the pure gold, unadulterated truth from him. He was a good and faithful friend who never changed his opinions to appease the prevailing winds.

The last time we met was in Waitrose, a week before he went to France. He was giving a small dinner party for some friends and asked me how to make potato latkes. I told him about the recipe my mother had used, and how you had to be sure to grate the potatoes when they're raw. I tried to post a written version through his door very early the next morning but the door opened as I was doing it and Lindsay, in his immortal dressing gown, asked me in for coffee. He did an awful lot of Jewish sighing that morning. I never saw him again. I hope the latkes went down well.

Years fly past and there is an absence of pain. Things look decidedly better than they used to. It has all been a long, and sometimes terrible struggle, but somehow I have survived. In my last twenty-five years I have written over thirty plays, made a living and raised a family. Who else can say more? What else is there? I'm one of the lucky ones. Some pay therapists to unload their fantasies, dreams and nightmares. I get paid for writing them down.

My grandchildren surround me and pull out what is left of my hair. There are ten of us now. I barely knew how to be a good father and now I'm trying hard to learn how to be a good grandfather.

I still dream of amber: shops with windows full of it, huge globes of glistening gold; great golden sunflowers reaching up to shattering orbs in the sky. Children dancing and giggling in a blazing afternoon. Strings that start from lemon and go all the way to treacle. The ten years I wasted and can never retrieve. The innocent past, gone forever. And the shots fired into the backs of those skulls in Riga.

My mother, stirring in the cosmic soup, reminds me of a story she heard a thousand years ago. Once an angel soared across the sky, clutching a mirror. It contained the whole truth, the meaning of existence. But as the angel soared higher she let the mirror slip out of her grasp. It fell and shattered, scattering all over the earth, and people, wherever they were, all over the world, each picked up a sliver and believed that they alone possessed the truth.

"What is truth?" asked jesting Pilate and never waited for an answer. I'm still waiting and still here, with all the questions and none of the answers. In Jewish terms I've achieved the greatest thing of all: grandchildren. It may sound strange to the non-Jewish world but a billion Chinese will understand. And I think I've finally written enough words. This book alone accounts for one quarter of a million, if you count the rewrites. "Face it, you'll drop dead writing. Your head will fall forward on to the keyboard, and that's how we'll know there will be one less person for breakfast," says Erica these days. Gallows humour never fails. We poke our tongue out at the Great Moloch and get on with our lives. There's that Jewish joke. An old man greets his daughter. "When I die, please scatter my ashes in Brent Cross shopping centre."

She is mystified. "Why there?" she asks.

"Then at least I know you'll visit me once a week."

So, who am I to complain? Every morning brings Erica who I never deserved; how lucky she was to find me. And the afternoon brings the whole family. All this out of nothing. The miracle remains. A flashback: Erica coming down those stairs in Bunjee's cellar in 1954 and suddenly there's a whole tribe of us.

My grandchildren are playing, giggling in the garden.

Also by Bernard Kops:

STAGE PLAYS
with year of first production

The Hamlet of Stepney Green 1956
Goodbye World 1960
The Dream of Peter Mann 1960
Change for the Angel 1960
Enter Solly Gold 1961
The Boy Who Wouldn't Play Jesus 1965
Stray Cats and Empty Bottles 1967
David it is Getting Dark 1968
On Margate Sands 1980
Ezra 1981
Simon at Midnight 1985
Kafé Kropotkin 1988
Sophie 1990
Moss 1990
Playing Sinatra 1991/2
Androcles and the Lion 1992
Dreams of Anne Frank 1992
    (winner of *Time Out* award for
    Best Fringe Play, 1992/3)
Who Shall I be Tomorrow? 1993
Call in the Night 1994
Jacob and the Green Rabbi 1995
Café Zeitgeist 1996

PLAY COLLECTIONS

Kops Plays One
    (*The Hamlet of Stepney Green,
    Playing Sinatra, Ezra*),
    Oberon Books, 1999
Kops Plays Two
    (*On Margate Sands,
    Dreams of Anne Frank,
    Call in the Night*),
    Oberon Books, 2000

TELEVISION PLAYS
with year of first broadcast

I Want to Go Home 1963
Stray Cats and Empty Bottles 1964
The Lost Years of Brian Hooper 1965
Enter Solly Gold 1968
Just One Kid 1974

It's a Lovely Day Tomorrow 1975
    (nominated for Emmy, 1975)
*The Geese that Shrieked and the Boy
Philospher* (adaptations from Isaac
Bashevis Singer) 1975
Moss 1976
Rocky Marciano is Dead 1977
Nightkids 1983

RADIO PLAYS
with year of first broadcast

Return to Stepney Green 1957
Everybody Likes Saturday Night 1958
Home Sweet Honeycomb 1962
The Lemmings 1963
Israel (Part One) 1963
Israel (Part Two) 1964
The Dark Ages 1964
Bournemouth Nights 1979
I Grow Old, I Grow Old 1979
Antlanta 1980
Ezra 1980
Over the Rainbow 1981
Simon at Midnight 1982
Moss 1983
Trotsky was My Father 1984
More Out than In 1985
Kafé Kropotkin 1988
Colour Blind 1989
Congress in Manchester 1990
Soho Nights 1992
Sailing with Homer 1995
    (winner of the
    Writers Guild Award, 1995)
The Jericho Players 1996
    (nominated for the
    Writers Guild Award, 1996)
The Jericho Players (Part Two) 1998
Your Ashen Hair Shulamit 1998
Loving Failure 2000

NOVELS

Awake for Morning 1958
Motorbike 1962

Yes from No-Man's Land 1965
The Dissent of Dominick Shapiro 1966
By the Waters of Whitechapel 1969
The Passionate Past of Gloria Gaye 1972
Settle Down Simon Katz 1973
Partners 1975
On Margate Sands 1978

AUTOBIOGRAPHY (Part One)

The World is a Wedding 1963, 1975

POETRY

Poems 1955
Poems and Songs 1958
Anemone for Antigone 1959
Erica, I Want to Read You Something 1967
For the Record 1971
Barricades in West Hampstead 1988
Grandchildren and Other Poems 2000

NON-FICTION

Neither Your Honey Nor Your Sting
     (Offbeat History of the Jews) 1985

Index

Aarons, Gerald, 191-3
Absolute Beginners, 105-9
Ackland, Joss, 52
Adler, Larry, 176
Adler, Mr (tailor), 77, 86
Aldermaston marches, 112-13, 163
All Night Bagel Shop, 208-9
Alvarez, Al, 123
amber necklace, 104, 157, 186-7, 227
American visa application, 180-1
Amis, Kingsley, 111
Amsterdam visit, 128
Anderson, Lindsay, 113, 163-5, 207, 226
   and *Who Shall I be Tomorrow?*, 223-5
   Lindsay, and *Yes from No-man's Land*, 164
anti-Semitism, 135-7, 218-20
   Pound, Ezra, 218
Archer, David, 14, 15-16, 17, 36
Arden, John, 59, 110, 115
Arts Council of Great Britain, 23-6, 60
As You Like It (café), 31
Athenaeum, 81-2
Auden, W. H., 54, 111
Auerbach, David, 17

Bacon, Francis, 17, 36
Baddeley, Hermione, 87, 92
Baldwin, James, 124-5
Barrymore, John, 62
Baza, 136-42
   hospital, 139-42
BBC, commissions *Stray Cats and Empty
                Bottles*, 105
Beatles, the, 69, 115
Beggar's Opera, The, 60
Belsize pharmacy, 191
Betjeman, John, 90-1
black bombers, 113-14, 193, 194
Bloom's restaurant, Whitechapel, 41
blues *see* speed
bomb, atomic, first play about, 87
Booth, James, 105
Botteghe Oscure, 16
Brahms, Caryl, 54
Brent, Peter, 122

Bristol Old Vic, writer in residence, 60,
                61, 62-7
Broccoli, Cubby, 168-73
Brothers of the Resurrection, Oxford
           halfway house, 201-5
Brown, Pete, 112
Brzeska, Gaudier, 220
Buchan, John, 136
Bunjee's, 227
Burton, Richard, 54
Bush, Alan, 57-8

Camberwell Green flat, 11
Cambridge Circus bookstall, 21, 32
Canetti, Elias, 122
Canfield Gardens flat, 153-4, 159-60
cannabis, as substitute for speed, 152-3
   bad trip, 120-30
Cantos (Pound), 218
Carlos Williams, William, 136
Centre Fortytwo, 118-20
Change for the Angel, 95, 97
Chava Queen, 36, 38
Chopin, Frederick, 135
Christie, Agatha, 136
CIA, and *Encounter*, 111
Civil Guards, 139, 143
Clifton suspension bridge, 65, 67
Cocteau, Jean, 20, 37
Cohen, Colman, 95-6
Cold War, 11
Colony Room, 34-5
Colquhoun, Robert, 35-6
Comédie Française, 82
Compayne Gardens, flat, 121-2, 127
Conway Hall symposium, 57-9, 70
Cosmo café, 122-3, 163, 178, 219
Crawford, Michael, 97
Crisp, Quentin, 30-1, 217
CV4 touring company, 211

Dale, Jim, 63
D'Arcy, Margaretta, 115
David it is Getting Dark, 126, 132, 133-4,
                  147
   in Paris, 165-7

David le Nuit Tombe, 165-7
Dayan, Yael, 162
de Freitas, Michael *see* Michael X
Deakin, John, 17
Delaney, Shelagh, 59, 109, 110, 162, 177
Dennis, Nigel, 111
Derek (neighbour), 222
Devine, George, 109-10
Diamond, Harry, 36
Dias, Georgie, 13
Dirty Charles, 215
Dissent of Dominick Shapiro, The, 151, 156
    Time Magazine fiasco, 156-9
Doctor No, 172
Dream of Peter Mann, The, 60, 62, 68, 72,
                                        83
    at Edinburgh, 86-90
    critics and, 89-90, 93-4, 109
    pre-Edinburgh tour, 85, 86
Dreams of Anne Frank, 225-6
Drinamyl, 136
drug-taking *see* Kops, Bernard, drug-taking
Dunlop, Frank, 63, 66, 71-2
    and *Dream of Peter Mann, The*, 77, 83,
                                        87-8

Eliot, T. S., 213, 218
Ellison, Rae, 144, 173
Emery, Jack, 217
Encounter, 111
Enter Solly Gold, Mermaid production,
                                176-7, 211
    to be on Broadway, 179-81
Ezra, 217-19

Feuillère, Edwige, 82
Fielding, Fenella, 54
Finchley Road, 121-2
Fings Ain't What They Used T'Be,
                    screenplay, 170-5
Fire Next Time, The, 124
FitzGibbon, Constantine, 111
Flecker, James Elroy, 60
Fleming, Ian, 172
Flowerdew, Don, 36
Frank, Anne, 128, 225-6
Fraser, John, 52
Fraser, Ronnie, 105

French Café, 13
Freud, Lucian, 15, 17, 36
Friday nights, 155
Furie, Sydney J., 172

Gallery One, 133
gas escape at Nerja, 182-3
Gascoyne, David, 14
Gay, John, 60
Georgie Girl, 162
Germans, attitude towards, 74-5, 129
    see also Olympia typewriter
Gerry Dearie, 42
Gielgud, John, 164
Ginsberg, Allen, 218
Giovanni's Room, 125
Golders Green Hippodrome, 86
Goldoni, Carlos, 63
Gordon family, 12, 104
Gordon, Gertie, dies, 183-4
Gordon, Max, 145-7, 185
Granada, 135
    Erica in hospital, 143-45
Graves, Robert, 84-5
Great Titchfield Street, flat, 115
Greek Cultural Centre, 118
Greenwich Theatre, 224
gypsies, Spanish, 75
    on road, 137-8, 139

Hackney General Hospital, 116
Half Moon Theatre, 217-19, 220
Hamlet of Stepney Green, The, 12-13, 69
    Littlewood and, 32-3, 42-5, 47, 48-9
    Lyric Theatre Hammersmith, 60
    MacInnes introduction to, 83-4
    Marvin and, 19-21
    Oxford Playhouse and, 48, 49, 52-5
    translations, 128, 129
Hard Day's Night, A 69
Hardy, Tim, 86-7
Harewood, Lord and Lady, 87
Harris, Richard, 164
hashish *see* cannabis
Hassan, 60
Hastings, Michael, 59
Hauser, Frank, and *The Hamlet...*, 48, 49,
                                        53, 55

Hayes, Melvin, 97
Heal, Joan, 64
Hobson, Harold, 20, 81-3, 92
Holloway sanatorium, 198-201
Holm, Ian, 218-19
Horovitz, Michael, 112
house fire in Nerja, 75-6
Huddleston, Trevor, 202-3

If, 164
Ionesco, Georgiou, 20
Ireland, Vicky, 225
Ironfoot Jack, 13, 36, 215, 217
Israeli protection, 219-20

Jack (ex-paratrooper), 50
Jacobs, John, 105
Jellicoe, Ann, 59-60
Joe Kops and the Hotshots, 17
John Barnes (store), 162-3
Jones, Mervyn, introduction to *The Hamlet...*, 85

June in Her Spring, 35

Kapital, Das, 77
Karlin, Miriam, 105
Kaye, Danny, 218
Keeley's Yard, 32
Keyser, David de, 97
Kingsbury, 193-4
Kops, Abigail, 150-1
   at Nerja, 182-3
Kops, Adam, 13
   and Potts, 28
   in Bristol, 62
   in Nerja, 182-3
   car accident, 138
   Erica pregnant with, 11-12
   rescued from drowning, 75
   witnessing withdrawal, 149
   writing poem in car, 135
Kops, Bernard
   and Centre Fortytwo, 118-20
   and reviews, 93-5, 96
   and Russians
      Embassy reception, 77-81
      Pavechenko, 98-103
   and socialism, 71, 77
      Conway Hall symposium, 57-9, 70

and Theatre Workshop, 41-5
at Bristol Old Vic, 60, 61, 62-7
Betjeman interview, 90-1
car accident, 138-46
drug-taking
   black bombers, 113-14, 193, 194
   burglary attempt, 193-6
   cannabis
      as substitute for speed, 152-3
      bad trip, 120-30
   Drinamyl, 136
   early, 12
   Holloway Sanatorium, 198-201
   increases intake, 184
   life with, 187-198
   Oxford halfway house, 201-5
   renounces, 174, 183, 193
      finally, 209
   returns to, 206
   sees doctor, 197-8
   speed
      after Edinburgh disaster, 89, 91-2, 96, 98
      at Royal Court conference, 109-10
      availability in Spain, 144
      effect on driving, 126
      effect on sleep, 126-7
      prescriptions from O'Flaherty, 150, 152
   renounced, 162
   withdrawal, 149, 150-3
   steals Max's prescription pad, 147-8
   suicide attempt, 206-8
   takes Erica's Dexedrine, 146
fails to write novel, 111-12
fears in Nerja, 132, 134
financial problems, 15, 104, 126, 187, 210
   borrows from bank, 157, 159, 185-6
grandchildren, 226-7
in Amsterdam, 128
in Bristol, 64-7
in Nerja, 72-7, 130-45, 181-3
in Paris, 165-7
in Vienna, 129
media exposure, 49-51
mental health, early, 12, 50
painting, 184

taxi, 169, 188-91, 207-8, 209
works
  listed, 229-30
  Change for the Angel, 95, 97
  David it is Getting Dark, 126, 132,
                  133-4, 147
    in Paris, 165-7
  Dissent of Dominick Shapiro, The, 151,
                  156
    Time Magazine fiasco, 156-9
  Dream of Peter Mann, The, 60, 62, 68,
                72, 77, 83
    at Edinburgh, 86-90
    critics and, 89-90, 93-4, 109
    pre-Edinburgh tour, 85, 86
  Dreams of Anne Frank, 225-6
  Enter Solly Gold
    Mermaid production, 176-7, 211
    to be on Broadway, 179-81
  Ezra, 217-19
  Hamlet of Stepney Green, The, 12-13,
                  69
    Littlewood and, 32-3, 42-5, 47,
                48-9
    Lyric Theatre Hammersmith, 60
    MacInnes introduction to, 83-4
    Marvin and, 19-21
    Oxford Playhouse and, 48, 49,
                52-5
    translations, 128, 129
  novels for Secker & Warburg, 175
  On Margate Sands, 211-15
  Playing Sinatra, 222, 226
  screenplay writing, 168-73
  'Shalom Bomb' (poem), 9, 112-13
  Stray Cats and Empty Bottles, 105
  Who Shall I be Tomorrow?, 223-5
  World is a Wedding, The, 117, 170
  Yes from No-man's Land, 164
Kops, Dave, 49
Kops, Debbie, 115, 116
Kops, Erica
  amber necklace, 104, 157, 186-7, 227
  and Bernard's distress, 12
  and Bernard's drug-taking
    concealed from, 91, 96, 98
    finds Oxford halfway house, 201
    finds speed, 125

    shares cannabis, 153
    stops drug supply from O'Flaherty,
                  152
    support during, 187-198, 206-8
  and Bernard's suicide attempt, 206-8
  and *The Dream of Peter Mann*, 83, 87-92
  and financial problems, 15, 104, 126,
                  187, 210
  and reviews, 94-5, 97
  and *The Hamlet…* introduction, 83-4
  car accident, 138-46
  family, 104
  gets job, 210
  on Baldwin, 125
  persuades Kops not to play David Levy,
                  44
  pregnant
    Abigail, 149
    Adam, 11-12
    Hannah, 123
    Rebekah, 162
  prescribed Dexedrine, 146
Kops, Essic, 76
Kops, Hannah
  at Nerja, 182-3
  born, 124
  car accident, 138
  gastroenteritis, 151-2
  in Granada, 145
  witnessing withdrawal, 149
Kops, Jack, 160
Kops, Joe (cousin), 128
Kops, Joe (uncle), 17
Kops, Joel, 17, 51
  escapes Nazis, 104-5
  marries Debbie, 115-16
  dies, 116-17
Kops, Phyllis, 116
Kops, Rebekah, at Nerja, 182-3
Kossoff, David, 176
Kustow, Michael, 119

L'Ouverture, Toussaint, 123
Lang, Harold, 52
Lasky, Melvin, 111
Lavrin, Beba, 118-20
Legrain's café, 68
Lessing, Doris, 59, 110, 115

Lillie, Beatrice, 87, 89
Linda (Legrain's waitress), 68
Linklater, Dick, 23, 60
Littlewood, Joan, and *The Hamlet...*, 32-3, 38-9, 41-5, 47, 48-9
Litvinoff, David, 24-5
   News Chronicle article, 49-50
Litvinoff, Emanuel, 24
   on Russian overtures, 100, 101-2
Logue, Christopher, 59, 119, 123
Lom, Dina
   and Kops's work, 89-90, 156, 158, 168-9, 176, 179, 214
   personal help, 143, 198, 201
Lom, Herbert, 157
Look Back in Anger, 12
Lorca, Federico Garcia, 72, 136
Louis' Hungarian Café, 122
Lumley, Joanna, 224
Lyceum Theatre, Edinburgh, 86-8, 91

MacBryde, Robert, 35, 36
McColl, Ewan, 119
MacInnes, Colin,
   Absolute beginners, 105-9
   and Adam, 123
   and black youths, 105
   and *Encounter*, 111
   and Irene Worth, 107-8
   and *The World is a Wedding*, 117
   at Colony Room, 34-5
   at *The Hamlet...* first night, 55
   at Torino's, 17
   introduction to *The Hamlet...*, 83-4
   on cure, 205-6
   on Theatre Workshop, 41-2, 47
   return and death, 213, 215-16
MacNeice, Louis, 17
Margate, mentally ill people in, 211-15
Martin, Kingsley, 170
Marvin, Mark, 17-21, 38, 69-71
Maschler, Tom, 198
Mason, Jackie, 179
Matisse, 135
Matthews, Francis, 224
Mayer, Tony, 19-20, 37
McDiarmid, Ian, 218-19
McDonnell, Darren, 222

McDowell, Malcolm, 164
McGowan, Jackie, 60
McGuire, Leo, 150
Melia, Joe, 176, 177
mentally ill people, in Margate, 211-15
Mercer, David, 177-8
Mermaid Theatre, 176-7
Michael X (de Freitas), 123-4
   becomes Muslim/ changes name, 129
   Compayne Gardens flat, 124, 129, 155, 159-60
   hanged for murdering girlfriend, 160
Miles, Bernard, 176
Milhaud, Darius, 20, 37
Millar, Jimmy, 119
Misquotation, 170
Mitchell, Adrian, 112
Molinas (of Torino's), 17, 26, 30
Monmouth Street flat, 30
Monty, Old, 219
Moody, John, 62, 69
Moody, Nell, 62-3
Moraes, Dom, 14
Mortimer, John, 60
Mossad protection, 219-20
Mr Love and Justice, 213
Muriel (Colony Room), 34
Musgrave, Victor, 133

necklace, amber, 104, 157, 186-7, 227
Nerja
   first visit, 72-7
   second visit, 130-45
   third visit, 181-3
New Directions, 16
New Statesman, 170
New York Times review, 157
News Chronicle article, 49-50
Nicky (neighbour), 94
Noble, Johnny, 30
Norman, Frank, 14-15, 170, 171

O'Flaherty, Tim, 150, 152
O'Toole, Peter, 60-1, 62, 66
Old Monty, 219
Olympia typewriter, 98, 101, 225
On Margate Sands, 211-15
Oresteia, The, 32

Orphée, 20, 37
Orwell, George, 135
Ove, Horace, 160
Owen, Alun, 68-9
Oxford Playhouse, 48, 49, 52

Paris, *David le Nuit Tombe*, 165-7
Parton Press, 16
Paul (student), 225
Pavechenko, Yuri, 98-103
Pember, Ron, 176, 211
Penguin, publishes *The Hamlet...*, 83-5
Perlmutter, Maurice, 113
Peter, Brother, 202-5
Pinewood Studios, 171-2
Pinter, Harold, 60
Plaschkes, Otto, 161-2, 163, 224
Playing Sinatra, 222, 226
Polka Theatre, Wimbledon, 225
Pool, Rosie, 127-8
Potts, Paul, 25-9, 31, 38, 217
Pound, Ezra, 135, 217-18, 220-1
Powell, Michael, 156

Quirk, Mrs (neighbour), 153, 154

Raffles, Gerry, 39, 41-2, 45
Randolph Hotel, Oxford, 53
Rasputin's Palace, 98
Red Shoes, The, 156
Richard, Cliff, 63
Roberts, Rachel, 164, 224
Rough and Ready Lot, The, 68-9
Rowton House, 25, 26
Royal Court Theatre, 12
Royal Court Theatre, conference, 109-10
Rudge, Olga, 220-1
Rush, John, 214-15
Russell Taylor, John, 56
Russian Trade Delegation, 98
Russians
   in Eastern Europe, 177-8
   overtures from
      Embassy reception, 77-81
      Pavechenko, 98-103

Sabbath, 155
Saint Denis, Michael, 63
Saltzman, Harry, 168-73

Sandra (secretary), 172
Sayers, Dorothy, 136
Schmidt, Peter, 24
Secker & Warburg novels, 175
Servant of Two Masters, The, 63
Seven Dials, 30
Shakespeare, Dorothy, 221
'Shalom Bomb' (poem), 9, 112-13
Shaw, Maxwell, 32
Sherrin, Ned, 54
Shulman, Milton, 177
Sierra Nevada, 135
Sigal, Clancy, 110
Simpson, N. F., 60
Sinatra, Frank, 222
Sinclair, Leonard, 151-2
Sitting on a Fortune, 133
Socialist Party of Great Britain, 36
Soviet *see* Russian(s)
Spain *see* Baza; Granada; Nerja
speed
   availability in Spain, 144
   effect on driving, 126
   effect on sleep, 126-7
   prescriptions from O'Flaherty, 150, 152
   withdrawal, 149, 150-3
Spender, Stephen, 111
Spiegel, Sam, 61
St Giles churchyard, 31
St Joseph's Hospice, 116
Stoppard, Tom, 64-5, 66
Stray Cats and Empty Bottles, 105
Sunday Times, 20
Swiss Cottage Library, 218
Sylvester, David, 111

taxi, Kops's, 169, 188-91, 207-8, 209
Terzief, Laurent, 165-6
Theatre of Reassurance, 87, 140
Theatre Royal, Stratford East, 41-5
Theatre Workshop, 41-5
Thirkell, Angela, 35
This Sporting Life, 224
Thomas, Dylan, 14
Time Magazine fiasco, 156-9
Times of India, The, 14
Torino's, 17, 24, 26, 30, 96
Toynbee, Arnold, 135

Trocchi (poet), 119-20
Turner, Tony, 58
Tynan, Kenneth, 70, 82, 93
Tynan, Kenneth, Conway Hall
                        Symposium, 57-9

Vismes, Eileen de, 13, 36
Vivaldi, 221
Voltaire, 135

Wanamaker, Sam, 19
Warburg, Freddie, 198-9
Waste Land, The, 213
Wesker, Arnold, 52, 59, 82-3, 96-7
    and Centre Fortytwo, 118-20
Wesker, Leah, 113
West Hampstead, move to, 121-2
White Lady of Wapping, 105
Whitechapel, 40
Who Shall I be Tomorrow?, 223-5
Wilson, Angus, 111
Wingate, Roy, 30
World is a Wedding, The, 117, 170
Worth, Irene, 105, 107-8
writer in residence, Bristol Old Vic, 60,
                        61, 62-7

Yes from No-man's Land, 164
York, Susannah, 224